21ST CENTURY WORKFORCES AND WORKPLACES

21ST CENTURY WORKFORCES AND WORKPLACES

The Challenges and Opportunities for Future Work Practices and Labour Markets

STEPHEN BEVAN, IAN BRINKLEY, ZOFIA BAJOREK AND CARY COOPER

Bloomsbury Business
An imprint of Bloomsbury Publishing Plc

B L O O M S B U R Y
LONDON · OXFORD · NEW YORK · NEW DELHI · SYDNEY

Bloomsbury Business

An imprint of Bloomsbury Publishing Plc

50 Bedford Square	1385 Broadway
London	New York
WC1B 3DP	NY 10018
UK	USA

www.bloomsbury.com

BLOOMSBURY and the Diana logo are trademarks of Bloomsbury Publishing Plc

First published 2018

© Stephen Bevan, Ian Brinkley, Zofia Bajorek & Cary Cooper, 2018

Stephen Bevan, Ian Brinkley, Zofia Bajorek & Cary Cooper have asserted their right under the Copyright, Designs and Patents Act, 1988, to be identified as Author of this work.

British Library Cataloguing-in-Publication Data

A catalogue record for this book is available from the British Library.

ISBN:	HB:	978-1-4729-0499-7
	ePDF:	978-1-4729-0501-7
	ePub:	978-1-4729-0500-0

Library of Congress Cataloging-in-Publication Data

Names: Bevan, S. (Stephen), author.
Title: 21st century workforces and workplaces / by Stephen Bevan [and three others].
Description: London ; New York : Bloomsbury Business, 2017. |
Includes bibliographical references and index.
Identifiers: LCCN 2017053845 (print) | LCCN 2017056733 (ebook) |
ISBN 9781472905000 (ePub) | ISBN 9781472905017 (ePDF) |
ISBN 9781472917508 (eXML) | ISBN 9781472904997 (hardback)
Subjects: LCSH: Work–History–21st century. | Work environment–21st century. |
Labor supply–21st century.
Classification: LCC HD4855 (ebook) | LCC HD4855 .B48 2017 (print) |
DDC331.1–dc23LC record available at https://lccn.loc.gov/2017053845

Cover image © Shutterstock

Typeset by RefineCatch Limited, Bungay, Suffolk
Printed and bound in Great Britain

To find out more about our authors and books visit www.bloomsbury.com. Here you will find extracts, author interviews, details of forthcoming events and the option to sign up for our newsletters.

CONTENTS

FOREWORD BY LOUISE FISHER

When I reflect upon the work and workplaces in my career so far, the ones I think about most fondly are not those with the best offices, canteens or even employee perks, it's the ones where I have worked with great teams, people whose company I enjoy, who help me work better and where I have grown as a person and as a professional.

I was given a senior HR job once because the Director I was going to work for said he saw I was always smiling and was fun to be around. Of course I had to be able to do the job too, but he turned out to be one of the best managers in my career. He was thoughtful, we had fun and did great work as a team. He also recognised my contribution and knew how to stretch me to do more.

In the 21st century we will still need to be led by good managers, to have the tools to do great work, to feel like we are contributing all we can and to have fun! We will want to know we are being treated fairly and have opportunities to grow and develop our careers if we want to. As I reflected, I realised that I worked better for people who took an interest in me and my well-being, who gave me helpful feedback, who stretched me and treated me fairly. Leading people is not rocket science but it's amazing how many people managers don't get it. They don't see this is their most important role and don't practice or ask for feedback about how they are doing it!

The people coming into the workplace for the first time will in the 21st century have more choices and more demands. They want to be able to work for organisations whose values match their own, they want to work more flexibly and they can happily work with modern technologies enabling them to work remotely and more flexibly. They socialise through technology and don't need people to be with them in the same office to feel a sense of belonging.

These younger workers (just like older workers) want to be trusted to perform without their supervisor or manager being ever-present. After all, these are the generations for whom technology, 'apps', instant (and constant) communication, immediate responses to questions (and decisions) are a way of life. They want this in their workplaces too.

Technology is everywhere already. I can't think back to a meeting I attended where at least one person wasn't on their mobile device 'checking in'. I am as addicted as the next person and I consider myself to be a Luddite regarding new technologies! But what's the cost of this new way of working on our health and well-being? If we are never off-line, resting, thinking and reflecting, how will this affect our energy, our productivity, our creativity and innovation?

We must consider this in our 21st century workplaces, we know we will all have to work longer – we need to build in longer periods of rest into our working lives or our health and well-being will be affected. The concept of the gap-year, the sabbatical, the career break – will resurrect itself and employers need to have policies in place to retain their best employees – or lose them to workplaces that have thought this through and allow the flexibility that is needed.

We already recognise we must create workplaces for the millennials and younger generations who are information-hungry and tech savvy, who won't want to work in the traditional hierarchies of old, who want to know instantaneously if they are doing a great job. Companies' HR and people practices will need to adapt to meet the needs of the changing workforce. Does the annual appraisal process support this or inhibit better performance and productivity? How dynamic are these traditional processes and do they excite the workforce and help everyone perform better? If they don't, they should.

In 1989 Charles Handy was writing about a world I now experience, 'the shamrock organisation'. Organisations have the traditional core of senior managers and professionals, they have the outsourced or contractor workforce and the flexible, seasonal and temporary workforce. Legislation in the UK is catching up to better define 'what is an employee', especially with so called gig workers. Even for the people in the third leaf of Charles Handy's shamrock, the flexible workforce has changed over the years. Certain industries like the hospitality industry have used zero hour's contracts for many years, successfully meeting both parties' needs. The CIPD's own research found many people are happy with zero-hours contracts; it suits them and their needs to be flexible and part time. I have used these types of contracts in the past and they are not all bad news, as long as they are used in a fair and respectful way.

Did the demographic time bomb ever really hit us in the way that we were warned it would? My sense is that enabling workers to move across geographies especially in the European Union, but also within other parts of the world has kept that at bay, perhaps temporarily. Older workers also help fill some of the skills gaps and many companies are helping employees ease into retirement through flexible working practices. Access to pensions while working and other pension freedoms have helped too. This gives older workers choices; they no longer have to retire at a compulsory age. If they want to and are able to they can work for as long as they like leading to five generations in today's workplaces.

One aspect of the workplace that is changing because of more transparency is the view of executive pay. Great performance should be rewarded. Too often we see high rewards for little or no improvement in performance. Publishing data on the ratios between CEO pay and employees' pay, along with equal pay data will start to see different conversations in RemCo's. I love the phrase 'the best disinfectant is sunlight.' In my view, greater transparency will bring fairer rewards. With fairer rewards we might start to see more Women and BAME representation on company boards and in senior roles. The younger generations expect this, but as soon as graduates start to progress we start to see differences in pay and opportunity. Why? What is it about the 21st century workplace that means we have still not addressed this issue?

This book uncovers a number of things that might help. The book highlights and reviews the 21st century work and workplace and uncovers the myths and the reality of the workforce. The authors look at employee productivity and review why it is that the UK lags behind other leading economies. Is it all about management and leadership and having better people skills?

The authors review the myths of globalisation and the impacts of immigration and technology which will impact the way work gets done. The authors, who are experts in their fields, review the impact on the health and well-being of the workforce and how we can be healthier and more productive.

They also look at pay and reward systems and argue for fairer, more transparent rewards. They finally look at the realities of the ageing workforce. They pose some interesting suggestions about how people could 'unretire' and how ageing workforces can become a strength to organisations.

Finally, the authors draw conclusions about the engagement of trade unions in the workplace, regulations for the protection of workers, senior management pay and workplace well-being. In my experience how organisations approach these topics tells you a lot about that organisation's culture. Getting it right so that people feel motivated and treated fairly, along with feeling like employees have a real say in the way the workplace is run has a big impact on the real engagement and productivity of the workforce.

This book brings new research, insight and thoughtful leadership, and challenges us to think differently about the way that work will get done and what the workplace will look and feel like in the 21st century. I am sure you'll find that the time you invest in reading it, will be of enormous value to you.

HR Director of Xerox and Chair of the CIPD Board, Louise is an experienced senior HR professional having worked at senior and board levels in a number of global organisations across a variety of industry sectors.

Introduction

This book sets out how work is today and how it could change over the next decade. It is centred on the workplace because that is where the big changes take place that impact directly and indirectly on a workforce of 32 million in the United Kingdom (UK) and over 580 million across the Organisation for Economic Co-operation and Development (OECD). These changes take place against a background where huge doubts about the future of work dominate the public debate, where concerns about wages, productivity, job security and the end of work through new technology are acute.

The first three chapters are concerned with setting the scene and dealing with some of the bigger picture issues in the labour market, focusing on productivity and the workplace, changes in the structure of the labour market, and the impact of global forces on employment. In Chapter 1 we argue that part of the solution to the 'productivity puzzle' lies in the workplace, around the quality of management, work practice and better use of skills, a difficult area neglected by policy areas that requires bridging the yawning gap between productivity as defined by economists (output per hour) and how productivity is interpreted by managers and workers.

In Chapter 2 we contest some common mythologies about how the nature of employment is changing: the permanent employee job is still the bedrock of the labour market, the length of average employment relationship has not fallen, the middle of the labour market is not being hollowed out and migrants are not taking our jobs.

In Chapter 3 we go global. We argue that no one's meal is in danger from the rise of China and India, globalization takes the rap for many things that are home-grown, we are more likely to face a global labour shortage than surplus, offshoring will not hurt overall employment and the robots are not coming for our jobs. New tech may enhance our ability to do more for longer at work, but that is still far off.

In the rest of the book we turn to look in more detail about the forces shaping the workplaces of tomorrow. Every day workplace decisions are being made that will change the way we work and are managed: the impact of new technology on how and where we work, the way we are rewarded, how we balance the demands of work and personal life, and how our well-being at work is determined. We look at what the results have been and what they are likely to be in the future.

In Chapter 4 we look at the workplace and office of the future. Put aside futuristic notions driven by over-excited extrapolations of current new tech and radical office re-design. The pace at which offices will change ultimately depends on the ability and willingness of people to adapt and that in turn depends on working practices catching up, slowly, with technological potential.

In Chapter 5 we look at the future of management, emerging as one of the critical factors in both organizational and wider economic success. Yet managers are under pressure, expected to manage increasingly complex workplaces. There is no magic solution, but we conclude that the core skills that managers need most today, and in the future, are 'people skills'.

In Chapter 6 we look at the health and well-being of the workforce, reviewing recent trends, setting out the business case for employer interventions, and outlining what those key changes ought to be if we are to have healthier and more productive workforces in the future.

In Chapter 7 we look at pay and reward where faith is in danger of trumping evidence. We argue that the march away from collective setting of pay towards greater individualization has created as many problems as it has solved. We argue for a new form of 'collectivization' of reward based on transparency, fairness and consultation.

In Chapter 8 we look at one of the big, universal and uncontested changes in the workforce – that of ageing. Workplace health and support have critical roles alongside introducing gradual retirement and the concept of 'unretirement' – but there are major barriers to making this a reality, and we set down five suggestions for how we can ensure future workplaces can turn workforce ageing into a strength.

Our final chapter brings this together. The biggest challenge is to make a reality of 'good work' across the workforce and not just some, and that requires simultaneous action across several areas to create more workplaces fit for the twenty-first century. These must include a more systematic engagement of trade unions outside the traditional bargaining agenda, modest re-regulation of the labour market to ensure fair protection of all workers, stronger action to inhibit underserved pay rises at the top, and stronger and more systematic improvements in workplace well-being.

Some may say that this the book represents a Panglossian view of the workforce and the workplace and that we have paid insufficient attention to what is going wrong. We would counter that it is based on solid evidence and we have presented a balanced view. Moreover, in our view so much of the public debate is based on misconceptions and exaggerations that we are in danger of making bad policy and practice.

In fact, as we make clear, there are significant areas that do require urgent attention, including many in permanent full-time jobs whose experience of work is not only far worse than the majority but, in some respects, is deteriorating. Weaknesses and unfair or misguided practices in management, in reward and pay, and in well-being at work are widespread and on some measures the progress we have seen appears to have stalled since the recession.

In the past, we have tended to disconnect questions of distribution and fairness from productivity and performance. We contend that the two are intimately connected, which is why so many of the proposals and ideas set out in these chapters are about improving the position and treatment of both managers and the people they manage.

Successive governments have, rightly, been focused on the productivity problem afflicting the UK and many other OECD countries. It is central to future rises in living standards and national prosperity.

Yet what happens in the workplace and the levers that might be directly or indirectly pulled has been strangely neglected, even though the outcomes that government want hinge critically on decisions made in the workplace. We hope that, if nothing else, this book helps make the case that the workplace matters and that there are practical actions that employers and others, with support from policymakers, can do to make a difference.

1

Productivity and the workplace

Introduction

We start this book with a brief chapter on productivity because the importance of productivity is hard to underestimate. It is central to improving living standards not just for the workforce but also for the population. Yet the past decade has seen productivity slow, in some countries like the UK average growth has been close to zero and economists have struggled to fully explain why. Theories have come and gone, disproved by time or subsequent research. Others seem to work for some countries and not others.

Many OECD economies have emphasized the importance of investment in research and development (R&D), the innovation infrastructure and higher-level skills in driving up productivity. Over the past decade OECD-wide investment in R&D increased from just over 2.1 per cent in 2005 to just under 2.4 per cent in 2015 (OECD, 2017a) and the share of those between the ages of 25 and 34 with a degree increased from 34 per cent to 42 per cent over the same period (OECD, 2017b). Yet productivity has fallen virtually everywhere. Either OECD economies are investing poorly, or something else needs to be addressed.

We contend that an important part of the 'something else' lies in the workplace, around managerial competences and workforce practices that are struggling to come to terms with the latest wave of new technologies. The rest of this chapter sets out some of the evidence to support this idea and looks at how productivity in the workplace is perceived by managers and workers. It is also a recurrent theme in later chapters about creating more productive workplaces through changes in workplaces, managerial practice, reward, well-being and meeting the challenge of workforce ageing.

The productivity challenge

The dire productivity performance of the UK economy and the consequences for wages can be seen in estimates from the Office for National Statistics (ONS). These show that had the pre-2008 trend continued, productivity levels would today be 20 per cent higher than before the crash. Instead, actual growth between 2007 and 2016 has been zero. This is shown in the left-hand chart in Figure 1.1. Real wages have fallen as a result, as measured by average weekly earnings, comparing 2007 and 2017. This is also shown in the left-hand side of the chart.

The historical record suggests this may be very unusual. The Bank of England has calculated annual average productivity growth for different historical periods, measured by total factor productivity, starting with pre-industrial Britain where it took a century to record a 10 per cent increase in productivity, moving through the Industrial Revolution from 1760 onwards and what the Bank terms a period of mass industrialization from 1850 onwards and the 'information revolution' from 1950 onwards. In each period productivity is significantly higher than in the preceding period. But from 2008 onwards the productivity growth record becomes negative. This is shown in Figure 1.2.

The historical comparisons should not be taken too literally. We are comparing very long averages with a much shorter recent period and the further

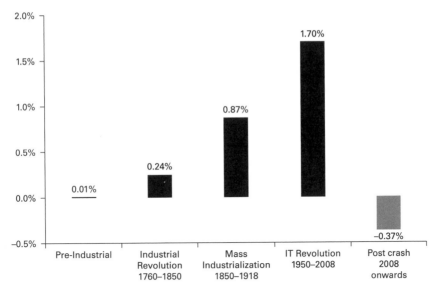

FIGURE 1.1 *The worst performance since records began.*

Note: All figures estimates of total factor productivity annual average growth UK.

Source: Productivity puzzles – speech by Andy Haldane, Chief Economist Bank of England, March 2017, Table 1.

http://www.bankofengland.co.uk/publications/Documents/speeches/2017/speech968.pdf

back we go the sketchier the economic statistics become. But it is certainly hard to find evidence of such a prolonged period of very low or negative productivity growth in the twentieth century, which seems to be afflicting so many OECD countries and maybe some non-OECD ones as well. So, what might have got us into this almost unprecedented position where productivity growth looks more like something experienced in the pre-industrial age?

Many have favoured the zombie firm explanation, where forbearance by UK banks and ultra-low interest rates allowed large numbers of marginal 'zombie firms' who would otherwise have gone under to survive and squander resources that should have been re-allocated to more productive enterprises. However, recent OECD research suggests that zombie firms accounted for a lower share of employment and capital in 2013 in the UK after the recession than they did in 2007, before the crash. Zombie firms in the UK may have been quicker to die off in the decade up to 2007 compared with the decade up

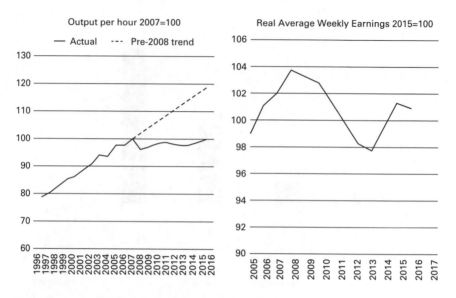

FIGURE 1.2 *Productivity and real wages stagnant.*

Source: ONS, April 2017.

https://www.ons.gov.uk/employmentandlabourmarket/peopleinwork/labourproductivity/bulletins/labourproductivity/apriltojune2017

https://www.ons.gov.uk/employmentandlabourmarket/peopleinwork/earningsandworkinghours/articles/supplementaryanalysisofaverageweeklyearnings/november2017

to 2017, so it may still have contributed to the productivity slowdown. But it does not look like a smoking gun.

The latest thinking from the OECD and others is that we are in the grip of a slow-down in the rate of technological diffusion – the rate at which new technologies are adopted and adapted across the economy. In all OECD countries, a small group of firms have successfully mastered the new digital technologies and have seen significant productivity gains (the leaders) while the rest have seen productivity languish at close to zero (the laggards). This goes back to before the crash – the OECD estimates that between 2001 and 2013 productivity growth among the leaders was around 40 per cent compared with 5 per cent for the laggards (McGowan et al., OECD, 2017a).

It is not unusual when waves of new technologies first appear for there to be a gap between early adopters and the rest, but the gap looks much bigger and much more persistent than in the past. There is no sign yet that the laggards are catching up. We may be in a position where many firms and organizations have exhausted the productivity gains from previous new technologies but are unable or are unwilling to make the jump to exploit the latest wave. The divergence in productivity growth looks much greater in the UK than elsewhere – we have a very long tail of underperforming companies, according to the Bank of England (Haldane, 2017).

JOHN CRIDLAND

PAY IS INTRINSICALLY LINKED TO productivity – how much value is created in each hour worked. It is one of the most important factors determining what pay rises firms can afford. The UK faces a productivity challenge as productivity fell during the recession and at the beginning of 2014 was still 16 per cent below where it would have been had the crisis not happened. The extent to which businesses can rise to the productivity challenge will determine wages in 2030 and the standards of living that they support.

This doesn't mean making people work harder. It's about finding new approaches that add more value or simplify things so that firms are more effective and their employees can work smarter and reap the financial rewards from it. The Confederation of British Industry (CBI) is calling for businesses to take a long-term approach to raising employee value-added, making it a firm priority. At the same time, government should ask the Office for Budget Responsibility to report on the UK's productivity performance to help better guide policymakers as they seek to support business in their endeavours.

The refocus on the workplace

An emerging theme in the discussion about why we are in such a difficult position is that the new digital technologies require a step change in complementary investments if they are to generate significant productivity gains, which few businesses appear capable of taking. The OECD has recently suggested that the competitive advantage for firms able to operate at the technological frontier (the leaders) has increased for exactly that reason, giving them bigger rewards and fewer competitors than they would have faced in the past.

> This stagnation could reflect the increasing costs for laggards firms of moving from an economy based on production to one based on ideas ... Indeed, the importance of tacit knowledge as a source of competitive advantage for frontier firms may have risen if increasingly complex technologies were to increase the amount and sophistication of complementary investments required.
>
> ANDREWS et al., 2016

There may therefore be good reasons why the laggards do not make the jump. Managing a simultaneous change in business strategy and work organization together with effective use of new technologies that requires big investments is a daunting prospect at the best of times and in periods of global economic uncertainty even more so. Moreover, in an era with ultra-low interest rates, sticking with what you have may still generate reasonable profits. The balance between organizational risks and rewards has shifted in favour of more of the same. This may help explain the otherwise odd behaviour of employers continuing to hire people in large numbers even though the additional workers are contributing nothing to productivity.

However, it may be that in too many countries, including the UK, the quality of management is becoming an increasingly severe constraint. Concerns about the quality of management once you move outside the top corporates and multinationals has been a long-standing worry in the UK, especially in family-owned firms that have lower productivity than firms that are professionally managed (Awano et al., 2017). In a recent speech, the Chief Economist of the Bank of England highlighted this as an issue, and suggested that substantial improvements could be gained by improving managerial quality:

there is a statistically significant link between the quality of firms' management processes and practices and their productivity. And the effect is large. This suggests potentially high returns to policies which improve the quality of management within companies.

ANDY HALDANE, speech, March 2017

Another important piece of the jigsaw are more general skills. We have one of the best-educated workforces in the OECD – by 2020 according to one projection over half the workforce will have a degree (UKCES, 2015). The UK higher-education system has a good reputation internationally and attracts large numbers of overseas students on that basis. But other indicators suggest that all is not well in the rest of the workforce and in the new generations of workers entering the workforce without a degree. A recent review by the Chartered Institute of Personnel and Development (CIPD) of the UK's skills record makes depressing reading (CIPD, 2017). It found that:

- Despite nearly 20 years of high levels of investment in the UK education system by OECD standards, the outcomes in terms of basic literacy, numeracy and computer solving skills are at best mediocre (this is also a finding for the United States (US)).

- Most indicators on vocational training and education for the workforce suggest the UK either does not compare well or is slipping behind other European economies.

- Even when skills are adequate, there is some evidence that they are poorly used, with the share of people at all skills levels saying they could do more is higher than in some other OECD countries.

Yet the true extent of the problem is still something of a guess, according to the review. Although the problems of over-skilling (where people say they could do more than their job allows) and under-skilling (where people say they need more to do their jobs properly) have been well known and documented for decades, we still do not have robust measures of either at both international and national level with wide discrepancies depending on definitions, methodologies and measures used. This is a glaring omission, and reflects an obsession with measuring educational outcomes in terms of qualifications rather than workplace skills – and as the CIPD report argues, it is the latter that matter more for productivity.

Improving performance at the workplace level rests on the actions of managers and the responses of employees. But we think there is a fatal disconnect between the productivity problem as perceived by policymakers and economists and the productivity problem as perceived by most managers and workers. We explore this below.

Managerial perspectives

We have many workplace and organizational surveys that regularly ask managers many questions about almost all aspects of their business, from reward packages to employment policies and about investment, output, sales and exports. Virtually none of them ask about productivity. If managerial surveys asking about productivity are rare, surveys of employees are on the endangered species list. Yet what we have reveals some disconcerting findings.

The CIPD conducted some major surveys in 2014 that showed that about two-thirds of managers said they measured productivity or that the term was widely used within the organization (CIPD, 2015). So we have perhaps a third of organizations, most likely to be smaller businesses, that might struggle to recognize the term let alone do much about it. Indeed, the CIPD–JP Morgan report *People Skills* (forthcoming) suggests that policymakers may have unrealistic expectations of this segment of the business population because they lack even rudimentary human resources (HR) capability. It would be a gross over-statement to say that HR capability is the solution to the productivity problem among this group of firms, but it is hard to imagine implementing some of the practices we identify later in the book without either in-house capability or access to effective external support which is often non-existent.

However, even among the two-thirds who recognized the term, there was little consistency of measure with most managers using some broad measure of business performance such as sales, profitability or cost control instead of the conventional economic measures of output per employee or output per hour worked. Most managers in the survey overstated the productivity performance of their organization. They were asked whether they thought productivity over the past year had gone up, gone down or remained the same. They were also asked about their relative performance compared with similar organizations. On both measures few managers thought their performance was below average (5 per cent) or had declined (10 per cent) even though the aggregate figures show that productivity growth was zero and therefore must be negative for a significant share of enterprises.

This is not new – the 2004 Workplace Employment Relations Survey (WERS) also found that managers over-reported on productivity and on financial performance (WERS, 2004). The 2004 WERS is distinctive in being able to match objective measures of workplace productivity performance and managerial perceptions of performance. There is an association between the two, so managers are not being entirely irrational, but the relationship was not statistically significant.

Employee perceptions

We have relatively little information on what employees think about productivity, but one survey published by the Smith Institute in 2015 gives us some insights (Welfare, 2011). The survey has strengths and weaknesses. It was very large (7,500 employees) but it is not representative of the workforce or the structure of the economy as respondents were trade-union members mainly from retail, media and communications, and the civil service.

Most said they knew at least something about their organization's approach to productivity or that their employer measured productivity. However, this was typically in relation to their own job through target and performance, in contrast to the managerial focus on organizational, workplace and team measures of productivity. There are echoes of the managerial survey, in that nearly half thought they were working more productively than two years ago, and 27 per cent thought they were working harder but not more productively. Many of those who thought they were more productive said they also worked harder. Only 13 per cent said they were more productive for the same or less effort – what has sometimes been termed 'working smarter'.

It is hard to avoid the impression that for employees it is hard to separate perceptions of being more productive from perceptions of working harder. Greater worker effort seems a much more common experience and that in turn is consistent with evidence discussed in later chapters that the share of stressful jobs has increased. Very few unambiguously reported being more productive in a way that would fit the conventional economic definition of increased output per hour worked.

While most thought that new technology could make jobs better and more productive, few thought improved productivity would lead to more pay and better working conditions. Although pay and productivity have historically been in close step at the whole-economy level, this may not seem the case at workplace level if the actual productivity of the workforce is being over-estimated by both managers and employees alike. In recent years, the sense of disconnection between pay packet and productivity may have been increased in the UK as non-pay labour costs have been rising, limiting the pay rise that employers feel able to concede.

What works at the workplace level

There has been a great deal published, often in one-off surveys, that makes some connection between changes in office design or workplace practice that will improve productivity, even though sometimes the claimed connection is somewhat tenuous. Hardly any demonstrate a statistically significant association and virtually none cause and effect. Finding a significant positive link with productivity is inherently challenging, partly because any one action is unlikely to have a measurable impact. Instead, significant productivity improvements may require several inter-dependent changes to be introduced at the same time. Moreover, some measures may depress rather than increase productivity.

The CIPD survey quoted above looked at which organizational characteristics were most strongly associated with managers who said they are doing better than the average on productivity. Three attributes were found to be statistically significant – a business strategy based on delivering quality services and products; a workplace culture that managers thought was 'right' for the business to succeed; and widespread investment in workforce training.

Working practices were more complex and suggest a complex relationship that could either be positive or negative. There is a wide range of literature that has found a statistically robust relationship between high-performance management practices and productivity, but also that such practices are not very common (WERS, 2011). And as we showed above, there is a clear relationship between improving managerial quality and firm performance, including productivity.

The CIPD survey also looked at many flexible working practices that many organizations have introduced or made available. This survey of HR managers used some relative performance indicators such as speed and effectiveness and response to competitors and relative performance rather than asking about productivity directly. However, as many managers tend to use these indicators as proxy measures of productivity, it offers some insights about potential linkage. None showed a statistically significant link – positive or negative – for all three measures, some of which were positive for speed or effectiveness of response but negative for relative performance.

The study suggests, however, that we should be cautious about putting too much weight on the results for individual measures, as the context in which they are delivered is likely to matter even more. For example, a workplace with poor employment relations or workplace culture may perform badly but have just as many flexible working practices as a workplace with good employment practices and a positive workplace culture. Moreover, the data cannot demonstrate cause and effect. There are no 'silver bullets' in workplace practice.

Building support for organizations and managers

There are some signs that the importance of the workplace is being reflected in the policy agenda and the beginnings of a network of intermediary institutions focused on workplace productivity. The November 2016 Budget included some modest funding for management training programmes and for the establishment of a business-led Productivity Leadership Group, following an initiative from Charlie Mayfield and other business leaders in autumn 2015, with a focus on practical measures to help industry and managers to engage more constructively with the productivity agenda (see www.bethebusiness.com). In 2016 ACAS launched a productivity tool to help both businesses and workers to adopt practices and procedures that will, in the right context, help drive productivity improvements (see www.acas.org.uk/index.aspx?articleid=5609). However, a focus on workplace productivity is still very much on the fringe of public policy thinking which remains resolutely focused on necessary but conventional measures such as physical and digital infrastructure investment and support for science, R&D and innovation.

Something is missing. Skills policy in many countries, but especially the UK, seems unable to focus on much beyond school-leavers. Measures that would support life-long learning for the workforce over 25 years of age are by comparison often marginalized and under-funded. But even this is no silver bullet unless and until more serious attention is given to the quality of management and working practices that will support the wider objective of increasing productivity. A good starting point would be to look seriously at improving managerial performance and addressing the key skill sets that managers will need to create more productive workplaces in the future. This challenge is addressed in Chapter 5.

2

The changing labour market: myths and reality

Many think the past decade has been one of exceptional change in the world of work. Some see a big shift in employment characterized by the rise of zero-hours contracts and low-paid self-employment in the 'gig economy' together with the increased use of agency workers which makes employment much less secure than it was in the past. Add in exceptionally weak real wage growth and a widely held belief that the huge rise in migration from the European Union (EU) since 2004 has depressed wages and reduced the employment opportunities for native Britons, and it is not surprising that many see the world of work becoming a darker place for many people, especially the young and those with fewer skills who live in areas of long-term industrial decline.

The Brexit vote, the election of Donald Trump as US president, and the apparent rise of anti-migrant sentiment and support for more populist political parties across the EU have all been linked to these developments, creating a protest vote by those suffering the long-term adverse consequences of globalization and new technology and the alleged indifference of 'metropolitan elite' policymakers and unresponsive political systems.

In this chapter, we look at the *evidence* from the official statistics, surveys (official and non-official) and from academic and other studies on how the world of work is changing rather than how some people think it is changing.

We will test out some of the more persistent views that the structure of employment has tilted towards more insecure forms of work and that the job for life is over with more frequent job changes. We will look at the evidence on the quality of work and how that has changed over time. Where possible we look at the international trends as well as national data to show both similarities and differences between the major OECD economies.

Our contention is that, contrary to expectations, the fundamental structure of the UK labour market has changed very little and that for most people their experience of work has improved. The share of 'good work' has increased and, on some measures, there is a reasonably good match between what people want from a job and what they get. However, these trends are not universal. For significant parts of the workforce work has become more insecure and the quality of working life was not high to start with and has worsened significantly over the past decade. And not all aspects of work have improved, even for the majority, with pay and progression remaining major sources of dissatisfaction.

Employment is becoming more 'contingent' and less permanent

The rise of zero-hours contracts and the 'gig economy' is seen as part of a tidal wave of insecurity with all the new jobs, so it is claimed, consisting of temporary jobs, casual work and self-employment. These non-permanent jobs are sometimes referred to as atypical.[1]

What we find is that the share of people in work in permanent employee jobs has changed little since 1997 and permanent employee employment remains the bedrock of the UK labour market. There are remarkably few significant changes, with an increase in self-employment balanced by a decline in the share of temporary employees, unpaid family workers, and those on government employment schemes. This is shown in Table 2.1.

TABLE 2.1 *Labour-market structure in the UK, 1997–2017*

Share of workforce in Q4	1997	2008	2017	Change 1997–2017
Permanent employees	78.9%	81.6%	79.4%	0.5
Full-time employees	63.5%	64.4%	62.6%	−0.9
Part-time employees	21.8%	21.8%	21.9%	0.1
Self-employed	13.4%	13.0%	15.0%	1.6
Temporary employees	6.4%	4.8%	5.0%	−1.4
Unpaid family/government schemes	1.2%	0.6%	0.7%	−0.5
People with second jobs	4.8%	3.9%	3.5%	−1.3
People on zero-hours contracts	–	0.5%	2.9%	2.4*

Notes: All figures Q1 in each year. Permanent employment is total employee employment minus temporary employee employment. *Zero-hours contracts are 2016. Change in zero-hours contracts between 2008 and 2016 is overstated, but levels in 2008 and 2016 are underestimated.

Source: Office for National Statistics: www.ons.gov.uk/employmentandlabourmarket/peopleinwork/employmentandemployeetypes/bulletins/uklabourmarket/july2017 (authors' estimates)

Among the major OECD economies there have been small declines in the share of permanent employee employment in Germany, France, Italy and Canada, and a significant rise in Japan. These shifts are hardly transformational and in most countries permanent employment remains the 'norm' for most people in work. This is shown in Figure 2.1.

This was a period that started with a recovery from a deep and prolonged recession in the mid-1990s and went through a deeper financial crash in 2008. It coincided with a step-change in the impact of globalization as China and India opened their economies and the EU expanded, with greatly increased flows of migrants to the UK and some other Western EU states. It also was the period when the new information and communication technologies took off, with profound changes for many in how we do our work. Industries have risen and fallen in response while the share of well-educated labour has dramatically

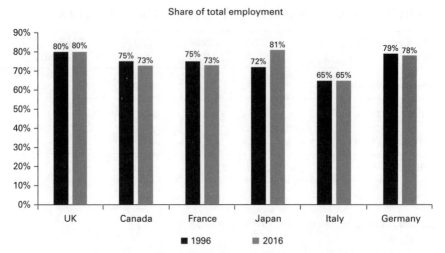

FIGURE 2.1 *Permanent employee jobs remain bedrock of labour markets.*

Note: Permanent employment is total employees minus temporary employees as share of total employment. Latest US official estimate is 2005, when permanent dependent employment was 84 per cent of total employment compared with 85 per cent in 1995.

Source: OECD database: www.oecd.org/els/lfs-jobdurationandworkingtime.htm (authors' estimates)

increased. And despite all that, the structure of employment has barely moved. There is a quite amazing resilience in the face of change.

An important caveat to these figures is that activity on the margins of labour markets is hard to measure from household surveys such as the Labour Force Survey. Sometimes the categories may cut across conventional definitions of permanent and temporary. For example, we know that a significant number of people on zero-hours contracts describe their job as permanent. We also know from work done by the ONS that a significant part of the rise in zero-hours contracts is because of increased awareness among those on them, following extensive publicity in the media and campaigning work by trade unions and others (ONS, 2017). And it is likely that even now, levels of zero-hours contracts may be underestimated, as separate estimates based on the number of contracts issued by employers show significantly higher levels than the number reported by individuals. Similarly, while the published statistics only present figures for temporary agency staff we know there are large numbers of agency workers who have permanent contracts and a small number who classify themselves as self-employed (Judge and Tomlinson, 2016).

We may also in some cases be overstating the extent of 'contingency' by focusing on employment status. In 2005 the US Bureau of Labor Statistics published research that counted all temporary jobs as self-evidently contingent, but otherwise ignored the employment contract and went directly to the heart of the issue by asking people whether they thought their job would last beyond a certain period (US Bureau of Labor Statistics, 2005). The Bureau reasoned that contingent and what they called 'alternative' forms of employment were different concepts and that people could be in stable employment relationships for many years as freelancers or subcontractors while those in notionally permanent jobs could face great insecurity. The Bureau came up with a range of between 2 and 5 per cent, much the same as in a similar survey in 1995.

The notion that nonetheless the nature of work is changing dramatically has a big audience in the United States, partly because no official statistics on what are called contingent and alternative work arrangements have been published for over a decade. Voices of sanity based on the evidence we do have unfortunately get less coverage and acknowledgement in the public debate because they deal in inconvenient and unexciting facts. A recent study by Annette Bernhardt concluded:

> we all share a strong intuition that the nature of work has fundamentally changed contributing to the deterioration of labour standards. Yet at least with aggregate national data, it has been hard to find evidence of a strong unambiguous shift towards nonstandard or contingent forms of work – especially in contrast to the dramatic increase in wage inequality.
>
> BERNHARDT, 2014

Much of the recent confusion has been generated by the US Government Accountability Office (GOA) which in a recent report said about 40 per cent of the US workforce was in 'contingent and alternative employment' in 2010 compared with 35 per cent in 2006 (US GOA, 2015). This figure has been widely quoted, invariably out of context, to imply that these workers were in a form of freelance work or part of the gig economy and that non-standard and non-permanent employee jobs were becoming an endangered species. The GOA report focused on access to benefits and conditions at work and (unhelpfully) included all permanent part-time workers in their definition because on average they got less access to company benefits than full-time workers. The reported increase was because of an increase in permanent part-time employee employment. The share of contingent labour excluding this group did not change at all over this period.

A recent study by Katz and Krueger which looked at employment growth in the US between 1995 and 2015 defined 'alternative work arrangements' as temporary agency workers, on-call workers, contract workers and independent contractors or freelancers (Katz and Krueger, 2016). This showed a rise in such jobs from just over 10 per cent of the US workforce to nearly 16 per cent, mostly over the past decade. Much of the increase was accounted for by contract workers; that is workers employed by a company but hired out to work elsewhere. As the authors note, some of the recent change might be driven by the temporary loss of permanent employee jobs over the recession 2008–2010.

What can we safely conclude from this saga? Perhaps the most important is that if a gap opens in the official statistics on a hot topic, then others will rush in to fill the information vacuum created. These alternative estimates vary from the exaggerated to the sound and respectable, making it hard for the casual observer to sort out the wheat from the chaff. We remain deeply sceptical that contingent and alternative employment is as high and has increased as much as some contend, but remain open to the idea that changing business models such as greater use of labour contracting companies may be impacting on the US labour market at the margin. Fortunately, we will have a definite answer when the next US Bureau of Labor Statistics estimate of 'contingent' working arrangements is published. The survey was conducted in May 2017 but at the time of writing a release date had not been set.

The end of jobs for life?

It is often asserted that the 'job for life' has gone, and people will have to get used to a working life where jobs do not last and several career changes will be required. Employers, it is said, are either no longer able or no longer willing to offer long-term jobs to most workers as new business models seek to minimize 'core' staff by large-scale outsourcing and offshoring and by tapping into networks of freelancers. Moreover, employers are sometimes told that new generations of younger workers, especially the better educated, are no longer willing to commit to employers for long periods (PwC, 2017).

In this alleged brave new world of unstable and transitory employment, the primary duty of government, employers and individuals is to give workers the skills to cope with more frequent job changes. This duty is in fact the right one but for the wrong reasons. Making a reality of life-long learning so workers can progress, cope with changes in technology and make the best use of their skills is central to improving work for most people. But the central premise that long-tenure employment relationships are on their way out is simply wrong.

The UK labour market has always required people to change jobs on a large scale as industries fall and rise, new technologies enter the workplace, consumer preferences and tastes alter, the fortunes of localities alter, new business models are developed and new sources of competition challenge incumbents both domestically and from overseas. Moreover, different groups in the labour market have experienced different trends – for example, average tenures have fallen for some men and increased for some women (Gregg and Gardiner, 2015). Yet despite this underlying dynamism the statistical evidence is that the average time people spend in an employment relationship with one employer has not greatly changed in nearly 40 years. In the UK previous research has also found little sign that job stability changed very much between the mid-1970s and mid-1990s (Burgess and Ress, 1996). And as we show below, there has been little change since then.

Before looking at the actual numbers, it is worth noting that the official statistics often refer to 'job tenure' and that is therefore the common description used in many accounts of labour-market change. However, the question asks how long people have been with their current employer and is therefore a better measure of how long employment relationships are lasting than how long jobs exist. In the UK, the average share of long-duration tenures – which we define as employment relationships that have lasted for at least ten years – have increased slightly from 30 per cent of all those in work to 32 per cent between 1996 and 2015, according to the OECD. The average job tenure has remained at around eight years. In other major economies for which we have comparable figures we find similar trends, with the share of long-tenure jobs increasing along with average job tenures. These trends are shown in Table 2.2.

TABLE 2.2 *Increase in long-tenure jobs and average tenures across OECD, 1996–2015*

	Share of long-term tenures (10 years)		Average tenures (years)	
	1996	2015	1996	2015
Canada	28.5%	29.2%	–	–
France	42.3%	46.0%	10.6	11.4
Germany	36.0%	41.2%	9.7	10.6
Italy	45.3%	49.8%	11.1	12.2
UK	30.0%	31.9%	7.8	8.0
US	25.7%	27.3%	–	–

Notes: Employment relationship is time with current employer, US, 1997–2012. No comparable data for Japan.

Source: OECD employment database: https://stats.oecd.org/Index.aspx?DataSetCode=TENURE_AVE

The belief that employment tenures have radically altered is partly because of the influence of a somewhat rose-tinted view of the past, where everyone had a job for life. This was never true for many manual workers and women workers. This narrative nonetheless fitted in with the prevailing view that the labour market was massively deregulated in the 1980s to promote greater flexibility – it wasn't, a point we discuss later in this chapter. A more recent influence may have been the rise of employment in digital services where employment tenures seen remarkably short even in companies which are widely regarded as highly attractive employers. One estimate suggested that the average tenure for an employee at Google was just over one year (Giang, 2013). However, such new tech giants do not directly employ many people and are much more the exception than the rule.

Job insecurity

Some have defined insecurity in terms of employment status and relative pay and tenure. More direct measures rely on individual responses to surveys. Some are measures of job security (how safe do people feel in their current job) and others measures of employment security (how confident do people feel about getting another job). Some definitions are so complex they defy easy or meaningful measurement, with the definition offered by the International Labour Organization (ILO, undated) a prime example:

> Job security is the possession of a niche in work, allowing some control over the content of a job, what the worker actually does and the opportunity he or she has of building a career. Another way of presenting job security is to refer to property rights in a person's work. In other words, whereas employment security refers to the sense of attachment to a current enterprise or establishment, job security refers to the sense of attachment to a particular job or range of tasks.

This is, quite frankly, a muddle of a definition. Job autonomy and progression are very different to job security. Some of the dullest jobs with little autonomy and chance of progression may be very secure. Similarly, jobs that offer a great deal of freedom and high levels of satisfaction and pay may be extremely insecure. Football managers are one of the more extreme examples. Others have invented new words such as the 'precariat' (a combination of precarious and proletariat) as a way of describing the rise of new social classes. This is, however, a hard concept to pin down and attempts to measure it have focused on wider and vaguer concepts such as access to economic and social capital, of which employment and job security are but part.

The OECD has recently developed an employment insecurity index based on more objective and understandable criteria, such as the probability and duration of unemployment and the relative generosity of unemployment benefits compared with the median wage (OECD, 2014c). The OECD index shows that in 2013 the UK (alongside the US) has one of the more insecure labour markets in the OECD, well behind other G7 economies such as Germany, Japan, Canada, France and Italy. This fits the conventional view that deregulated labour markets are insecure labour markets.

However, when UK workers are asked directly about job insecurity, their answers seem to contradict the idea that the UK is an inherently insecure labour market compared with the rest of Europe. The EU's Sixth European Working Conditions Survey (Eurofound, 2015) asked whether people thought their job might be lost in the next six months, with fairly similar results for the UK, Germany and France with much higher levels of concern in Italy. The Survey also asked whether they think getting another job at a similar wage would be easy or hard and workers in the UK were significantly more optimistic than workers in Germany, France and Italy. We always must be a little careful with responses to international surveys, as we may also be picking up differences in national expectations. Nonetheless, there is little here to suggest that UK workers feel more insecure than their European counterparts.

TABLE 2.3 *Perceptions of job and employment insecurity in 2015*

Might lose job in 6 months	EU	UK	Germany	France	Italy
Agree	16%	12%	10%	13%	21%
Disagree	69%	74%	80%	78%	58%
Neither	15%	14%	10%	9%	21%
Easy to get new job same wage					
Agree	36%	49%	38%	40%	22%
Disagree	43%	35%	39%	47%	50%
Neither	20%	17%	23%	13%	28%

Source: Eurofound (2015).

One of the reasons why the worker survey results do not seem to square with the more objective measures of employment protection and security is that the relationship between employment protection and worker insecurity is not straightforward. The basic argument is that flexible labour markets like the UK allow labour to move reasonably quickly from activities where employment is contracting to areas where employment is expanding. This is much less true in labour markets where legal restrictions make it much harder and costly to lay off workers and firms are consequently more cautious about new hires. Sometimes such restrictions create 'dual' labour markets of insiders and outsiders, with permanent full-time insiders protected at the expense of younger, part-time and temporary workers. Some research suggests that, perversely, insiders in more protected labour markets can feel more insecure about future employment prospects because they know it will be more difficult to find another job that offers the same pay, security and benefits (OECD, 2014c).

Job quality

When we look at other indicators of labour-market quality from the same survey the same apparent contrariness of UK workers continues – when asked about good working conditions, satisfaction with work–life balance, satisfaction with the job or whether they had good prospects then the UK tends to sit just below a group of small advanced Northern European economies (the Nordics and the Netherlands) but ahead of Germany, France and Italy, and well ahead of most of the economies of Southern and Eastern Europe.

The Sixth EWCS confirms previous analysis by the CIPD that on most individual indicators of job quality and workplace experience the UK compares well with countries like Germany and France (CIPD, 2015). The EWCS provides two index measures based on answers to several questions to capture what the survey calls 'trust, co-operation and fairness' and 'management quality' which draws on worker perceptions of how their managers treat them. The index scores on both these measures are comparable with or better than the scores for Germany, France and Italy. The portrayal of the UK workplace as producing worse outcomes and poorer-quality jobs than European counterparts is not true.

One reason is that the UK has a lot of good-quality jobs compared with the rest of Europe. Professor Francis Green has used the 2010 Survey data to categorize jobs into four categories – good and well paid, well balanced, poorly balanced and poor (Green and Mostafa, 2012). The UK had a high share of the former and a low share of the latter compared with most other European labour markets. For example, about 65 per cent of jobs might be described as 'good' in the UK (good and well paid plus well balanced) compared with 49 per cent in Germany, 51 per cent in France, and 54 per cent in Italy. More recent UK research from the 2015 British Social Attitudes Survey (BSAS) (McKay and Simpson, 2016) shows that the share of 'good jobs' has increased from 57 per cent to 71 per cent of employee jobs between 1989 and 2015.[2]

TABLE 2.4 *Worker perceptions of workplace fairness and managerial quality in 2015*

Index (0 to 100)	Fairness, Cooperation, Trust*	Management quality**
EU	75	73
UK	75	76
Germany	78	70
France	71	70
Italy	71	68

Notes: *questions on whether treated fairly, whether appreciated, trust between managers and employees, resolving conflicts fairly, fair work distribution and cooperation; **questions on whether managers were respectful, provided praise and recognition and feedback, promoted working together, were helpful, encouraged development.

Source: Eurofound (2015).

Why, then, despite the evidence, do the myths around the quality of work in the UK – and especially in comparison with other major European economies – persist? Professor Francis Green suggests one factor is that that the focus of much research has been on employment protection legislation and its impact on labour markets, with the presumption that less protection must mean worse outcomes (Green, 2013). For some individuals that will be true. But it is a big jump to the conclusion this must also be true for the labour market. Professor Green points out that richer economies tend to have more highly skilled, better-paid jobs, and the UK has an unusually high share of corporate managerial and professional jobs by European standards.

However, even if the UK compares better than some think, it would be wrong to portray UK workplaces as happy places full of enlightened managers overseeing fulfilled workers. The EWCS shows that there are significant minorities – between a quarter and a third of the workforce – where workplace practices are a long way removed from the ideal and the quality of jobs are in some sense poor. For these workers, their jobs offer little satisfaction, they do not have a good work–life balance and they have little in the way of supportive or consultative managers. Moreover, measures of insecurity around employment status – such as fear of arbitrary dismissal, discrimination and victimization in the workplace – all increased between 2000 and 2012, suggesting that for a minority of workers things may have got worse (Gallie et al., 2016).

The BSAS quoted above also suggested that it is not the young, but some groups of older workers who have been at the wrong end of changes in the quality of employment in recent years. Some 70 per cent of those under 34 said they had a good job and 77 per cent said they had a secure job, compared with 63 per cent and 54 per cent of older workers. Indeed, the survey suggests that it is older workers in more routine jobs vulnerable to replacement by technology who have lost out in almost all dimensions – since 2005 feelings of job insecurity have increased (in contrast, they fell for younger workers), a higher share report they are stressed most or all the time and they have less say at work than in the past.

The BSAS also asked people what they wanted from work and whether they thought their job delivered. There was a good match between what people want and what jobs deliver in terms of working independently, helping others, being useful to society and personal contact. However, there were significant gaps on job security and interesting work where over 90 per cent of people rated these as important job attributes but only 65 and 75 per cent respectively said their job provided them. There was, however, a yawning gap between those who thought good prospects of advancement were important (81 per cent) and those who said their job provided this attribute (31 per cent). There was also a significant gap between those who thought a high income was important (66 per cent) and those who thought their job provided one (26 per cent). This is harder to interpret as most surveys suggest most people tend to think they should be paid more than they are, but given that most people will also have experienced falling real wages since 2008 it is perhaps also signalling substantial and growing discontent over wage levels. So, while the quality of work has improved in some dimensions, this is not true for all those in work and for many there remains a big gap between what they think is important in a job and what that job is delivering.

The myth of deregulation

The most commonly held belief is that Anglo-Saxon labour markets like the UK have been extensively deregulated over the past 30 years, leading to a growing divide with the more regulated labour markets of Europe. As a result, it is said, Anglo-Saxon economies have high employment rates and less unemployment, but at a cost of employment becoming more insecure with a high share of poor-quality work and less content workers whose bargaining positions have been undermined by the decline in collective bargaining coverage. As we have shown, the evidence does not support this contention, as least in terms of employment structure or on most dimensions of the quality of work.

The fact is that UK workers have never had high levels of protection by international standards. The OECD publishes an annual index showing the relative strength of employment protection. Between 1985 and 2013 the index shows little change. An updated index covering more recent periods shows a slight strengthening of protections from 2000 onwards which were reversed in 2010. Indeed, with a few exceptions, there has been relatively little change in most OECD countries over the past 20 years.

The big changes in the UK and some other OECD labour markets have been driven much more by the reduced power of trade unions, the deregulation of product markets and extensive privatizations, the rise in educational qualifications, changes to the welfare system and more recently immigration. The deregulation of product markets – such as reducing state control and ownership of industry, and removing barriers to entrepreneurship and foreign trade and investment – across the OECD has been much more extensive and significant than the deregulation of labour markets.

Moreover, employment protection is only part of the regulatory environment that governs the employment relationship and, in many ways, it is significantly more regulated now than it was in the mid-1980s. We have, for example, seen stronger anti-discrimination legislation, new requirements to provide pensions, extensive health and safety requirements (with an enviable workplace safety record as a result), and the introduction of regulations on minimum wages and working time. Controls on employing some non-UK nationals have been introduced and will significantly increase once the Brexit negotiations have been completed to include all non-UK nationals. There may be new regulations governing the employment rights of the self-employed and the obligations of 'gig economy' platform providers to individuals who provide services through their platforms.

The retreat of organized labour as measured by the share of union members in the workforce is often portrayed as a unique achievement of Margaret Thatcher and the Conservative Party administrations of 1979 to 1997. In fact, trade-union membership has been in decline in almost all industrialized economies over the past 30 years. Across the OECD just under 33 per cent of the workforce were trade-union members in 1983 and in 2013 it was down to 17 per cent. Only a handful of countries have bucked the trend (Iceland, Belgium, Spain) (OECD, Trade Union Density). We look at the impact of the retreat from collectivization in the UK in more detail in Chapter 7 on reward and pay.

Self-employment and the gig economy

The rapid rise in self-employment and the creation of many micro-businesses over the past decade in the UK – and especially since 2008 – has been interpreted in different ways. Some see it predominantly as an indicator of structural change towards an economy where small and flexible firms especially those in knowledge-intensive service activities will become more important and offer a credible alternative to more conventional employment opportunities. Others see it as driven by high unemployment and the lack of alternatives, especially in localities where there has been little or no job creation (TUC, 2014). Other evidence based on direct surveys of the self-employed suggest most of the increase in self-employment has been voluntary (Dellot, 2014). As unemployment has fallen since these surveys were conducted, it is likely that most people entering self-employment today do so out of choice.

Despite the recent surge in self-employment, the increase in the share of the workforce who are self-employed over the past 20 years has been modest – up from 13.2 per cent in the first quarter of 1997 to about 15 per cent in the first quarter of 2017. The growth of self-employment in the UK is against the general long-run trend in the rest of the OECD. Between 1995 and 2015 the share of self-employed in the workforce declined in the US, Italy, Japan and France, and remained relatively stable in Germany and Canada. This is shown in Table 2.5.

Most of the increase has been in one-person businesses and there is little direct evidence that this is associated with a new-found enthusiasm for enterprise. A recent analysis by the ONS shows that the flow of people into self-employment has remained much the same over the past 20 years (ONS, 2014b). What has changed is the outflow – people are staying in self-employment for longer. Over the past five years outflows as a share of those in self-employment fell to 23 per cent compared with the long run average of between 32 and 37 per cent.

New forms of self-employment: the gig employment

If prizes were to be given for the gap between hype and reality, the gig economy must surely be in the running for top prize. It is not helped by a variety of

TABLE 2.5 *Self-employment rates across the OECD, 1995–2015*

	1995	2015	Change 1995–2015
Italy	29.3%	24.7%	−4.6
UK	14.9%	14.5%	0.4
Japan	18.3%	11.1%	−7.2
Germany	10.7%	10.8%	0.1
France	10.8%	9.7%	−1.1
Canada	8.6%	8.6%	–
US	8.5%	6.5%	−2.0

Notes: Includes unpaid family workers; US and Canada exclude incorporated self-employed; France is 2011.

Source: OECD: https://data.oecd.org/emp/self-employment-rate.htm

names and labels, some of which are positively misleading. The 'sharing economy' is widely used, but is a contradiction in terms. We share with families and friends and through charitable donations. The economy consists of transactions where goods and services are exchanged for money. A better name is platform economy, by which we mean digital platforms that link providers and customers in different ways. The gig economy is part of the platform economy, where labour services are demanded and supplied through platforms. These labour-service platforms are distinct from capital- and asset-based platforms that allow people to rent property (e.g. Airbnb), sell finished goods (e.g. eBay, Etsy), or provide capital for new ventures (crowdfunding).

Because so much of the increase in self-employment is among people who employ no one, some have seen the rise of the gig economy as a key driver. There is no direct statistical evidence to demonstrate this. Moreover, the impact on employment levels is ambiguous. By creating new markets and expanding existing ones, the platform economy may be adding to total employment by providing new ways in which people can enter work through self-employment.

But it could also just be substituting for old ways of working. In practice both processes are likely to be at work.

Some of the gig economy is concerned with the delivery of physical services such as taxi-driving, shopping, delivery, handyman services, cleaning and babysitting. Online platforms may have allowed a new way of bringing providers and customers together, but it is not obvious this is a revolution in the way we work. Such services have in the past often been delivered by the self-employed and transplanting them onto digital platforms does not change the nature of the service or, often, the employment status of the provider.

Broader concerns that the rise of the gig economy has been at the expense of fewer permanent jobs is not supported by the aggregate figures. However, we cannot rule out some substitution at the margin for minimum-wage employee jobs. A recent survey of Amazon Mechanical Turk workers in the US found that a very large share of the business placed on the site by the private sector came from a very small number of firms who were having the work done at hourly rates paying less than the federal minimum wage (Hitlin, 2016). Nonetheless, the lack of any clear signs of the gig economy in the employment statistics – such as a rise in the number of second jobs – suggests that cannibalization of existing forms of self-employment is likely to be the most important impact on the labour market.

Our view on the available evidence is that the gig economy is growing, but remains small and in the US and the UK largely consists of marginal low-paid work, often undertaken as a supplement to the main household income (Brinkley, 2016). The most recent survey in the UK found that just 4 per cent of people in work had undertaken any form of gig type activity in the last 12 months (CIPD, 2017). This figure cannot be directly compared with employment statistics which ask people what they were doing in the week of the survey. The share of people who in any one week were undertaking gig economy work will be a fraction of this total, especially as people tend to dip in and out of the gig economy as their needs and incomes from other sources fluctuate. US surveys that have attempted to estimate gig-economy activity for much shorter periods come up with figures of less than 1 per cent (Bernhardt and Thomason, 2017).

The gig economy is therefore likely to have a very modest impact on the number of jobs and hours worked in the UK and US labour markets, and an even smaller impact on the number of people in work is modest. In that sense, the labour market is not being subjected to 'Uberization'.

Whether it grows much beyond its marginal status depends on several technological, market, social and regulatory factors that can operate in both directions. For example, technological advance may open more markets and services that can be delivered through online platforms. They may, however, also eliminate some of the low-value-added work that is at present too difficult to computerize or offshore. In the longer term, advances in driverless cars and delivery drones may also reduce some physical services delivered through online platforms, although realistically this is decades away. It has yet to be conclusively demonstrated that the business models that underpin some gig-economy companies is sustainable for the long term in terms of growth and, above all, profitability (Colley, 2017). Regulation could constrain growth in some areas to protect incumbents or enforce changes in employment status (one of the unintended consequences of Uber-style business models is that minicab drivers who would otherwise have remained self-employed will gain greater employment rights as 'workers' in the future).

Choice and atypical work

In this chapter, we have reviewed some of the evidence on the growth of atypical work such as temporary, zero-hours, gig-economy and labour-only self-employment. These have often been inherently inferior to permanent employee jobs because they offer fewer employment rights and confer more bargaining power to employers, leading to greater exploitation. This had led to calls for them to be either banned or severely restricted. A closely related assumption is that workers only enter such contracts out of necessity, not choice, and therefore radical intervention is required to either ban or restrict them. There are indeed many cases of exploitation and patently unfair employment contracts detailed in cases highlighted by the Citizen's Advice Bureau and trade unions, albeit many workers in permanent employment also suffer from abuse at work.

However, it is typically only a minority who say they are in these sorts of contracts because they could not get regular work or because the alternative was unemployment. A combination of the latest official statistics and one-off surveys carried out by different organizations between 2013 and 2017 describe a much more nuanced position than the critics of such working arrangements allow. About 30 per cent of zero-hours contract workers, temporary workers and the self-employed were in these arrangements because of necessity, not choice, while 14 per cent of gig-economy workers said they could not find regular work and 11 per cent of part-time workers said they could not find a full-time job (CIPD, 2017). Most people doing atypical work either appear to be exercising some sort of choice or are indifferent to their employment status. Of course, it is possible that some people responding to such surveys may think such work is the norm and therefore the notion of choice does not arise. Even so, it is hard to imagine possible mis-measurement being so large that it would significantly change the overall picture.

This makes constructive intervention more challenging than the simplistic notion of simply banning some forms of atypical work such as zero-hours contracts, despite the apparent popularity of such measures. It is hard to square the idea of maximizing choice for individuals over how they work over their working lives with such heavy-handed intervention. However, we cannot go to the opposite extreme and say that workers who want regular work should be denied the opportunity just because the majority seems satisfied with their status. Moreover, gig-economy workers seem to be remarkably tolerant of very low rates of hourly income (CIPD, 2017), and it is hard not to conclude that their willingness to work is being taken advantage of by some.

There are measures that can be taken to improve quality and promote choice, such as giving workers a right of conversion of zero-hours and temporary contracts to regular or permanent positions after a period. Efforts to improve worker voice through formal trade-union organization, professional bodies and social media forums all have a role in strengthening bargaining power and improve mutual knowledge of existing employment rights and provide the confidence to seek redress. The latter can be assisted by state organizations and by reducing the cost of access to employment tribunals.

Overall, the way forward is not through crude bans on forms of atypical work but a concerted effort to increase the degree of choice and the quality of work, regardless of employment status. The key tests should be not whether a job offers permanent employee status, but does it offer good work, a strong voice and a genuine choice for the individual supported by minimum standards enforced through employment law.

The role of small firms

The idea that employment is shifting towards small firms is a persistent one, often given credence by general assertions that small firms are 'the backbone of the economy'. Non-pecuniary motives such as being their own boss seemed much more important. A small proportion of new firms and a small proportion of small firms – sometimes termed 'gazelles' – do go on to grow strongly and make a big contribution to job growth. These are, however, very much the exception not the norm for the small-business population (OECD, 2016).

Unfortunately, the state of small-firm statistics makes constructing a consistent measure over time challenging, at least for most European

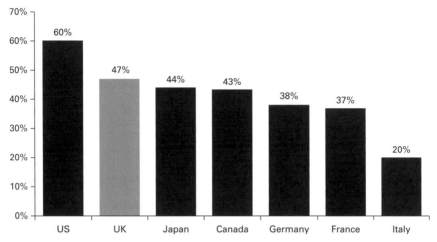

FIGURE 2.2 *Share of business employment in large firms in 2013.*

Notes: Share of all private-sector employment in businesses that employed at least one person. Large firms defined as those with 250 or more employees. All figures 2013 or nearest year.

Source: OECD (2016b).

economies. The best guess for the UK is that the share of employment in small and medium-sized enterprises (SMEs) with at least one employee has not changed much since 1994. Latest estimates from the OECD show that the UK also has one of the highest shares of employment in large firms, at 47 per cent, compared with 38 per cent in Germany and just 20 per cent in Italy. The US, however, has an even higher share of employment in large firms, at around 60 per cent. This is shown in Figure 2.2.

Lovely and lousy jobs

A common criticism of the change in employment is that too many of the new jobs are low paid as well as being insecure. Another common view is that the middle of the labour market is contracting as manufacturing contracts and other routine jobs are lost through automation. As a result, job growth has been concentrated among higher-skill and lower-skill jobs – so both the share of low-paid jobs and the share of higher-paid jobs have increased over time. This trend has been called 'hollowing out' or the 'hourglass labour market' with the equally eye-catching title of 'lovely and lousy' jobs first coined in a research paper by Goos and Manning (2003).

As with most labour-market change, however, the reality has been more complex. While the changes described have indeed taken place they are only half the story. In more recent periods the overall shape has moved away from the hourglass of the 1980s and 1990s to something more like a cocktail glass with net job growth increasingly concentrated in the higher-skill categories. This is shown in Figure 2.3.

However, looking at occupational change is not straightforward as jobs content change, new jobs are added and old jobs drop out and as a result the

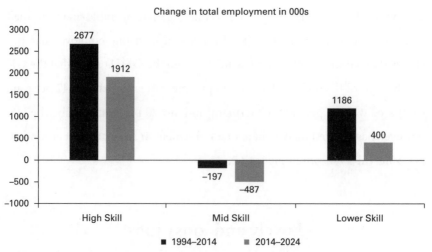

FIGURE 2.3 *Polarization – from hourglass to cocktail glass.*

Notes: high skill is top three occupational categories; mid-skill is skilled manual and administrative and secretarial; lower skill is operatives, sales related, personal and leisure services, unskilled.

Source: UKCES (2014a).

way jobs are classified in the official statistics changes over time. If the shares of both higher-pay employment and lower-pay employment are growing side by side we would expect there to be a clear link with growing wage inequality, but many recent studies find the link at best inconclusive. A recent review of the literature by Business Innovation and Skills (BIS) found that job polarization is not being accompanied by wage polarization and that 'there are as many jobs in the middle percentiles of the wage distribution as ever, just different jobs' (BIS, 2013). A recent study of the US labour market between 2000 and 2007 comes to much the same conclusion: the traditional middle of the US labour market made up of mainly production and clerical workers had indeed contracted but it had been largely replaced by a new middle made up of technical jobs in health care, maintenance and repair, managers in hospitality and retail, and sales reps (Holzer, 2015).

JOHN CRIDLAND

THE STRUCTURE OF THE UK's economy has changed in many ways. Manufacturing has become a highly skilled sector and services businesses have grown substantially. This has supported a growth in the number of professional and highly skilled jobs, replacing middle-skilled and routine jobs. It is the right choice for the UK – we must compete internationally on quality, not cost, and doing so has supported rising wages for workers – but there is a risk of an unhealthy divide between the relatively low-skilled, domestically focused sectors and the relatively professionalized, highly skilled and internationally tradable sectors unless there are clearer routes to gain the skills that help workers to move up.

Businesses, colleges and universities must work together to create more and better ladders that help workers into higher-skilled, higher-paid jobs. In particular, greater focus is needed on vocational routes to in-demand higher skills, and part-time study routes that allow workers to learn and earn at the same time.

Portfolio working

At one stage, it was fashionable to argue that people would develop 'portfolio' careers, holding a multitude of jobs with different employers or combining self-employment with an employee job.

Second-job holding increased in the UK up to the early 1990s, although even then it was not extensive, but has been in decline as a share of the workforce ever since as shown earlier in this chapter. Today, second-job holders make up just 3.5 per cent of the workforce. The trends in the rest of Europe show some increase in second-job holding, especially in France and Germany, but the share of employment has remained low, edging up from just under 3 per cent to just over 4 per cent across the EU15 between 1996 and 2016 according to Eurostat. The portfolio worker, alas, is yet another mix of old wine and wishful thinking of how the world of work ought to be. Many second jobs either reflect long-established working practices or less well-paid individuals trying to increase total income. For some the portfolio career is a reality, but the true portfolio worker imagined by some is still a rare beast.

24/7 working

There is a widespread assumption that unsocial patterns of work must have increased, reflecting the demand for some services to be supplied 24 hours a day and the growth of sectors such as hospitality, retailing and leisure services where many services are required in the evenings and the weekends. It has become cheaper for employers with the erosion of special pay rates for unsocial hour working, with far fewer restrictions on opening hours. In addition, new technologies and globalization have increased the need for people to be available around the clock to service financial and other markets overseas and the development of online shopping may require distribution centres to be in operation on a 24-hour basis.

There has in fact been a significant reduction in unsocial hours working in the UK over the past 20 years, according to the European Labour Force Survey. For example, in 1996 44 per cent of people said they never worked evenings, but this increased to 63 per cent in 2016. For night work, 76 per cent said they never worked nights in 1996 and by 2016 that increased to 84 per cent. The changes of weekend working were even greater – only 35 per cent of the workforce said they never worked on Saturdays, but in 2016 that had increased to just over 60 per cent. For Sunday working, the share who said they never worked increased from 56 per cent to 73 per cent. The trends are more mixed in the rest of the EU, for example, working unsocial hours has also fallen in France and Italy, but increased somewhat in Germany. The UK has become more like our EU neighbours – unsocial hours working was much more extensive in the UK in 1996, but by 2016 the differences had largely vanished.

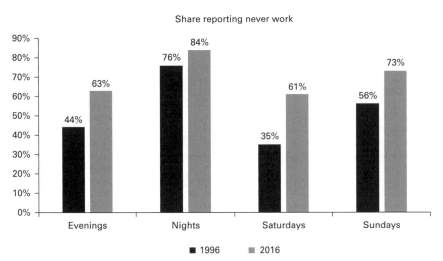

FIGURE 2.4 *Unsocial hours working falls in the UK, 1996–2016.*

Sources: Eurostat: http://appsso.eurostat.ec.europa.eu/nui/show.do?dataset=lfsa_ewpsun& lang=en and http://appsso.eurostat.ec.europa.eu/nui/show.do?dataset=lfsa_ewpsun&lang=en

Part of the explanation in the UK is that unsocial-hours working was common in industries such as manufacturing, mining and agriculture – and these sectors employ fewer people today than they did in 1996. In the remaining high-value manufacturing industries nightshift working may also have become much less common. This decline has helped offset the increase in demand for people to work nights, evenings and weekends in service industries. Moreover, some unsocial-hours work will have been offshored to overseas call centres. Other factors may be the sharp decline in the 'Saturday job' for some young people (UKCES, 2015b). Some 24-hour services can be delivered with relatively small numbers of staff. For example, supermarkets and call centres offering 24-hour access do not need the same level of staffing as they would in peak periods. Finally, it is also possible that while fewer people are involved in unsocial hours, those who do so are working more intensively with more hours than in the past.

The perception of a rise in unsocial-hours working is likely driven by two factors. One is that unsocial-hours working in production sectors such as manufacturing is much less visible than in consumer services. The second is that new technologies make it harder than ever to draw a clear line between work and home. We live in a time when some workers will check and respond to emails outside normal office hours. This intermittent and casual use is also much more difficult to measure than more formalized arrangements.

Migrants are taking our jobs and cutting wages: the myths of Brexit

Public concerns about migration have been with us for decades, if not centuries, with each new wave of migrants causing concerns amongst natives who fear that the new arrivals will deprive them of job opportunities. Immigration has been increasing as a salient issue over the past decade, in part driven by larger-scale migration from the newer EU states. The share of non-UK nationals in the workforce has roughly doubled from just over 7 per cent to just over 11 per cent between 1996 and 2016, according to the ONS, an increase of just over 1.5 million or 72 per cent.

These movements have given rise to concerns that foreigners are taking all the new jobs. Rather contradictory, it is also feared that migrants are coming to take advantage of the UK's more generous unemployment benefits. Concern has also been expressed that they undermine training effort, as firms can recruit skilled labour from overseas rather than making efforts to train up native workers. Additionally, it has been argued that they undercut the low skilled by being willing to work for very low wages while being seen by employers as having a stronger work ethic.

It seems at times as if the popular discourse is that migration has been an unmitigated disaster for the UK labour market. To the extent that this view has driven the Brexit vote, it has also had a huge political impact on the position of the UK in the world, the future regulation of the labour market and prospects for growth and employment. As we show below, few areas illustrate the gulf between the populist view and the economic evidence than on migration.

A recent review of the evidence for the UK by the London School of Economics (LSE) provides a fair summary of the consensus view of migration on employment, unemployment and wages:

> we can confidently say that the empirical evidence shows that EU immigration has not had significantly negative effects on average employment, wages, inequality or public services at the local level for the UK-born. Nor, it should be said, are there large positive effects. Any adverse experiences of UK-born workers with regard to jobs and wages are more closely associated with the biggest economic crash for more than 80 years.
>
> WADSWORTH et al., 2016

The OECD (2016b) published a review of many international studies on the impact at local level on wages, employment and unemployment. This echoes the findings for the UK. Most show either no statistically significant impacts on the employment or wages of natives or very small positive or negative impacts. A recent review of some of the literature by NIESR identifies several channels by which migrants can plausibly contribute to both innovation and productivity growth. The results broadly reflect those for employment, with mildly positive impacts for the UK (Rolfe et al., 2013).

The November 2016 report by the Office for Budget Responsibility (OBR) set out some of the potential costs from Brexit. The OBR forecasts for future growth factor in the impact of net inward migration on overall population growth and on the participation rate – the share of people of working age in work or actively seeking work. The OBR estimates that expected slower growth in migration means that growth will be 1 percentage point lower between 2017 and 2021 as a result. Gross domestic product (GDP) per capita is expected to be 0.3 percentage points lower.

> in the absence of the referendum result we would have revised up cumulative potential output growth by 1.0 percentage point due to higher net migration. On a per capita basis, cumulative growth would have been 0.3 percentage points higher because net migration adds proportionately more to the working-age population than to the total population, thereby boosting the employment rate too.

It remains the case that any institution or commentator who pronounces confidently on the wider impact of Brexit on the labour market is probably going to be proved wrong. Indeed, until we know the shape of UK migration policy, have better insights into whether significant numbers of migrants are going to vote with their feet, and what additional or alternative public policy and employer responses might be forthcoming we cannot say for certain what the economic impact will be. The balance of evidence so far is that it will be negative, but whether it is a marginal impact or something more significant is at present unknowable.

We know that migration has made a significant contribution in terms of employment levels and the employment rate and that contribution has increased over the past decade. The UK is likely to remain an attractive destination for EU migrants from Eastern and Southern Europe given significant differences in unemployment rates and wage levels. Nonetheless, to the extent that the voluntary choices of migrants and the future shape of migration policy reduce labour supply this will show up in economic growth and average living standards being somewhat lower than would otherwise be the case.

It is also likely that a reduced supply of migrants will further increase levels of unfilled vacancies, already at record highs, and skill shortages may become a more serious problem. It is possible that the future supply of high-skilled labour via EU students attending UK universities will decline. As the negative impact of rising migration on the employment prospects and wages of UK citizens has been almost non-existent, we would equally expect any decline in migration to have little or no positive impact at the aggregate level. However, we also expect very little impact on aggregate productivity, as the overall impact of migration has been at best modest.

The impacts will not be felt evenly, and sectors and localities where migrants form an above-average share of the workforce may experience more severe consequences. As migrants tend to be drawn to expanding industries and localities, any significant constraints on future growth in these sectors and areas will hamper the effective operation of the UK economy and labour market.

In principle, many of these negative impacts could be offset by increasing employment growth and the employment rate among UK citizens further compared with the significant increases already achieved over the past decade. We will, however, need to see what additional or alternative policy measures will be forthcoming from future governments to achieve this. It will also depend on the effectiveness of the employer response in retaining migrant labour, developing alternative sources of supply when this becomes necessary and investing in the remaining workforce.

In the final section of this chapter we look at two major trends that will persist over the next 20 years – the non-myths of the labour market. We have touched on how the shape of the labour market is changing with the increasing dominance of high-skill jobs. Below we look at the OECD-wide rise of knowledge-based industries and the professional jobs that go with them. And we also look at the greying of the workforce, as employment rates for older workers start to close the gap with the rest of the workforce – a major change discussed later in this book in more detail.

A knowledge-based world of work

The concept of a knowledge-based economy has been around for decades, and achieved a political profile as the EU set its objective to become the most knowledge-based economy in the world by 2020. The term is now out of fashion and this is a pity as it captured and still captures many of the big changes in both our industrial and occupational structures. Analysis of long trends shows that since the 1970s the share of knowledge-intensive services has increased in all OECD economies; the share of manufacturing employment has fallen and the share of less knowledge-intensive services has remained roughly the same (Brinkley, 2008). The same trends are evident in more recent times. Between 2008 and 2016 employment in knowledge-intensive services (as defined by Eurostat) increased by nearly 9 per cent across the EU27 compared with an increase of less than 1 per cent in total employment. The share of knowledge-intensive service-based employment consequently increased from 37 to 40 per cent of total employment across the EU. In 2016

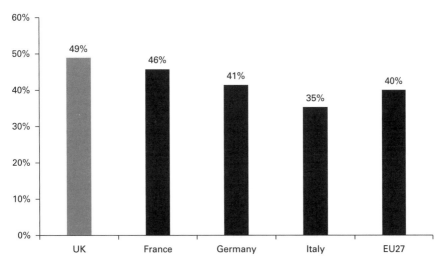

FIGURE 2.5 *Share of employment in knowledge-based services in 2016.*
Source: Eurostat: http://ec.europa.eu/eurostat/cache/metadata/EN/htec_esms.htm

the UK had the second highest share of employment in knowledge-intensive services (behind Sweden) at 49 per cent of total employment. France was on 46 per cent, Germany 41 per cent and Italy 35 per cent.

The rise and rise of the professional classes

The past 20 years has seen the rise of the professional and associated professional worker. Professionals have been one of the biggest drivers of new jobs and have become the biggest single occupation group. Professional regulation and professional style regulation of many non-professional jobs – especially those classified as 'associate professional and technical' – through qualifications, certification and licensing is becoming a critical means of regulating the labour market through both statutory and non-statutory mechanisms.

The UK is not alone in this trend. Between 2011 and 2014 professional and associated professional and technical employment across the EU28 went up by 2.6 million while the employment of skilled and semi-skilled manual workers went down by 2 million. The most important reason for why we have so many professionals is the relatively high share of knowledge-intensive service industries where we have comparative advantage. In Germany and France, the share of professionals in the workforce is between 17 and 18 per cent and in Italy 15 per cent against the UK's 24 per cent. This is shown in Figure 2.6.

Other contributory factors may be the UK's lopsided educational and training system, with a strong higher-education system and weak vocational and technical systems. Germany, for example, has a low share of professionals but a high share of associated and technical workers, reflecting a bigger

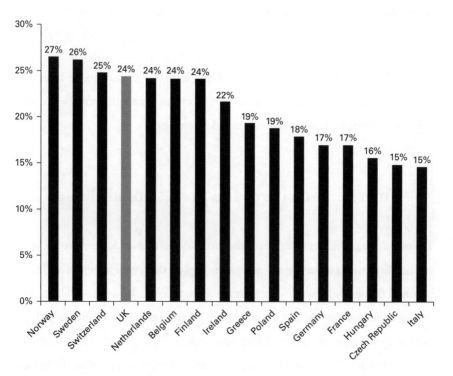

FIGURE 2.6 *Professional jobs as share of total employment in 2016.*

Note: all figures share of people classified as professionals under International Standard Occupational Codes as share of total employment.

Source: Eurostat: http://appsso.eurostat.ec.europa.eu/nui/show.do?dataset=lfsa_eisn2&lang=en

manufacturing base, a smaller knowledge-intensive service sector, and a stronger emphasis on good-quality vocational and technical skills across the economy. But the rise of professionals in the UK workforce may also reflect the desire for both old and new occupational groups to acquire professional status to improve reputation and standards, but also to raise pay and status. Increasingly it is hard to find a group in the top three occupational classifications *not* represented by some form of trade association that claims to promote 'professional' standards.

Regulation by professionalism

Professionalism provides guarantees of appropriate qualifications and by implication a degree of consistency in the delivery of high-quality services, especially where professions are formally regulated. There is good news also for both new and old professional bodies whose membership is likely to expand and whose regulatory role in the labour market – whether backed by statute or not – will increase. However, while some restrictions are both necessary and desirable, making entry too restrictive can reduce labour-market efficiency, increasing wages for those on the right side of the qualification, licensing and certification line at the expense of fewer job opportunities for other workers and higher prices for some businesses and consumers. As more jobs and more occupations become closed for those unable to obtain the 'right' qualifications and meet the requirements for entry, we may be seeing the development of a two-tier labour market where the dividing line is not the employment contract but a mix of statutory and non-statutory entry requirements.

Evidence on the extent of regulation and its labour-market implications is hard to come by, especially outside the United States, but one recent study (Koumenta et al., 2014) by researchers at Queen Mary College (QMC) undertaken for BIS defined regulation as including licensing, accreditation and certification covered by the EU Regulated Professions Directive (although in fact this can also apply to workers in non-professional jobs). In 2012 the UK regulated 131 professions – more than in most others in the EU – but many of these were relatively specialist and there is some evidence from an earlier study commissioned by UKCES that occupations the UK in the past has regulated less intensively than in some other EU states – though the evidence is very out of date (Forth et al., 2011).

The QMC study showed that the share of the UK workforce covered looked in line with other EU countries, but the lack of data meant that researchers had to give an upper and lower estimate on the share of the workforce professionally regulated with the accurate figure lying somewhere in between the two. The UK professional regulated workforce was somewhere between 10 and 21 per cent. However, for some countries the range is huge – 13 to 43 per cent in Denmark and 4 to 31 per cent in Germany for example. The UKCES study cited above covered all occupations – including relatively newly regulated occupations such as security guards and child-care workers – and found that 'at least' 28 per cent of all jobs were subject to some form of 'professional' regulation in 2010 but that the true figure could be anywhere between 33 and 50 per cent. In truth, we do not know what the extent of professional-type regulation is, how fast it is growing and what its aggregate impact will be – but clearly it is likely to be significant.

US studies suggest that professionalism has, in some cases, resulted in higher wages and prices than would otherwise be the case. Not surprisingly, professional groups have typically been big advocates of licensing, even for occupations where it is not self-evident why the state should be regulating entry at all. For example, some US states require interior designers to have a licence. A recent study (Gittleman and Kleiner, 2013) concluded that professional regulation now covers a bigger share of the workforce and extracts a bigger wage premium than was ever the case for trade unions. In 2008 about

28 per cent of all US workers in a survey said they required a licence to practise compared with 12 per cent who said they were union members (and 17 per cent covered by collective agreements).

We are not yet at that point in the UK, although the trends are clear – the trade unions of the twenty-first century will be a mixture of the traditional trade union and professional organizations exercising influence on wages and employment with and without the sanction and support of the state. Getting that balance right between protection of the public, ensuring confidence and security, and not imposing excessive entry requirements on jobs that do not require universally high levels of qualification remains a major challenge.

The grey workforce

ELLA BENNET

I THINK THE IDEA OF a large ageing workforce is a myth. True, life expectancy is increasing and the period 'after work' needs to be financed – and at present governments and society in general can only think of working longer, to an older age. This is ignoring the undoubted impact of game-changing technology (second half of the chess-board issue – we are starting to see the real impact of geometric rather than what has felt like linear progression in the impact of technology on daily life). The real question is more to do with how society copes with us all living longer.

However, in the short term, a longer working life might be useful, as it alleviates some of the pressure on knowledge transfer.

Recognizing the risk of knowledge loss though redundancy or retirement is not new – and much has been done to develop approaches that ensure knowledge is captured and shared. Additionally, we know that younger people (such as our apprentices and graduates) are less likely to be concerned by change than many 50- to 60-year-olds in the current workforce. These younger people are already living comfortably with ambiguity and have the expectation of (technology-driven) change. (As an example, most

50-year-olds dread having to change their mobile phone or computer; younger people queue up all night to buy the newest iPhone, as they see it (correctly) as simply a device to connect to their (and other people's) data in the cloud ...). Recognizing and using this gives an organization such as Fujitsu an opportunity and an advantage – that of reverse mentoring – or to put it more emotively 'learning from the young'.

One of the bigger underlying changes in the workplace is that the workforce is getting older and people over 50 are now much more likely to be in a job than in 1997. In 1997 the employment rate (the share of the population in work) for those between the ages of 50 and 64 was just under 59 per cent. For over 65s it was just under 5 per cent. By 2017 the employment rate for these two age groups was just over 71 per cent and just over 10 per cent respectively. As a result, the share of the workforce over 50 has increased from 23 per cent to 32 per cent. The increase of older women in the workforce has been even more pronounced, with the employment rate for those between the ages of 50 and 64 increasing from just over 50 per cent to 66 per cent. The share of older women in the female workforce over 50 has consequently increased from 21 per cent in 1997 to 31 per cent today.

These trends are also evident across most OECD economies. The international data for comparison is for the age group 55 to 64 rather than 50 to 64, as in the UK national data, but the overall picture is the same. Employment rates for older workers have increased in all major economies, sometimes dramatically. For example, the employment rate for 55- to 64-year-olds in Germany has increased from 38 per cent to 69 per cent between 1996 and 2016. In contrast, the increase in employment rates in the US has been very modest, up from 56 per cent to 62 per cent, but in contrast to most other OECD countries employment rates for 'prime age' workers in the US have been falling.

In Chapter 8 we look at the reasons behind these trends and the implications for the workplace and workforce, and how we need to adapt both policy and practice to minimize the challenges and take advantage of the opportunities that an ageing workforce brings.

Conclusions

Many of the assertions that through repetition seem to have become established 'facts' are nothing of the kind. Over the past 20 years there has been no significant shift towards contingent labour and average employment relationships are growing not falling. The formal boundaries between office and home remain stubbornly resistant to change, and the 24/7 society has had little impact on unsocial-hours working. There has been no shift towards low-wage work. We are not becoming a more entrepreneurial society. And migrants are not taking the jobs or reducing the wages of native workers.

What is happening is that we are shifting towards an economy where knowledge-intensive services and knowledge-intensive activities – especially focused on the promotion of professionalism – are growing. The workforce is greying, making the concept of the conventional working age cut off at 64 redundant. There is little sign of the workforce turning back to collective organization in the workplace as a response to the Great Recession. And the possibility is opening that we may be able to return to the full-employment labour market of the past – provided a second global economic downturn does not intervene.

There nonetheless remains a huge gap between the perceptions of what is happening to the labour market and what the aggregate national data tell us, not least on migration. Why should that be so? We suggest at least three reasons:

- First, dynamic labour markets create winners and losers and the position can look very different depending on what you do and where you live. The view from the depressed seaside towns and older industrial areas of England is inevitably going to be radically different to that from the booming metropolitan economies of London, Manchester and Leeds. This was clearly shown in the recent Brexit vote. Even within these cities we find huge discrepancies between haves and have-nots. The general rise of inequality over the past 40 years in many OECD economies has widened the gap between those who gain and those who lose out.

- Second, some gains are widely spread and taken for granted but losses are highly concentrated and very visible. For example, many people benefit from automation and globalization delivering better services and lower prices – think of internet shopping and cheap consumer electronics. But those who lose their job in retail and manufacturing as a result are bound to be less sanguine and are unlikely to be comforted by rising living standards for those in more secure jobs and the generation of new jobs in other parts of the economy which they may not be qualified to reach. This disconnect between gains and losses has been intensified by an unprecedented period of falling real wages, so that the benefits from globalization and other changes to the economy have become even less tangible to a majority of the workforce.

- Third, the 'lump of labour' fallacy – the belief that there is a fixed number of jobs – has a strong grip on the popular discourse because it seems to accord with ordinary experience. Hence, more migrants *must* mean fewer jobs for native workers, and older people staying on in work *must* reduce opportunities for the young. In the past similar arguments were used to say that married women should stay at home and not take jobs way from breadwinning men.

Significant changes do of course happen – the rise and fall of industries can be rapid in response to changes in technologies and markets and sometimes big economic shocks. Yet in some ways the basic structure of the UK labour market has changed slowly over time: it is better described as a 'steady-eddy' than a 'hurricane'. But it is inside the workplace where often the more significant changes in the organization of work are taking place – often beyond the reach of regular statistical measure. It is change in the workplace that is the focus of the rest of this book.

3

The global workforce

This chapter looks at some of the big changes that are operating on a global level (by which we mean they tend to affect large numbers of countries, whether in the OECD or across the emerging economies) that could impact on the world of work and the levels of employment and unemployment over the next decade or so – though sometimes we take a longer time perspective because some of the changes will only play out over the next 20 to 30 years.

As in Chapter 2, we have based our insights on current evidence, which is sometimes dull. We intend to spare the reader silly titles or using the word 'Great' or 'Mega' to describe a trend. Self-styled 'gurus'[1]and 'futurologists' also have no place in our book, at least not to be taken seriously (Appleyard, 2014).

Readers will perhaps have already seen that from Chapter 2 we are sceptical about claims that the structure of work has changed radically. We therefore expect many of the features of the labour market of today we summarized at the end of that chapter to also be present in 2025. Where things are changing, they are often well established and well known such as the growth of higher-skill work and the ageing of the workforce.

The biggest area of uncertainty is the rise and fall of industries and activities within them where technological disruption and the impact of global markets is at its greatest. The corporate landscape may be different, as existing incumbents in fast-moving industries are toppled by new challengers which are just as likely to be coming from China and India as the US or Europe. We still expect the overall share of employment in more knowledge-intensive industries to increase but expect a lot of coming and going below the aggregate level in some parts of the private sector.

We look at the following major trends:

- the rise of the BRICS who may or may not be coming for our lunch (Connor, 2011);

- the 'Great Doubling' and other 'Greats';

- population ageing and the 'Great Shrinking' (only joking);

- will all the jobs be offshored?;

- the coming of the robots and the second machine age;

- human enhancement (we indulged in one speculation).

The rise of the BRICS

People could be forgiven for thinking the world is about to be taken over by the BRICS (initially Brazil, Russia, India and China, with South Africa added in 2010) and other regional groupings with equally catchy sets of initials. In the 1990s, we had the Asian Tigers – small fast-growing economies that some pundits argued were the template for the future. As the Russian, Brazilian and Indian economies all stumbled, the focus switched to other potential candidates such as Turkey, Indonesia and South Africa – though at the time of writing India had crept back into fashion again. India and China at least share the common characteristic of having very large populations and China has been growing very strongly. That these economies will have a higher share of world GDP in the future is as near as a certainty as we can imagine.

This is in line with historical experience – faster-growing newcomers will take a bigger share of world trade and output, as they always have and always will. This shift will have important implications, not least in international economic and political relationships, but the issue we focus on is whether the rise of BRICS (or some other combination) depresses living standards and employment in the current OECD economies. So relative GDP per head is a better indicator of whether we will prosper or not in a future world economic system that gives equal weight to China, India and some other economies as it does today to the United States, Japan and Europe.

The economist Andre Sapir has undertaken some work for the OECD in 2014 looking 50 years ahead based on current endowments and trends on what will happen to shares of world trade and GDP per head in 2050 (Sapir, 2014). The shift in the share of world trade is confirmed – in 2011 about 66 per cent of world trade was accounted for by the current OECD and in 2060 this is expected to decline to 42 per cent. The share of India and China increases from 22 per cent to 46 per cent, most of which is accounted for by the increase in China's *domestic* economy.

In 2011 the top 20 economies in the world were a familiar list of Northern and Western Europe, North America and Japan. And in 2050 the picture is much the same. Individual economies move up and down, partly reflecting the comparative severity of permanent economic losses from the 2008 crisis and more fundamental problems such as ageing populations. The main losers are the Southern European economies with France, Italy, Spain, Greece and Portugal all falling down the rankings. The UK remains at 14th place in both years. But what about the BRICS? What we see in the projection is China closing the gap, so by 2050 it squeezes into the top 30 (and in doing so overtakes many of the Southern European economies on their way down). The rest remain where they currently are – Russia just outside the top 30, Brazil and India just inside the top 40.

Of course, these projections can just as easily be criticized as no more than speculative. Sapir himself thinks they are too conservative and conventional, and dominated by recent economic events such as the 2008 crash. They cannot easily take account of the impact of another global financial disaster, climate change or political instability. Some individual countries could improve their rankings by undertaking far-reaching internal reforms and others might start to drift down the rankings because of unwise decisions. It will be interesting to see whether the recent election in France of a reform-minded president and the UK's pursuit of Brexit have any impact on the relative positions of France and the UK. However, nothing published since Sapir's original work suggests that the overall picture is going to be very different. The idea that the prosperity of the average citizen in the existing OECD economies is under threat from the rise of the non-OECD G20 economies over the next, say, 20 years is not very plausible.

TABLE 3.1 *BRICS and the G7 OECD economies by GDP per head, 2011–2050*

OECD	Rank in 2011	OECD	Rank in 2050	Change
United States	2	United States	2	0
Canada	9	Canada	7	+2
Germany	12	Germany	13	−1
UK	14	UK	14	0
Japan	17	Japan	11	+6
France	18	France	23	−5
Italy	21	Italy	29	−8
BRICS		**BRICS**		
Russia	32	Russia	32	0
Brazil	37	Brazil	39	−2
China	40	China	27	+13
India	41	India	41	0

Source: Sapir (2014).

Even so, it has long been argued that globalization – by which we mean greater international trade – poses a threat to jobs and the quality of work in many OECD economies. In this world, transnational corporations can take advantage of global labour markets awash with well-educated labour to drive down wages and reduce the autonomy of all but a relatively small elite of workers in the West.

There is, however, no historical association between greater trade and rising unemployment in the West. Instead we have seen the reverse. In most OECD economies, the unemployment rate has fallen over the past 20 years despite a big increase in the importance of trade as a share of GDP. Unless we think the relationship between employment and trade is going to change in some fundamental way, there seems no good reason to think that more trade over the next 20 years is likely to be associated with higher unemployment.

The OECD, in a book published in 2013 (Huwart and Verdier, 2013), concluded that while globalization could have some negative impacts on jobs in the West, overall it had created more jobs than it has destroyed especially over the period since 2008. Moreover, the OECD says that while globalization can create greater wage inequality, the impact of new technology and domestic policies such as welfare, labour-market regulation and support for collective bargaining together have bigger impacts. Globalization gets the blame for many adverse trends in labour markets which are essentially home-grown within the rich economies of the world or are driven by entirely different causes.

The 'Great Doubling' (and other 'Greats')

Richard Freeman in an influential paper published in 2006 entitled 'The Great Doubling' argued that the opening of the BRICS to international trade had effectively doubled the size of the global labour force but added relatively little to the global stock of capital (Freeman, 2006). With cheap labour so abundant, bargaining power would inevitably swing to capital undermining employment conditions and threatening jobs. Freeman was, however, rather more optimistic than this summary might suggest. He argued that:

> by bringing modern technology and business practices to most of humanity the triumph of global capitalism has the potential for creating the first truly global labour market. Barring social, economic, or environmental disasters, technological advances should accelerate, permitting huge increases in the income of the world and eventually rough income parity among nations that will 'make poverty history'.

This was of course written before the financial crash of 2008 when global capitalism demonstrated its more destructive side. Moreover, even if the benign impacts of new technologies and modern business practice came to pass, it would take many decades for them to have positive impacts on the global labour market, argued Freeman. In the meantime, how the OECD economies handled the transition – for example, through policies on education and skills, investment in new technologies and science, stronger collective bargaining institutions and better social welfare nets – would determine the impact on their labour markets.

It is easy to be impressed by the huge numbers when talking about the Chinese and Indian labour markets. Indeed, the global workforce could be 3.5 billion strong by 2030 according to an estimate by the McKinsey Global Institute (Dobbs et al., 2012), a number so large it is hard to imagine. However, much of this labour is poorly educated and effectively disconnected from the global labour market in any meaningful sense. The International Labour Organization (ILO) has recently estimated that over 80 per cent of the workforce in low-income countries and over 50 per cent of the workforce across mid-income countries are made up of own account and informal family workers, compared with about 10 per cent across the OECD (ILO, 2015). The same McKinsey report quoted above estimated that by 2020 about 1 billion people in the global workforce will still lack any secondary education.

Of course, the share of wage and salary workers who might potentially compete with Western workers is undoubtedly increasing in non-OECD economies as people leave agriculture and rural areas and move to industry and service-sector jobs in the cities. But also, according to the ILO the share of workers employed in global supply chains in non-OECD economies is not increasing. This is partly because some export-facing enterprises and activities are capital rather than labour intensive and partly because employment growth in domestic activities has been faster. The creation of truly global labour markets through the 'Great Doubling' and the creation of truly global labour markets is likely to be a slow process.

Moreover, while it is commonplace to highlight the fact that China and India are producing far more graduates than the West, it is a big mistake to assume that they are also of a similar quality. The Indian National Association of Software and Services Companies notes that while India has vastly expanded the number of places for engineering graduates to around 1.5 million, about 75 per cent of technical graduates and 85 per cent of general graduates are said to be unemployable in India's own high-tech services industries and are even thought to be unsuitable to work in call centres (Anand, 2011). A study published by researchers at Stanford University in 2013 found that graduates produced by the BRICS economies had more than doubled between 2000 and 2010 to some 40 million. However, in India and China most were coming out of lower-quality mass institutions rather than the elite institutions that can match the better Western universities (Donald, 2013). A more recent article by the Associated Chambers of Commerce and Industry of India suggests many of these concerns remain (ASSOCHAM, 2016).

This of course will and is changing as educational quality rises in China and India. Chinese institutions are already appearing in the top ranks of global indices of university excellence and more will follow. This will add to the global stock of knowledge and the capacity to exploit it – the pace of new scientific discovery and the refinement of what we think we know already will increase. The ability to forge strong connections between Chinese and other top institutions in the emerging economies and Western universities will therefore become even more important. However, this will not happen overnight and for the foreseeable future there will be continued strong demand from the middle classes of China and India to educate their sons and daughters at top educational institutions in the West. Moreover, many of the better graduates from China and India will be in high demand by Chinese and Indian companies to serve their own huge domestic markets as their own economies restructure towards more knowledge-intensive activities.

If competition from the massive expansion in highly skilled labour globally was having adverse impacts, we might expect it to show up in the wages of Western graduates compared with non-graduates. We can see no such effects. The graduate wage premium has remained constant or has even increased in most OECD economies. Across the OECD, graduates earned just under 50 per cent more on average compared with those with a higher secondary education in 2000 and 55 per cent in 2014 (OECD, 2014a, 2016a). The idea of a big threat to the wages and jobs of graduates in the West from the expansion of well-educated workforces in the rest of the world is hugely exaggerated.

A world of labour shortages

In the previous chapter we looked at the ageing of the workforce in the UK. The demographics apply even more in the future, with a divide within both the OECD and amongst the emerging economies between economies where the workforce could contract and countries where it is likely to expand, according to the Boston Consulting Group (BCG) (Strack et al., 2014). Between now and 2030 the workforce in countries such as Germany, Japan and Italy is expected to shrink, while the US, UK and Canada will continue to expand. Among the emerging economies, the workforces are expected to shrink in China and Russia and expand in India and Brazil. The McKinsey Global Institute report quoted above estimates that by 2050 the working-age populations of Russia, Japan, Germany and Poland will have shrunk by around 30 per cent, China and Italy by between 15 and 20 per cent. So, the 'Great Doubling' will in some countries turn into the 'Great Shrinking'. Even in countries where the workforce continues to expand, the BCG estimates the demand for labour will start to outstrip supply. By 2030 most of the world will be facing labour shortages. This is not good news for the growth rate and the improvement in living standards unless we can find other sources of labour supply or improve the average productivity of each worker employed.

These projections are of course just that – they are based on UN population estimates and assume no great change in current participation rates or rates of migration and use past performance on productivity and growth as an indicator of what will happen over the next ten to twenty years. These could change – countries facing shrinking workforces could adopt policies to encourage more older workers and women to enter the workforce, they could increase net inward migration rates or they could increase the productivity of existing workers. Social and economic changes can influence the birth rate. Long-term demographic projections are therefore just as likely to be wrong as long-term economic forecasts.

Some of these variables are easier to change than others. Participation is probably the least challenging. As we noted in the last chapter, retirement ages have been increasing in most OECD economies. Many economies have also successfully increased the participation of women. In contrast, domestic resistance to large-scale migration has become an almost universal political reaction across the OECD. Improving productivity across the OECD has also proved a challenge – indeed, since 2008 the productivity growth rate has declined significantly. A recent report from McKinsey (Manyika et al., 2015) claims to have identified major opportunities to improve productivity in most major OECD and emerging economies. Historical experience tells us it is easier to identify opportunities than to exploit them in a way that increases the productivity performance of the whole economy.

It can be hard to imagine a world where we worry much more about labour shortages than whether there will be enough work for everyone, especially when looking at high unemployment rates and under-employment across the world today. Indeed, the two may persist side by side, with acute labour shortages in some industries and activities and large numbers of unemployed who reside in areas of industrial decline or lack the education, skills or experience to fill the vacancies that exist. Policies that address both the spatial distribution of employment and workforce mobility, as well as investment in education and training are likely to be even more badly needed in the future.

All the jobs will be offshored

When concerns at offshoring were at their height, some seemed to think that services would be hollowed out in the same way as manufacturing with claims that up to 20 per cent of US jobs were in danger of being offshored (Levine, 2012). Other assessments have attached the label the 'Great Unbundling' to a series of related changes driven by globalization and new technologies that once again would threaten employment in advanced industrial economies (Baldwin, 2006). In recent US presidential elections, the export of US jobs to low-wage economies became a major issue for the leading contenders. The language can certainly be colourful, with offshoring described as a bigger threat to the US than terrorism and at the root of many of America's economic and social ills (Roberts, 2010).

One problem is that offshoring is an elastic term, sometimes called offshoring in the commonly understood shift of services to low-wage economies such as call centres and back-office processing centres. But a broader term, offshoring outsourcing, embraces both the decline of largely blue-collar employment in sectors exposed to international competition which has been affecting most OECD economies for decades and the newer shift in service-based employment enabled by new technologies and rising levels of education. It can also cover jobs lost because of competition with relatively high-wage economies (the car industry) and jobs lost to low-wage economies (some consumer electronics, call centres, back-office processing services).

In 2007 the OECD undertook an extensive study (OECD, 2007) that concluded that the offshoring of services did not have the adverse impacts on overall employment that were claimed, but in some cases it did accelerate the shift towards higher-skill job generation and like all changes in trade patterns and technologies it caused disruption in labour markets. However, while the dis-benefits of offshoring can be glaringly obvious – for example, a large company announcing it is cutting jobs because some activities are being offshored to India – the benefits to the economy from lower prices and higher productivity are much more general and harder to quantify.

Popular concerns about offshoring seem to have faded somewhat in Europe, as the evidence suggests that offshoring is neither as extensive or as destructive of overall employment as had been feared (*The Economist*, 2013). In recent years there has been some limited 'reshoring' of jobs as companies move facilities back to domestic markets to take advantage of shorter and more manageable and responsive supply chains in fast-changing consumer markets. The Engineering Employers Federation (EEF) found that one in six UK manufacturing companies had reshored at least some of their activities in recent years (Hopley, 2014). However, it has proved hard to come up with a reliable figure for exactly how many jobs might be affected. The best guess is that it is likely to remain modest. A recent assessment from the Ditchely Foundation concluded that:

There was a near consensus that re-shoring had been hyped in the media, that it was still too soon to conclude that it was a major trend (the evidence was mostly anecdotal so far), and that there were more important and interesting things happening in the world of manufacturing.

THE DITCHLEY FOUNDATION, 2014

The bigger changes within manufacturing sectors across the OECD are much more likely to be driven by two changes that will push in opposite directions. First, manufacturers typically want to locate production closer to their biggest markets and in the future the focus will still be on the growing economies in non-OECD Asia. So new investment and the jobs that go with it will be drawn overseas. However, in most OECD economies the line between manufacturing and services is blurring, so that the share of jobs in manufacturing that are service based is increasing – jobs such as management, design, marketing, and research and development. In 2012 around half of all jobs in manufacturing in France, the UK, Germany and the US were service based, according to the OECD (De Backer et al., 2015). These are typically harder to shift overseas than production jobs.

The robots are coming for our jobs

Much attention has been given to a recent academic report (Frey and Osborne, 2013) that suggested up to 50 per cent of jobs in the US could be affected by automation, including the introduction of robotics. An estimate by the Bruegel research centre has applied the same methodology of the original US study quoted above to the EU (Bowles, 2014). Surprisingly, the share of jobs at risk does not seem to vary very much for most EU states, at between 50 and 55 per cent. This is despite countries having very different economic, employment and industrial structures and very different capabilities when it comes to technological change. Less responsible commentators have ignored the cautions and caveats of the original authors, and stated that work as we know it is under threat from extensive automation. This plays to a widespread fear of the potential employment impact of robots, sustained by 'surveys' of dubious scientific value.

A more sober and soundly based but less well-known OECD study suggested that the pace of technological change is much slower than some had assumed (OECD, 2016b). It is not enough for something to be technologically possible. It must be produced at the right price and perform reliably and safely under actual conditions. It must pass official regulatory barriers to show it is safe and complies with all relevant regulations and controls. There must be a market demand and public acceptability (TNS Opinion & Social, 2012). In some circumstances, large-scale complementary investments may be required. Driverless cars are a good example of a new technology that is barely at the starting gate in overcoming all these barriers to implementation on a significant scale, and yet has prompted claims that US truck and taxi drivers will be put out of work in large numbers over the next decade.

The OECD also points out that it is comparatively rare that a job can be automated entirely. It is much more common for some tasks to be automated in jobs that are otherwise hard to automate. Looking across 21 countries, the OECD finds that on average about 9 per cent of jobs might be automated. In the US, the figure is 10 per cent compared with the 47 per cent in the study quoted above. Where they both agree is that full automation will have much bigger impacts on people with low education and on low-income households.

If there has been one consistently wrong prediction over the past 40 years, it has been that robots would be widely used not just at work but also in the home. Robots have indeed become an increasing presence on production lines and in some processes, but are still a long way from the dreams of science-fiction writers. More generally, new technologies which automate processes previously carried out by people have in the past been seen as heralding the end of work or at least the end of work as we know it. In every OECD economy, however, the number of people in work has continued to rise despite the adoption of successive waves of new tech. Experience suggests new tech is not a jobs killer for the economy.

But what new tech undoubtedly can be is a major disruptive force. Some analysts are concerned that the next wave of technologies will reinforce an existing trend towards 'skill-biased technological change' but potentially affecting different groups than in the past. The argument is that new technologies reward some workers with the relevant skills, such as cognitive and creative abilities, but displace others for whom the only alternative is much lower-paid and lower-skilled work. New techs do indeed kill off some jobs, even if they allow others to flourish. They can push the wages down for some groups of workers and drive up the wages for others. They can open sectors to international competition previously shielded and intensify the pressure on those already operating in the global economy. They can cause radical changes in industrial structure, with the rise of new industries and activities and the fall of others. They cause widespread changes in organizations as conventional business models fall apart and must be re-thought. And the pace at which they are being introduced is speeding up across the globe.

How well or badly economies and societies handle these changes will often determine the extent to which they cause lasting damage – the sort of policies that would ensure a 'good transition' from the threat of low-wage competition would also help achieve a better outcome for those on the receiving end of technological change.

The adverse impacts of disruptive technologies can be mitigated by effective and responsive systems, institutions and organizations that provide retraining for workers with redundant skills, and equip young people and others with relevant skills for the future. Such measures can also attract new investment to the areas worst affected and help those who can to move to new areas of opportunity.

We can get some sense of the dynamics of the labour market from a recent OECD study that looked at the impact on jobs at different educational levels of new technologies, trade and consumption. Technologies and trade destroyed about 9 million jobs in the UK economy between 1995 and 2008, but technology and trade also helped drive total employment by creating new markets, increasing living standards through lower prices, and boosting innovation. As a result, consumption created nearly 13 million new jobs over the same period, providing a net boost to employment of just under 4 million.

These trends were different for those with high levels of educational attainment (a university degree) and everyone else. New technologies had a positive impact on the employment of those with degrees and trade had a relatively small impact, so trade and technology together created just over 1 million jobs for those with degrees in the UK between 1995 and 2008, and consumption another 3 million. For those with low educational attainment, the story is less positive. Trade and technology destroyed 7 million jobs and while consumption added 4 million jobs, it still meant a net loss of 3 million jobs for

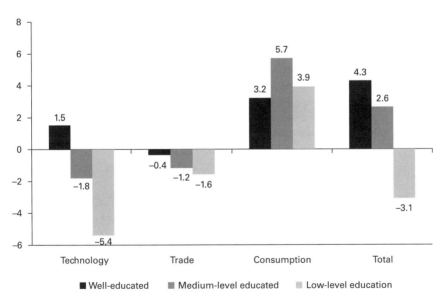

FIGURE 3.1 *Impact of technology, trade and consumption on jobs in the UK, 1995–2008 (millions of jobs by educational level).*

Source: Los et al. (2014).

those who are poorly educated. This is the basic arithmetic that has seen the shift of employment in most OECD economies away from those with low educational attainment and towards those with high educational attainment.

Neither of these trends should be thought of as exceptional. It is how dynamic labour markets work. The pace of change may be accelerating, especially in fast-changing areas associated with the digital and internet economies, but the nature of that change is not fundamentally different from the past. There are differences between OECD economies – consumption effects have, for example, been very weak in Japan reflecting the long-standing period of economic stagnation in that economy.

The second machine age

Some see the new technologies as genuinely transformative, offering a significant boost to growth and productivity and ultimately to employment, albeit with the disruptive impact we described above. The decline in productivity performance across most of the OECD in recent decades is characteristic of previous waves, where an initial fall is followed by a rebound. One recent book by Andrew McAfee and Erik Brynjolfsson talks about a second machine age where as the authors argue:

> Many have concluded that the era of large-scale technological unemployment has finally arrived. For these observers, labour trends visible in many countries – declining real wages and social mobility; rising inequality and polarisation; persistently high unemployment – are only going to accelerate as technology races ahead. But the world is not ready to give up on human labour. Humanity is entering a second machine age. The first, spurred by the industrial revolution, was mechanical; this one is digital. The first augmented our muscles; the second, our minds.

Others take a more pessimistic view, and suggest that the big innovations from new technologies have all been exhausted and that the next wave are so far away they can have no impact on the economy for many years. An article in *The Economist* asked the question 'Has the ideas machine broken down?' before concluding that it had not (*The Economist*, 2013a). Ultra-pessimists can nonetheless argue that the next big wave of new technologies will drive growth but not jobs, so we get mass technology-driven unemployment; or the lack of big-scale technological change means growth and productivity languish and unemployment remains high and living standards fall.

For this to happen would require some fundamental changes in the basic dynamics of economic and technological change we have outlined for new technologies to destroy jobs faster than they can be created. It is hard to disagree with the conclusions of the US economist David Autor who reaches back to the 1960s debate about how new technologies were going to create mass unemployment:

> I recall the observations of economist, computer scientist, and Nobel laureate Herbert Simon (1966), who wrote at the time of the automation anxiety of the 1960s: 'Insofar as they are economic problems at all, the world's problems in this generation and the next are problems of scarcity, not of intolerable abundance. The bogeyman of automation consumes worrying capacity that should be saved for real problems . . .' A half century on, I believe the evidence favors Simon's view.
>
> AUTOR, 2015

Look far enough ahead to the creation of full artificial intelligence and highly advanced robotics, and all bets are off, leading to either a dystopian or utopian future depending on the assumptions made. Science-fiction writers are very good at imagining what such futures would look like, and we should leave such speculation to them. Whether we call it a second machine age or some other catchy label, the prospect of mass unemployment caused by new technologies is remote on any reasonable time-scale.

Human enhancement

However, one area that may be more significant is sometimes called 'human enhancement' and it is potentially moving us into unknown territory when it comes to work, as a recent report from some UK-based scientific institutions makes clear (The Royal Society, 2012). The report from the Royal Academy and others says:

> Work will evolve over the next decade with enhancement technologies potentially making a significant contribution. Widespread use of enhancements might influence an individual's ability to learn or perform tasks and perhaps even to enter a profession; influence motivation; enable people to work in more extreme conditions or into old age, reduce work-related illness; or facilitate earlier return to work after illness.

As ever, such debates have already attracted rather confusing labels such as bio-conservatives and techno-progressives.

Some enhancements are familiar and have a very positive impact – for example, improvements to mobility, hearing and eyesight allow people to perform a wider range of tasks in the workplace, extend working lives and provide new opportunities for employment. Successfully applied on a large scale, future development of such enhancements could help significantly increase the employment rates for those suffering from some form of physical disability. These will not however be limited just to those with disabilities. For many years plastic surgery has been used not just to correct for physical abnormalities or improve mental well-being, but to enhance physical looks in the belief that this will improve the chances of employment and success in some creative activities.

Few people would have concerns about restoring lost or impaired functions so that people can work or retain employment, and have better and fuller lives. However, the possibility exists that technological advances could mean that movement, sight and hearing for some could be better than the human norm. Indeed, the most recent improvements in laser eye surgery can give some patients better than 20/20 vision (Stern, 2013). It may be a little far-fetched to think a future job advert would say 'enhancement an advantage' but clearly some jobs could be done for longer and more efficiently by enhanced workers. Even more controversial is the use of drugs to improve memory and concentration. Some such as Ritalin are used by some students today. The impact of the drugs available today seems to be modest, with widespread scepticism that they really help even among some student populations, according to the Royal Academy report. In Chapter 4 we look at the implications of enhancement for the future workplace in more detail.

Conclusions

The world is changing, as it always has. But if we fast forward to, say, 2025 or even 2050, what would we expect to see? China closing the gap with the rest of the OECD and most others struggling to make headway? More new technology in workplaces and automation spreading into new areas, creating new jobs and destroying old ones? An ageing workforce with more people working beyond normal working age? A world of growing labour shortages and the return to something like full employment in some OECD economies, including the UK? More jobs offshored and a few reshored? Technological and medical advances allowing more people with physical and mental disabilities to participate in the workforce – and perhaps throwing up new challenges for employers? If some of it sounds familiar then it is.

Of course, we have no idea what the economic position will be in 2025 – we could be in the grip of a second financial crisis or enjoying the benefits (and facing the different challenges) of full-employment labour markets. But we tend to a more optimistic interpretation of the long-term impact of technology and education on the labour market. For us, the two big challenges are distributional – how well can we respond to the endless disruption of changes in business practices, new technologies and markets that create both winners and losers, and how do we tackle deep and long-standing problems (the share of low paid workers in the UK has been essentially unchanged for 30 years).

It is not, I admit, quite as exciting as some accounts partly because we have not used labels such as 'Great' or claimed that the future will be a sharp and universal break from the past. Our only defence is that historical trends that defy the frequent ups and downs and disruptions of modern dynamic economies and societies probably deserve some respect. This of course can be challenged as being hopelessly backward looking and uninformed about how big the disruptive changes coming down the track will be. Both we and others who entirely disagree with our analysis and insight will be wrong to some degree – the question is which account is likely to be least wrong and that judgement we are content to leave to the reader.

SOFIAH UMAR, VP HR STRATEGY, SHELL INTERNATIONAL B.V.

THE COMPANY MENTIONED IN THE contribution is fictional and the views are based on future predictions.

It's a typical Tuesday morning for Li, a company manager. On her regular commute to work she uses her phone to scroll through various industry news feeds, work emails and her company's and competitors' performance metrics. They inform her that new international safety regulations will affect most of her offshore facilities, including those with a long list of planned works to ensure continuity of operations. By the end of today she will need to make a decision on how to manage any associated risks and provide an informed update at a stakeholder meeting involving offshore team leads, onshore engineers and representatives from health and safety, legal, external affairs, HR and finance.

A couple of other emails update Li with the status of geopolitical instabilities that have erupted in one of the countries of operation, putting her projects there on hold. Her employees on those projects are working virtually, but HR's advice is that these employees should be quickly moved to other projects and they have suggested some alternatives requiring their capabilities. She will attend to this today too.

Another email from Agnieszka, her HR partner, provides Li with on-boarding information for a new science graduate. Attached to this same email is a resourcing plan for an engineering project. Agnieszka suggests filling two remaining technical vacancies with a retiree and a third-party contractor. Li promptly clicks the 'agree' button, triggering an online resourcing process that means she can expect them to be on-seat within a week. Also in the same email, Agnieszka reminds Li that everyone in her company, regardless of their employment contract, is required to complete the mandatory social network training available via a massive open online course (MOOC). This is important to Li, as she still carries fresh and painful memories of her own team's contribution to a thread of comments heavily criticizing the company's presence in areas affected by the latest border disputes. This conversation later featured on other social networks, long after the damaging LinkedIn threads had been addressed. Li considers coaching her team to rebuild their affiliation to the company's purpose, when she realizes her 30-minute commute has, once again, passed quickly. She rushes to ready herself for getting off at the next stop and head into the office.

Li's activities during the commute may seem like an everyday occurrence for someone in her position today, but this is happening in 2025. So what are the differences in ten years' time?

Li goes through varied and numerous subjects within a fairly short time frame. She has no choice. Competition has intensified in her industry as inexperienced or non-traditional players have now matured their capabilities. This intense competition has led to a more complex environment with competing priorities. Li's role is to try and simplify these complex messages, so her team can focus on the key deliverables. This means she must decide her team's priorities quickly, while her agenda is driven by sudden changes in the external environment. A growing concern for Li, though, is around the limitations placed on the mobility of workers, especially those with key technical and critical skills. With more demand for technical skills than there is supply, multinationals are already grappling with how to place resources in challenging locations. While technology allows for increasingly flexible working arrangements by 2025, a more creative solution will be required to move workers to the challenging places where they are needed. Then her company can build local capability, better understand the localized situations and create effective partnerships.

Much of her leadership has required Li to go 'back to basics' on supervisory skills, an integral part of which is coaching. Not only is coaching continuing to be used as the main conduit for transferring skills and knowledge, but also to instil resilience as businesses have had to make tough choices during the difficult economic times of previous years. Employee affiliation has become an increasing challenge, and Li's role has been to ensure her people feel affiliated to the company and that those feelings are sustainable, whoever leads the organization. Li knows that those who affiliate with the company's defined purpose and its contributions to the local and global community will demonstrate more discretionary effort than those who do not. However, Li's main reason for honing her supervisory skills to increase affiliation is because she is managing a team under five different types of employment contract, not including the contingent workforce under three independent contractors, whom she needs to ensure deliver and perform in an integrated manner. Can you imagine the risk management she is dealing with on a daily basis?

Within this complex environment, Li is required to meet with various parts of her organization, as shown by the numerous stakeholders at the meeting on new international safety regulations for offshore facilities. Although Li works in the technical part of the business, many of Li's internal meetings are with people from non-technical areas of expertise, and she must rely on their information when it comes to her external engagements. Li has also learnt that successful collaborative relationships are a key enabler for her company to perform well. Internally, Li is managing more interfaces than the leaders of her company did a decade ago. Back then, companies like Li's were investing in the efficiency and effectiveness of end-to-end processes that touched on different parts of the organization. Continuous improvement methodologies and integrative and collaborative skills have become increasingly essential to ensure the effectiveness of the company.

Given the global business environment, Li relies on the strong support of her HR and other function partners in the service centre. Advances in IT have led to timely advice and fast transactions, making it easier for Li to work with her service-centre colleagues. Continued simplification and speed will be the mantra going forward, resulting in the application of off-the-shelf solutions like MOOC, rather than the company creating its own customized tools. Making processes increasingly efficient has seen more technology solutions and a decade of investments, requiring employees to become more self-sufficient. The hollowing out of 'middle' jobs to offshore locations or outsourcing altogether has resulted in non-traditional career paths for functional roles. One specific dilemma is how to progress graduate talent. With the offshoring of middle jobs there are fewer options for graduates to grow in places like head office. Plus given that graduates do not yet have specific skills, it's not easy obtaining the necessary work permits that allow them to go and work in an offshore service centre.

Another difference in 2025 for Li is the increased usage, and at times intrusion, of social media at work. True, social networks have continued to play a positive contribution in the workplace, providing easy access to new connections, sourcing valuable information and allowing employees to be advocates for the company. However, in the years up to 2025, erroneous information on social networks has taken on a life of its own, with employees using social media to air their grievances against their company. Li expects more regulation in this space to protect individuals, organizations and people's privacy.

Li still works in her office. Her company has found the physical environment reinforces a sense of community and corporate identity, while stimulating creativity. An element of fun within the workplace is required though, to encourage that sense of community and sustain the younger generation's interest in the office. A fun workplace is also seen as key to stimulating creative minds, a valuable differentiator when a company's competitive edge is based on its innovation and technology.

Li's organization also pays heightened attention to employee health, as staff work longer hours and to a greater age than previous generations. In 2025, a holistic view on health has been embedded. An example of this is the financial-planning awareness her company now provides to all new hires, because of the impact an employee's financial choices can have on their mental well-being. Working longer has had its benefits though, such as helping to address the shortage of experienced technical skills, plus older workers tend to be more mobile. Keeping older generations active is also regarded as making a positive contribution to society.

4

The future workplace

There have been some very avant-garde and engaging characterizations of the 'office of the future' in literature, film and journalism in the last century or so. Some have been far-fetched or aspirational. For example, ideas such as the so-called 'paperless office' have become the subject of ridicule (Gladwell, 2002) because, despite the proliferation of information and communication technology (ICT), the amount of paper we use at work seems to have grown exponentially. Indeed, the average US office worker uses 10,000 pages of paper each year. That's the equivalent of 4 million tons across the US every year. Others have pondered the changing nature of the physical space we might work in, with some employers already showing the way by installing slides or helter-skelters to get employees from one floor to another, or installing artificial grass floors to add variety and 'wackiness' to working environments where creativity is being promoted and others erecting treehouses, games areas or fire engines into collective spaces to encourage 'downtime' and to emphasize that work can be 'cool' even when the pressure to do more with less becomes more intense than ever.

Other visions for workplace innovation have been more prescient. For example, in 1945 Vannevar Bush wrote an article in the *Atlantic Monthly* (Bush, 1945) in which he described the development of various technologies that would eventually become hypertext, voice recognition, online encyclopaedias and personal computers. He envisaged a 'Memex' machine – a device in which people could compress and store all of their books, records and communications, 'mechanized so that it may be consulted with exceeding speed and flexibility'. Today and, almost certainly, into the future the ways that businesses capture, share and exploit both codified and tacit knowledge as a source of efficiency and competitive advantage will be a major area of focus and technological investment. This is not just about improving data storage and analytical tools, but using technology and workplace innovation to support the development of 'insight', learning and value creation.

Overall, the recognition that workplaces need to be designed, equipped and managed in ways that maximize the productive capacity of the people who work in them is an old idea that has had a modernistic makeover. The use of robotic and automated technology in modern car plants and in warehouse and logistic operations such as those run by Amazon have focused not just on the clever use of software, big data and Global Positioning System (GPS) but also on the quality of the jobs these innovations allow workers to have and, indeed, the number of jobs these innovations will eventually destroy. The hypothesis underpinning the famous Hawthorne studies of 1925–32 – in which researchers (Mayo, 1949) wanted to see if improving the quality of lighting among assembly workers would increase productivity – has come full circle with the impact of natural and artificial light now a major area of focus for ergonomists and work psychologists (Pachito et al., 2016). Of course the Hawthorne studies are now more famous for showing that intense scrutiny of work performance by researchers can have more impact on productivity than changes to the working environment, but we now know that factors such as light quality, ambient temperature and noise can all have a measurable effect on the quality of our working lives and on our productivity. This means that the concepts of 'design' are now part of the way we seek to configure modern workplaces.

Thus, the physical properties of workplaces, the technology they host, the productive potential of the interface between 'man and machine' and the effectiveness with which these innovations are implemented and managed are some of the more visible ways that our concept of the workplace of the future have been conceived. But in many sectors it will be the more intangible assets of the organization and the people who work in them that need to be nurtured and harnessed, and this can only be done in limited ways by having pinball machines in lounge areas or delivering coffee to your hot desk by drone (McGuinness, 2014).

In this chapter we *will* look at the impact of physical space and technology on work and on workplaces. But we will also look at equally important drivers of workplace effectiveness and ambience such as working time, flexibility, the psychosocial work environment and the concept of 'sovereignty' over space, time and task. We will argue that, looking beyond the world of luminous plastic office chairs, standing desks and social-media mediated collaborative platforms, we will still need workplaces of the future to nurture social capital and allow the people who work in them to be the masters rather than the slaves of the gadgets they will be using to do their jobs.

JOHN CRIDLAND

PEOPLE STILL TURN UP TO work in offices and factories, and a full-time job is still typically 9–5 on weekdays. In this regard, the workplace today doesn't look all that different to the workplace two decades ago, but the work we are doing and the ways we are doing it have changed dramatically and there is no reason to believe that they will stop changing in the future. A more flexible and individualized package of work and reward has emerged, driven by new technologies, societal and economic changes and an increasingly individual employee voice.

New technologies will continue to change our work in ways that we cannot foresee, but how businesses respond to three challenges and opportunities will have a significant bearing on the nature of work in 2030. Firms are challenged to raise productivity so that they can afford higher wages for all. They must make the wider pool of talent in an ageing and more diverse workforce a competitive advantage for the UK. And they must work with education providers to create more ladders into higher-skilled work.

Liberation technology: a broken promise?

Trawling back through newspaper and journal articles on the impact of automation on jobs shows us that alarm bells were ringing even in the early days of industrialization. French workers put their wooden shoes (sabots) into new-fangled machinery to undermine or 'sabotage' the relentless march of mechanization in the eighteenth century. They knew that machines meant less work for them both in the short and long term. Even eminent voices like John Maynard Keynes and Albert Einstein could not resist the temptation to link the mass unemployment of the 1930s to the growth of automation. Of course, there has also been a temptation to politicize the debate, with wranglings over what the wider diffusion of machines and ICT means in the long term for the substitution of labour by capital, especially in a so-called 'knowledge economy'. Ever since, as Chapter 2 showed, most of the subsequent and recent commentary on this topic has been apocalyptic, with hyped media reports of more qualified research suggesting that nearly half of all jobs were in danger of being lost through automation. Chapter 2 also highlighted research by the OECD showing the job-loss figure was closer to 10 per cent, though this more reasonable estimate has been often ignored in the public debate.

The interesting thing about this OECD analysis is that their estimates of the number of jobs whose scope, content and skill demands will be altered by technology was far higher – as much as 47 per cent. This has, perhaps, been a neglected part of the debate but it seems logical that, instead of focusing obsessively on the impact of automation on the *number* of jobs, we might do better to look at the nature, content and *quality* of those jobs.

The widespread adoption of mobile technology by individual citizens in every developed Western economy has brought about a fundamental – and probably irreversible – change in the way people consume digital content and interact with each other. It has also had a major impact on the way that many of us conduct business and do our jobs. When, where and how we work is now far less constrained or prescribed than even a decade ago, raising the prospect that the very nature of work itself, and the concept of 'the workplace' as a meaningful entity may be in need of a rethink. But are we ready for such a fundamental 'disruption' to our conventional conceptions of work? Are these changes, in reality, technology-driven rather than a rational response to the way work gets done and how communication, collaboration and transactions actually work most of the time? How much will we need to adapt our thinking about job design, working time, performance management, labour productivity and trust?

The data on the ubiquity of mobile technology show us, of course, that the only choice left is not whether we adopt it but how (and to what ends) we harness and embed it. Here are some examples of the picture in the UK (Garner et al., 2016):

- A 2015 survey found that 80 per cent of UK adults had either fixed or mobile broadband and 86 per cent of adults (and over 96 per cent of 16–44-year-olds) went online using any type of device in any location. It is worth bearing in mind, however, that even in 2016, 10 per cent of UK adults (5.3 million people) had never used the internet.

- By the end of 2016 it was expected that the number of mobile broadband users would exceed the number of PC broadband users.

- It was estimated that 73 per cent of 'millennials' expected to be able to modify and customize their work device and that a third of them would choose social-media freedom over a higher salary.

- Over 60 per cent of workers reported that their employer had no 'bring your own device' (BYOD) policy, however.

- Over 80 per cent of workers who did not have the option to work remotely would do so if they were given the opportunity.

- Those who did work remotely were tending to work longer hours, with 45 per cent of mobile workers reporting an increase in their working time. Recent research has shown that individuals who work 55 hours or more per week have a 33 per cent increased risk of stroke compared to those who work between 35 and 40 hours, and a 13 per cent increased risk of coronary heart disease. There is concern that some remote workers have an elevated risk of developing obesity, musculoskeletal conditions and even mental health problems as they are less likely to take exercise, may be vulnerable to poor diets and may become socially isolated.

Managers are one group of employees who seemed to have embraced mobile technology. In a recent survey (Garner et al., 2016), management-level employees were asked to report their responses to mobile working. The results appear in Figure 4.1. Here, 54 per cent reported that they got more work done, 46 per cent reported that their work–life balance had improved and 41 per cent said they felt empowered. However, only 49 per cent felt trusted, 45 per cent said they worked longer hours and only 37 per cent reported that it had reduced their travel time.

FIGURE 4.1 *Managers and perceptions of mobile working.*
Source: Garner et al. (2016).

So the results are mixed, and the extent to which mobile technology is a force for freedom or increased work intensity goes on. However, even with a substantial body of research (van Mierlo et al., 2006) that shows that giving employees more autonomy and control leads to productivity growth, the UK trend in the last decade has been moving in the opposite direction. Duncan Gallie and his colleagues found strong evidence of declining 'task discretion' and a significant reduction in autonomy (Gallie et al., 2004). Michael White, Stephen Hill and colleagues suggest that while employees may have more freedom to decide how they deliver their targets, employers now operate more rigorous regimes of accountability through sophisticated performance management systems and extensive surveillance (White et al., 2006). Both studies show that some workers have less control in their jobs than was the case a decade ago.

In some cases, the use of information technology in the workplace is one of the most important areas where autonomy has been eroded. Some workers express concern that technology is used as a performance tool that undermines trust. In the UK, service engineers in both BT and British Gas, for example, have been concerned that tracking devices in their vehicles allow their movements to be continuously monitored, and the amount of time they take to travel to and complete customer visits to be measured. As one BT employee said: 'Our cabs are fitted with a "tracker" device. It's a spy in the cab to see where we are, when we're on the move, and when we're not. They won't trust us to get on and do a job we've done well for years.'

In sharp contrast, there are examples where employees have been spectacularly liberated through the introduction of new technology. The Work Foundation tracked hundreds of workers at Microsoft in the UK as they were first given access to smartphones and to broadband at home. Aside from their general – and not unexpected – excitement about getting access to new 'kit', and the impact it had on their ability to check emails on the move and work more flexibly, about half of those involved reported that their work productivity had increased by between 50 and 100 per cent. Many also reported that access to this technology enhanced their perception of Microsoft as a 'cool' place to work (Sullivan and Diffley, 2003).

So, new technology pulls in two directions: sometimes constraining and reducing autonomy, sometimes empowering and creative. The key for employers is to consider what the impact is likely to be for employees in practice. And, again, where a climate of distrust or cynicism already exists, it is reasonable to assume that the technology will be received with distrust by the workforce. Research examining how ICT is introduced and used all too frequently finds that there is typically very little consultation with staff (Jones and Williams, 2005). Yet, going back to the example of the tracking devices in vans, when there is a dialogue about the commercial rationale of a new system – such as the need for full utilization of the fleet, speedier customer service and competitive advantage – it is possible to introduce the new technologies into the organization much more smoothly. It may be that, in the final analysis, digitization is not so much a technology issue as an organizational and cultural issue. The implication of this is that we may have more choice over its impact than we think.

Homeworking, flexibility and the rise of the laptop warrior

One promise of technology at work that remains largely unfulfilled is the one that convinced us that the widespread adoption of mobile ICT would reduce commuting and work-related travel. In most European cities, the commuter train carriages on wet winter mornings are often full of people who look bleary-eyed, haunted and silently resigned to the ordeal of delays, overcrowding and the effort of avoiding eye contact. And all this is before they get into the office. With a report (TUC, 2015) showing a 72 per cent increase in the number of people spending more than two hours travelling to work each day, it looks like many more people are opting – willingly or not – for working days book-ended with the joy of rush-hour travel. Most strikingly, the same report showed that there has been a 130 per cent increase in the number of women commuting for more than three hours a day since 2004. It can hardly be said that this part of the average working day enhances our quality of life, and yet for many it seems an increasing necessity.

In the south-east of the UK, for example, there is clearly a 'London' effect with house prices and rents still growing at a faster rate than elsewhere, forcing more people who need to retain their London salaries to find homes further out of the city. This effect is visible too in many other large cities around Europe and beyond, and it means that a higher proportion of our working days is being spent just getting to work and home again.

As might be expected, longer commutes can have all sorts of negative side effects. A 2011 Swedish study looking at the health consequences of longer commuting found a negative impact on sleep quality, stress, self-reported health and exhaustion among those commuting for more than an hour to work by car, bus or train compared with those walking or cycling to work (Hansson et al., 2011). Other studies have highlighted that work–life balance can be affected too, and with the high cost of child care, longer commutes can be both costly and disruptive to family life.

So, what of the promise of technology-enabled remote working? Wasn't that supposed to be weaning us off the idea that 'work is a place'? If anything, technology has played a part in intensifying rather than alleviating work pressure with large numbers of us checking emails at home and even on holiday. It wasn't so long ago that we were being told that the high cost of office accommodation was encouraging more employers to allow more people to work at home and attend meetings via Skype to reduce office occupancy. And what of the idea that remote working is a 'greener' alternative to having huge armies of commuters in NO- or CO_2-emitting transit day after day? Or the idea of 'staggering' start and finish times to smooth out the congestion of the rush 'hour' and allow people more time 'sovereignty'? If only a small proportion of the breathy journalistic commentary and the transformative impact of mobile technology on work comes true we can be assured that the way we conduct business, work in teams and conduct our lives outside work will continue to change unrecognizably.

Table 4.1 shows clearly that there has been limited change (between 1996 and 2016) in the proportion of the workforce in the six largest European countries who are now working 'usually' or 'sometimes' at home with somewhat different trends between countries.

The overall rates of working 'usually' at home are highest in France, with 4.4 per cent of the workforce reporting that they do this and this is also the most significant increase of the selected economies shown in the table. The incidence of 'usually' working at home has increased in the UK and Spain (and across the EU15 as a whole) but has fallen in Germany and Italy. With the exception of France, the overall proportion represented is in low single digits. This is hardly

TABLE 4.1 *Changing patterns of 'working at home' for employees, 1996–2016*

Usual	1996	2016	Change	Sometimes	1996	2016	Change
France	0.6	5.0	4.4	UK	23.1	17.6	−5.5
UK	0.9	2.0	1.1	France	–	11.4	–
Spain	0.3	1.8	1.5	Germany	6.1	6.2	0.1
Germany	2.5	1.6	−0.9	Spain	0.4	1.0	0.6
Italy	2.2	1.0	−1.2	Italy	1.6	0.6	−1.0
EU15	1.9	2.9	1.0	EU15	6.5	9.7	3.2

Note: no comparable data available for France before 2016 for 'sometimes' working at home.

Source: http://ec.europa.eu/eurostat/web/lfs/data/database

evidence that more widespread use of mobile and remote technology has led to a revolution in home-working.

The figures for the proportion of workers who 'sometimes' work from home also show a variable picture. Workers in the UK, according to these data, are much more likely to report working 'sometimes' from home – as many as 17.6 per cent and nearly 8 percentage points higher than the EU15 average. However, the high figure for the UK in 2016 represents a decline in the rate for 1996, when almost 1 in 5 UK workers reported working 'sometimes' from home. Italy also shows a slight decline over the same period whereas Spain and Germany show increases. There are no comparable figures for France before 2016, but in that year France had the second highest incidence of home-working of the major EU economies.

These data are sobering because they run counter to expectations and suggest that, while there has been an undeniable 'boom' in the use of mobile and networked technology by workers in contemporary workplaces, significant barriers remain to achieving the vision of many commentators of a transformation of how and where we work.

Perhaps part of the answer lies in the fact that the prevailing culture of most modern workplaces is still not ready to trust people to work remotely and out of sight. Maybe we still value 'inputs' more than 'outputs' or that many managers can't cope well with the idea of managing people they don't see every day, or that remote working is regarded as no more than an indulgence for those 'knowledge workers' (unlike their support worker colleagues) whose work is not location-dependent. In what may be a sign of the times, in 2013 the chief executive officer (CEO) of technology company Yahoo!, Marissa Mayer, made headlines by discouraging home-working in her workforce to improve collaboration and because 'speed and quality are often sacrificed when we work from home'. There remains a debate about whether this decision was about efficiency or trust. Whichever it was, Ms Mayer was probably articulating the private concerns of many more bosses, which is an indication of how much more we need to do to help our organizational culture catch up with technology at work.

Perhaps the Yahoo! example illustrates a more fundamental concern among employers about whether increasing the accessibility of flexible working – whether facilitated by technology or not – is becoming a demand that is primarily about accommodating the needs of a more diverse workforce rather than the need to deliver value to customers and drive value creation. But is the choice about flexible working correctly characterized as a binary choice or a zero-sum gain? Does offering 10 per cent more flexibility in working time result in a 10 per cent reduction in the quality of customer service? The simple answer is that, no, it does not. Indeed there is increasing evidence that customers also want flexibility from the way businesses deploy their employees because they too want access to goods and services at speed and during non-traditional hours. This opens up the possibility that, among smarter businesses, there may be a strong case for adopting flexible working practices that optimize the benefits both for employees and customers rather than trading off the needs of one against the needs of the other. Figure 4.2 illustrates how businesses could benefit by more creative adoption of this blended approach.

Let us take a simple example to illustrate how this mutuality principle might work in practice. Most large supermarket businesses know that empty shelves reduce service quality, customer choice, spend and, ultimately, loyalty. Yet they also know that a large-scale effort to replenish shelves during peak times also irritates customers whose smooth transit around the store is impeded by cages and staff blocking the aisles. These businesses also employ a diverse staff profile from young workers, working mothers, casual staff and students. Many of these find working non-traditional hours helps them balance their work and non-work commitments, whether these are about family care, study or leisure. Offering shelf-stacking shifts very late at night or early in the mornings can, if organized well, allow the store to ensure shelves are filled with minimal customer disruption by staff for whom a late-night shift fits in neatly with the

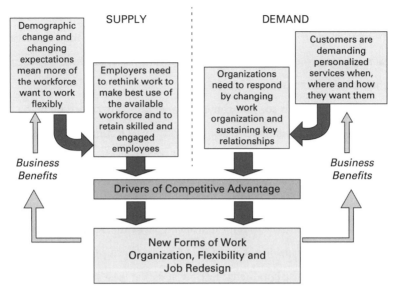

FIGURE 4.2 *Mutual benefit in the adoption of flexible working practices.*
Source: Jones et al. (2007).

way they wish to organize their non-work time. In this case, flexibility benefits everyone.

It isn't hard to think of other models where mutual advantage might be secured. Businesses who use a distributed network of employees, freelancers and specialists to give them both numerical and functional flexibility in the way they deliver projects, client work, software, consultancy or other services may find that remote technology and a mix of flexible contractual arrangements and employment 'deals' delivers cost-effective and high-quality work by adopting work styles that also meet the needs of the employees. In addition, the cost of accommodation might be reduced, and the utilization of capital investment in technology can be more fully realized.

Both now and in the future, of course, the types of work that are most likely to match this model of flexibility of both time and place will vary considerably. Thus, hairdressing will, for the foreseeable future, remain a service where production and consumption will need to be 'co-located'. No amount of technological innovation will change this. One way of assessing the scope of technology-enabled flexible working to be assessed and planned therefore is, for each job role, to determine where they sit on a matrix of time and location dependency, as illustrated in Figure 4.3.

In this figure, we can see that some job roles are constrained by being both time and location dependent. Thus, in addition to hairdressers, roles in the lower-right quadrant are less likely to be able to be performed remotely or at a time of the employee's choosing. However, roles in the diagonally opposite quadrant, including jobs that are time and location independent, are much more likely to be amenable to remote working at a time determined by the job holder. While this model is not intended as a prescriptive tool to decide which jobs can and cannot be conducted flexibly, it can at least help both employers and workers to explore the practical limitations of technology-enabled remote working and to negotiate mutually beneficial arrangements.

It is worth thinking about the number of increasingly lengthy, costly and stressful commuter journeys that might be avoided in the future if we could

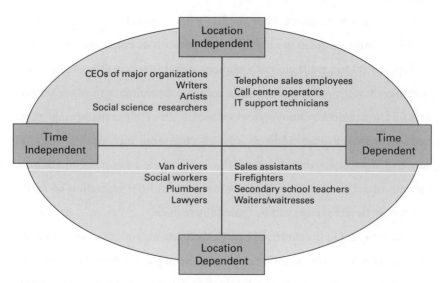

FIGURE 4.3 *Time and location dependency and flexible working potential.*
Source: Equalities and Human Rights Commission (2007).

get our cultural and technological 'act' together and to trust people to do a good job even if we can't scrutinize their every move. But it could be that, like so many others who have pondered this question, we are being naively unrealistic. Perhaps work is a place after all.

Human enhancement: wearables, implantables and 'smart' drugs

Perhaps we can find some more positive examples of technology or innovation that help workers to improve productivity and performance at work more directly and with their involvement and consent. Again, this is not a new idea, but one that is still not as widespread as it might be, and that is changing rapidly. Back in the 1950s, for example, a study was published looking at the relationship between the adoption of mining equipment and the productivity of the miners who used it to extract coal in longwall mines. It noted that, despite the clear advantages of the new technology, the way that work had been organized, jobs designed and workers involved in its adoption and use were having a negative effect on overall performance. Eric Trist and Peter Bamforth (1951) concluded that it was important to look at ways of achieving what they called 'joint optimization' when introducing technological advances into work and that the so-called 'socio-technical systems' approach to industrial production – in which considerations of work autonomy, sovereignty and task discretion should have complementary consideration to technological innovation – was the best way to maximize the value and the 'return on investment' from such technologies.

Here in the twenty-first century the principles of 'joint optimization' can be seen in ways that industrial psychologists such as Emery and Trist may never have envisaged. It may be in our relentless focus on robotics and on ICT we have neglected other innovations such as wearable or implanted devices and 'smart' drugs.

Advances in wearable technology are of great interest not just to consumer electronics companies but also to health-care providers, insurance companies and – increasingly – employers. Innovations in e-health and telemedicine, for example, allow patients to be connected remotely to clinicians who can monitor vital signs and even the rate of healing of broken bones via wearable technology. A team at McGill University has developed a so-called 'smart' shoe sole that can remotely monitor the recovery, gait, weight distribution and rehabilitation of patients recovering from hip fractures (McGill University, 2016). Many of us are also now familiar with the 'black box' technology used by some motor-insurance companies to monitor the speed and driving patterns of customers in order to inform the setting of premium levels and to differentiate between safe and reckless drivers. And those of us who use one or more of the bewildering array of wearable technology to monitor our physical activity, heart rate, sleep quality, nutrition and even our mood will be aware of the potential of such devices and apps to capture, record and analyse more about our activity, whereabouts, habits and well-being than we – or anyone else – would ever need to know. Of course, the fact that technology allows us to do these things, does not necessarily mean that we should. Perhaps as long as the purpose is benign and the uses to which the data is put remain life-enhancing and in the control of the subject then this is likely to command wide consent and be regarded as progress. For example, the more widespread use of virtual reality headsets in staff training and in simulation can help prepare employees for environments and situations before first-hand exposure in reality itself.

However, there is always a dystopian dimension to cutting-edge technological developments and it may be that the workplace and worker-productivity enhancement will prove more controversial if they shift control from the worker to the employer, and if 'consent' and other tacit components of contemporary 'joint optimization' become the first victims of the relentless progress of human augmentation by wearable or even implantable technology.

We already see this process in action. Amazon distribution warehouses, for example, now require employees who are picking orders to use wearable technology that automatically calculates the quickest route around the warehouse so that the list of items in a customer order can be collected in the most time-efficient way. The technological elegance of this system is undeniable, though it results in a Pac-Man-like procession of order-pickers walking mechanically along and between aisles of shelves at the behest of a pre-programmed algorithm which snuffs out any remaining autonomy or decision-latitude on the part of the worker. This technology, of course, can monitor speed, efficiency and productivity, and can check and report on toilet and other breaks.

From this, many believe (or fear) that the next step is the use of hardware implants to enhance both performance and surveillance. In 2017 the injection of tiny 'chips' the size of a grain of rice into the hands of Swedish employees gave the world a glimpse a view of how a not especially new technology can take on a potentially sinister new meaning. The Swedish start-up 'hub' called Epicenter – host to a number of small and mainly tech employers – has been offering to inject volunteer employees with the kind of chip that has been used to tag pets and to track parcel deliveries for a few years already. These chips, which are injected quite painlessly into the web of soft skin between the thumb and forefinger, allow staff to open locked doors, clock on or off, and order and pay for a skinny latte in the cafeteria. This example, where in excess of 150 employees have already been 'chipped', has been reported extensively in the press as one of several innovations that are likely to be part of the way that modern workplaces will operate within the near future. The coverage is often careful to accentuate the benefits to employees – for example, not having to remember four-digit security codes for multiple doors. While there is also discussion of the potential downside risks of this technology in the wrong hands (pun intended), we are only just starting to explore the potential of these advances to re-frame a number of aspects of the established order and the fundamentals of the employment relationship. It may be that, as with the indifference of many younger users of social-media platforms to issues of data security, that the 'threats' to privacy represented by some implantable devices are overblown and exaggerated. As one employee in the Epicenter hub who had volunteered to have a chip injected in her hand reportedly said with a shrug and a laugh, 'I just want to be part of the future'.

As with most historic workplace innovations from the flying shuttle in machine weaving to the implantable technology of today, these include trust, control, power and dignity. However advanced and mind-boggling the technology, these issues will need to be accommodated if the promised advances of the technology are to be fully realized. Indeed, perhaps the debate will focus less on the ethics and more on the efficacy of these advances. This is where we now seem to be in the field of cognitive enhancement.

It is widely accepted that the supermarket trolley was a great leap forward in labour productivity in retailing in the 1950s and 1960s. In a knowledge-based economy, the next 'great leap' for many enthusiastic futurologists lies in the use of cognitive enhancements to improve our concentration, allow us to work longer without sleep, to improve our memories, to reduce impulsivity or to improve our ability to plan.

These are all enhancements that are claimed for some smart drugs – and they mean going way beyond having an extra shot of coffee in the morning or a high caffeine energy drink before an exam. In general, these smart drugs are products already being used in clinical settings but whose effects are thought to enhance some aspect of cognitive function. For example, Modafinil (brand name Provigil) is normally prescribed for sleep disorders, Ritalin (given to people with ADHD) and Adderall (a mixture of amphetamine salts, not licensed in the UK) are all drugs that have been reported as being used by students hoping to get better results or by people in high-pressure jobs. They are often available on the internet and – despite patchy evidence for their effectiveness and probably insufficient data on their side effects – they have a growing reputation and a loyal following among those who claim they work for them.

The use of such smart drugs, however, raises a number of ethical issues. Professor Barbara Sahakian and colleagues, at the Unit of Brain and Mind Sciences at Cambridge University, have been examining their use for over a decade. In her book *Bad Moves: How Decision Making Goes Wrong, and the Ethics of Smart Drugs*, co-authored with Jamie Nicole LaBuzetta, she expresses concern about the 'lifestyle' uses of these drugs and the fact that there is no long-term data on their unintended impact.

A BBC report on smart drugs found that, even among those who use them, there are concerns about the implications of their more widespread use:

I want one as a student, but I don't want criminals on cognitive enhancers running around.

The drugs would get stronger and stronger due to increased demand of performance. Addictions would ensue. People would not be able to live without them. Employers would demand their employees to be constantly using them.

So there are practical, ethical and biochemical concerns about smart drugs and, in 2016, a report by the British Medical Association (BMA) provided a damning assessment of the evidence. It concluded that the evidence of positive impact was very weak but that for significant harm it was plentiful. The report provides a fascinating history of the use of smart drugs by elements in the Third Reich, by parts of the US military and, most recently, by students. But rather than enhancing cognitive ability in a controlled and safe way in workplace settings, the evidence is that the over-confidence and disinhibition that can result can have dangerous and undesirable consequences.

Perhaps advances in cognitive enhancement among workers that are less reliant on psychoactive drugs are in the pipeline and that the cul-de-sac of smart drugs may only be a temporary setback for those determined to augment the intellectual and cerebral raw material of employees. In the meantime, it is likely that other – more traditional – avenues for productivity enhancement will continue to be explored.

Work space

If work, for most of us, is going to continue to be a *place* as well as an *activity,* what are employers of the future going to do to make the physical space in which we toil as congenial and productive as possible? For many organizations the cost of accommodation in the form of offices, factories and warehouses can be second or third only to the cost of the people working in them. Despite the recognition that creative and innovative workspace design can have productivity benefits, perhaps these cost pressures will continue to win out in the battle between short-term expediency and longer-term investment. Looking at the evidence, it seems that the benefits of investment in creative workspace design can certainly accrue substantially for some employees in some organizations but that realizing these benefits requires both a vision and a plan to overcome some familiar cultural barriers.

For many years the ergonomic benefits of imaginative workplace design have been well established and the business case proven. For example, work-space layout that places tools or components in easy reach of the workers and that minimizes stretching, twisting, placing joints and muscles under undue strain all have proven benefits in terms of productivity, efficiency and the prevention of physical or mental health problems (Tappura et al., 2014). We also know that appropriate lighting, noise, temperature and even odour can have performance- and ambience-enhancing effects (Pachito et al., 2016).

There are, of course, other reasons why employers choose to invest in work space that is modern, technologically advanced and engaging – especially in knowledge-based sectors where the know-how, expertise and discretionary effort of bright employees can be a long-term source of competitive advantage and sustained performance. Part of this is intangible – the desire to have 'funky' or 'cool' work space is usually more than a childish indulgence. If the image or brand that a business has needs to be engaging to clients, customers, collaborators and colleagues then such investments are likely to be justifiable and effective. Attracting high-quality recruits and projecting a professional image to clients and partners each has an economic value.

For example, imaginatively designed work space can help to optimize some of the intangible assets of the organization such as the flow of communication and ideas and the energy and innovative potential of cross-functional teams. It can also maximize the serendipity of informal work conversations and interactions between colleagues who rarely work together. In these workplaces the layout, positioning of printers, coffee machines, storage, toilet facilities, meeting rooms and social space can be planned in detail to ensure that employees can get the best out of the opportunity to interact and collaborate with each other.

Researchers such as Max Nathan and Judith Doyle, however, have long recognized that the rhetoric and reality of office space for most twenty-first-century workers can be very different. In their 2002 study *The State of the Office*, they highlighted examples of both 'leading edge' innovation in office design as well as (many) more prosaic examples of workplaces that were poorly lit, cramped, technologically backward and both physically and psychologically hazardous. They suggested several reasons for this gap between the 'shiny' promise of the office of the future and the more downbeat everyday reality.

First, they concluded, work space is changing more slowly than work itself and unless the notable lag between changes in working practices, technology, customer demands and employee needs, and the capacity of work space to adapt, then the physical working environment will always represent an impediment to productivity growth and value creation.

Second, work space is still responding to the need to centralize, secure, monitor and discipline a white-collar workforce that operates, communicates and manages in a limited, time-bound, hierarchical, functionally siloed and risk-averse way.

Third, the way most businesses measure the return on physical assets and their preoccupation with cost-minimization only takes account of tangible assets with traditional models of depreciation. Yet the value created in many modern businesses with high-quality work space is intangible but vital to competitiveness.

Fourth, and despite the democratizing potential of shared and open work space, Nathan and Doyle found that status and the high value placed on privacy are strong drivers of the way work space is designed and allocated. Indeed, in recent years there has been something of a backlash against the use of open-plan offices. In her book *Quiet: The Power of Introverts in a World that Can't Stop Talking* (2012), Susan Cain argues that open plan is only rarely likely to be the design format of choice for introverts, for example. In fact, she argues that open-plan offices are 'associated with high staff turnover. They make people sick, hostile, unmotivated and insecure.'

The bottom line is that the physical working environment of modern workplaces and those of the future need to balance the need for efficiency, aesthetic appeal and flexibility. This means working as an environment that optimizes performance and productivity for most employees most of the time. Research by Haynes and Price (2004) illustrates how difficult this can be. Their data shows, in Figure 4.4, that there is a range of components of workplace design that employees report as having either highly positive or highly negative effects on their performance and productivity. Paradoxically, perhaps, the aspect that is regarded most positively by the largest proportion of employees (34 per cent) is 'interaction' whereas the dimension reported to have the most negative effects by the highest proportion (59 per cent) is 'distraction'. One characteristic of open-plan design is that it can combine both of these characteristics. However,

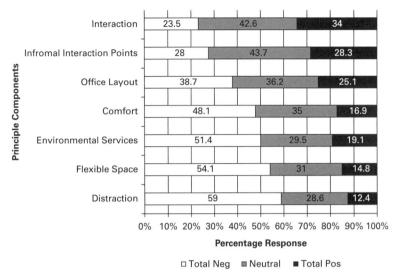

FIGURE 4.4 *Employee responses to components of workplace design.*
Source: Haynes and Price (2004).

if the negative effects of 'distraction' cancel out the positive effects of 'interaction' then an unsophisticated, inflexible and undifferentiated open-plan design might prove sub-optimal for most employees – even the extroverts.

Like so many other areas of work design, building in some autonomy, control or work-space 'sovereignty' that allows employees the chance to customize or personalize their work space is most likely to deliver engagement, contentment and performance benefits. The Haynes and Price data suggest that if open plan by itself is not a sufficiently sophisticated way of delivering opportunities for 'interaction', providing 'informal interaction points' around the workplace might go a long way towards helping to mitigate the risk of an uncontrollably distracting environment. However, researchers examining the way innovative workplace design is implemented also conclude that, as with information and communication technology, the transformative potential eye-catching 'kit' can have the life sucked out of it if the culture of the organization conspires to neuter its impact. Nathan and Doyle (2002) interviewed employees in a service-sector business that had invested in aesthetically designed shared social space and a café. During a tour of the space they were told:

> This is the café, but we don't use it. First it's colonized by IT people who spend all day playing pool. We don't mix with them. Also, it's quite far from where we work – bosses tend to wonder what you're doing when you sit in the canteen – there's a definite presumption that you're skiving.

So, to paraphrase Peter Drucker, 'culture eats innovative work space for breakfast'. If employers are to continue to invest in novel work-space design in the future, and if they are to avoid being disappointed that the results they get are short of what they expected, they should be clear that technology, art, pastel colours and beanbags will only turn the 'funky' into the 'productive' if the cultural attributes of the organization are also aligned and receptive.

The future workplace: a false promise or a false start?

There is a constant flow of ingenious and arresting technical innovation being produced by imaginative individuals working either for themselves or for 'edgy' businesses. This technology has an almost unlimited capacity to transform the way we create, curate, share and exploit knowledge, data, know-how and insight at work. The amount of data produced in the world is said to double every two years and by 2020 is expected to reach 44 Zettabytes, or 44 trillion gigabytes (Turner, 2014). Although Vannevar Bush could not have envisaged the sheer volume of data that modern workplaces would be processing only 75 years or so after his vision of the 'Memex' machine, it seems true to say that our capacity to embrace and integrate our modern versions of data storage, processing and communication technology has not advanced as quickly as the technology itself. As we have seen, for many workplaces, the dominant story is one of unfulfilled potential, cultural and attitudinal barriers to the wholehearted and efficient integration of productivity-enhancing technology into workspace design and working practices.

The pace of technological development will accelerate still further in the next few decades, offering us many further opportunities – especially at the leading edge of adoption among some businesses – fundamentally to alter the way humans function in and out of work. Developments in artificial intelligence, driverless vehicles, crowdsourcing algorithms, 3-D printing and many others will continue to spark apocalyptic speculation that we are approaching the 'end of work' or, at the very least, a transformative re-shaping of how, where and when most of us work. History tells us, however, that this transformative potential is often dramatically overstated. This is only rarely because the technology under-delivers, however. It is more commonly a reflection of the inefficient absorptive capacity of the majority of employers and the risk-averse and low-trust nature of too many organizations and their leaders. If the future workplace and, more specifically, the capacity of these workplaces to take maximum advantage of the technological innovations being made available to them the barriers that need to be overcome are wholly within our control. The role of managers in navigating their way successfully through these challenges will be critical. The next chapter looks at the role of managers in the workplace and how management skills can be improved for the future.

5

Better managers in the future workplace

Introduction

Ask many social, economic, political, technological and organizational observers about the nature of change in the last decade, and I am certain that common themes will be constant change, rapid development in certain aspects (e.g. technological developments – not all of them necessarily good) and uncertainty. We are still in a fragile state of recovery after the last financial crash, and the results of the European Union referendum and the outcome of the US presidential election have left us in yet further uncertain times, as the full implications for the economy, migration and productivity are yet to be fully determined. Chapters 1 to 3 set out some of the myths and realities of these changes. What is clear, however, is that the role of managers is going to be pivotal in whether UK workplaces prove resilient in a world of uncertainty and contribute to solving some of the massive challenges in making workplaces more productive.

Organizations still need to be able to adapt and function in these uncertain times so they can respond to meet the changing conditions in the external environment, over which they have very little, if any, control. How organizational resources are therefore deployed and developed could be very influential for productivity, and it can be argued that employees are an organization's most valuable resource. Anne Mulcahy[1] famously said: 'Employees are a company's greatest asset. They're your competitive advantage. You want to attract and retain the best; provide them with encouragement, stimulus, and make them feel that they are an integral part of the company's mission.' It seems therefore that organizations need 'good management' now more than ever, to drive growth, implement technology and draw out the talents of their workforce, to be able to survive (and survive profitably) in what can be difficult times ahead (CMI, 2014).

The word 'management' conjures up a lot of imagery. We all have our own ideas and expectations about what 'good management' consists of; for example setting goals, encouraging and engaging employees, implementing practices and procedures, and overseeing organizational change by ensuring that employees are still motivated and productive. In a *Harvard Business Review* article, Mintzberg (1990) wrote: 'If you ask managers what they do, they will most likely tell you that they plan, organize, coordinate and control. Then watch what they do. Don't be surprised if you can't relate to these words'. This encapsulates the difficulties that organizations have for choosing, developing and 'doing' management and indicates the vague objectives of what managers should do in their organizational roles, but not necessarily having the skills or the organizational culture in which they can manage effectively.

As has been discussed in previous chapters, the ways in which we are working, what the workplace is and the diversity of the workplace that managers need to manage are changing, and thus expectations about what managers should be doing and how they do it becomes increasingly challenging. Employers are aiming for increased productivity from their staff, optimum engagement and continuous innovation from their employees, and to do this it is clear that effective managers need to be developed, promoted or recruited. However, employees may look for alternative management characteristics – a manager who is able to listen to their concerns, who they can disclose to, who provides adequate and timely feedback on their performance, and who rewards and treats them fairly in the workplace. The two views of management are not, however, diametrically opposed, with evidence available to suggest that people management is now as important a contribution to organizational success as financial, marketing and sales management (Wong et al., 2009).

This chapter aims to discuss the essence of what 'management' is, understanding that it is a term that still defies an accepted definition, but has clearly led to a vast array of both academic and practitioner research about why it is important for organizational and individual outcomes. As will be discussed, organizational productivity not only depends on the environment in which people are found in, but the way in which they are managed, and thus the prominent theory of the psychological contract and the employee relationship will be discussed as a lens through which management can be developed and improved. The role of the psychological contract is important in one particular managerial relationship – the first line manager – which this chapter will look at in relation to employee productivity. The chapter will discuss how well management is 'working' in the UK currently, and discuss what challenges the future of the workplace will have for management practices and therefore what skills managers will have to acquire, and whether these skills are widely different to the skills required in the workplace now. Ultimately, the chapter aims to contribute to the debates about drivers for developing the management skills needed to contribute to economic and organizational growth.

What is management?

The question 'What is management?' is one that has been fiercely debated among academics and practitioners alike for a number of decades, and still continues today. One of the main bones of contention is the difference between leadership and management in organizations, especially where these terms are used interchangeably. It was Zaleznik (1977) in his *Harvard Business Review* article 'Managers and leaders: are they different?', who first started to distinguish between the characteristics of leaders and managers, and what each offers organizations. In brief, Zaleznik argued that whereas leaders can tolerate chaos and a lack of structure, managers like to seek order, control and a rapid resolution of problems. Additionally, as Lunenburg (2011) summarized, Zaleznik advocated that leaders are concerned with understanding the beliefs of the people whom they are leading, and gaining their commitment, whereas managers carry out responsibilities, worry about how to get things accomplished and therefore exercise authority to ensure this happens. Regarding the personality of a manager, Zaleznik (1977: 3) noted that 'whether their energies are directed towards goals, resources, organisational structures or people, a manager is a problem solver. The manager asks: What problems have to be solved and what are the best way to achieve results so that people will contribute to this organisation?' As a result, managerial characteristics need to include: persistence, tough-mindedness, hard work, intelligence, analytical ability and, as Zaleznik argues (if these characteristics and capabilities are not enough), most importantly tolerance and goodwill. With all of this, it is hard to imagine how we have any good managers at all!

The differences between leadership and management roles and how they can be applied in practice as argued by Zaleznik has been clearly separated into a number of themes, as can be seen in Table 5.1.[2]

Kotter (1990) believed that management and leadership are two distinct yet complementary systems for organizations – with the specific distinction being that leadership focuses on coping with change, whereas management copes with organizational complexities. Lunenburg (2011) suggested that, for Kotter, leadership involved: developing organizational visions; aligning employees to this vision through communication; and motivating employees to act towards this vision through empowerment and the basic need for fulfilment. As a result

TABLE 5.1 *How managers and leaders differ as argued by Zaleznik (1977)*

	Managers	Leaders
Attitudes towards goals	Take an impersonal, passive outlook. Goals arise out of necessities and desires.	Take a personal, active outlook. Shape rather than respond to ideas. Alter moods; evoke images, expectations. Change how people think about what's desirable and possible. Set company direction.
Conceptions of work	Negotiate and coerce. Balance opposing views. Design compromises. Limit choices. Avoid risk.	Develop fresh approaches to problems. Increase options. Turn ideas into exciting images. Seek risk when opportunities appear promising.
Relations with others	Prefer working with people, but maintain minimal emotional involvement. Lack empathy. Focus on process, e.g. how decisions are made rather than what decisions to make. Communicate by sending ambiguous signals. Subordinates perceive them as inscrutable, detached, manipulative. Organization accumulates bureaucracy and political intrigue.	Attracted to ideas. Relate to others directly, intuitively, empathetically. Focus on substance of events and decisions, including their meaning for participants. Subordinates describe them with emotionally rich adjectives, e.g. 'love', 'hate'. Relations appear turbulent, intense, disorganized. Yet motivation intensifies, and unanticipated outcomes proliferate.
Sense of self	Comes from perpetuating and strengthening existing institutions. Feel part of the organization.	Comes from struggles to profoundly alter human and economic relationships. Feel separate from organization.

of this leadership process, feelings of uncertainty and change can emerge in organizations. It is consequently the role of the manager to: plan and budget; organize staff; control and problem solve to reduce organizational uncertainty; and develop a sense of stability, in an attempt to ensure an organization remains productive and achieves its organizational aims. Consequently, management involves co-ordinating staff to handle the day-to-day changes when implementing the vision and direction of leaders.

Therefore, it is important to note that both leaders and managers make a valuable contribution to how organizations work, but how different the roles are is still being debated. Toor and Ofori (2008), in their synthesis on this issue, reported the scholarly differences of opinions in the management vs leadership role. They highlighted that leadership and management are two distinct and opposing styles of employee supervision, both being used in organizational settings, and both are popular (Kumble and Kelly, 1999). Others believe that managers and leaders are two sides of the same coin, are complementary in their actions (Bryman, 1992), although they both have their own organizational functions and activities that characterize their roles. Mangham and Pye (1991) argued that how the roles have been defined results in the imagery that leaders and leadership is something special and precious, and undertaken by 'important people', whereas managing then becomes something mundane, merely looking after the 'nuts and bolts' of an organization.

The resulting confusion has led to the conclusion that in organizational practice, many 'managers' may perform leadership roles and many 'leaders' may manage (Toor and Ofori, 2008). More worryingly, Kotterman (2006) noted that the ambiguity and blurring in the definition of leadership and management has implications for practice in how managers can be assessed, hired, developed and promoted effectively to ensure positive organizational productivity. Kotterman also was resigned to the fact that although this debate will continue amongst academics in the literature, organizations will continue to need both leaders and managers in organizations, and develop methods through which both effective leaders and managers can be developed – because, as will be explained, managers are important, and when management is not effective, there are resulting negative consequences.

FRANCES O'GRADY

THE TRADES UNION CONGRESS (TUC) has long argued that British management is characterized by mediocrity and short-termism, and that more firms should take a 'high road' approach to growth. But decades on from when we first raised this concern, the same problems remain, with multiple recent analyses identifying poor management as part of the UK's productivity challenge. We need to blow the dust off the boardroom. Without a new approach to corporate decision-making, and a decisive shift to an increased focus on long-term results rather than short-term share fluctuations, the high-investment, high-productivity model that British business desperately needs will remain elusive.

Achieving progress needs substantial reform of the UK's corporate governance regime. The TUC is pushing for reform of directors' duties, voting restrictions for short-term shareholders and the introduction of worker representatives on boards. These form part of a package of changes designed to ensure that companies place a greater emphasis on the views of stakeholders beyond shareholders, and that businesses are encouraged to focus on the longer-term gains that higher investment could bring. Improving management training, increasing the value that businesses place on good management and recognizing the right of workers to be managed well would help deliver real returns on a high-productivity approach to growth.

More broadly, too often the voice of employees is ignored or excluded in the workplaces. There is a strong case for UK employers to harness the benefits of new models of management with more inclusive approaches to decision-making at their core. The ambition should be to humanize work and give people more say, both in day-to-day issues affecting their particular job and more strategic issues. This would require both strengthened collective consultation procedures (which could be achieved through reforming information and consultation regulations) and also a change of attitude on the part of many managers.

The imperative for action is clear. Future jobs growth is forecast to be both in low- and high-paying industries, and if the UK is to remain competitive the importance of improving management performance will be even greater in years ahead than it is today.

Why is management important?

The poor productivity reported in the UK since the end of the recession, has resulted in a number of commentaries from economists and policymakers concerned with the 'productivity puzzle'. The Department for Business, Innovation and Skills (as it was known then) in 2012 produced the document *Leadership and Management in the UK – The Key to Sustainable Growth*, where it was reported that the failure of both public and private organizations to achieve their full potential may be as a result of managerial shortcomings and a lack of strategic thinking, including weaknesses in managerial capability in creating a culture of engagement, confidence and resilience to external challenges to productivity, and organizations failing to invest in the development of managerial skills. As Chapter 1 showed, current thinking is that the roots of the productivity puzzle lie in a stalling in the diffusion and effective use of the latest technology in the workplace and that improving the quality of management could make an important contribution to solving the puzzle.

This idea regarding persistently low productivity and managerial performance was discussed by Tamkin (2004), who cited numerous reports suggesting the fairly simple link between economic performance and the UK's deficit of good management. Some questioned whether more work should be conducted into this complex relationship; for example Porter and Ketels (2003) questioned whether the quality of UK management was the most important determinant of economic performance, or if other organizational factors held more importance. They concluded that room for improvement is always needed, but efforts to improve management alone would not achieve the sustained improvement and productivity that the UK needs to remain competitive.

So why is management so important? The BIS (Department for Business, Innovation and Skills, 2012) study proposed two ways in which businesses could benefit from good management:

- improved business performance;
- improved employee performance.

Improved business performance

In 2002, Bosworth et al., as part of the Department for Education and Skills research paper 'Managerial qualifications and organisational performance', identified a number of findings regarding why managerial performance could have an impact on organizational outcomes. These included:

- Managers who were highly and better qualified were associated with a better qualified workforce.

- Managers who were highly qualified were more innovative in their approach when adopting organizational strategies (e.g. the introduction of higher-quality products, technology or work practices into the workforce, or improving the quality of the products already available to the organization). In comparison, managers who were less qualified were increasingly focused on increasing the efficiency and the production of existing services, products and technology.

- Managerial proficiency and organizational performance appear to be positively linked (however, this could be a two-way relationship).

Although this research made that intuitive link between management practices and resulting economic productivity, up until recently there had been little empirical evidence to suggest this is actually the case. However, the work of Bloom and Van Reenen from Stanford University and the Centre for Economic Performance (CEP) at the London School of Economics has led to developments in the understanding of this relationship (Tamkin and Ni Luanaigh, 2016). Bloom and Van Reenen have sought to apply economic techniques to explore how management contributes to a firm's performance as the existing literature had little methodological rigour, lacked the systematic collection of data and did not include representative samples.

Tamkin and Ni Luanaigh (2016), in their review 'The relationship between UK management and leadership and productivity', provided an overview of the CEP survey tool developed to measure management practices. This is explained briefly below:

- A survey tool was developed that uses a range of open questions about the quality of management practices within an organization (public, private and service sectors). The responses are then compared to a marking framework that provides individual practice scores which can then be aggregated to an overall score.[3]

This instrument measures 18 managerial practices along three dimensions:

1   performance monitoring (how performance in an organization is tracked, reviewed and discussed);

2   target setting (what targets are provided for performance and the degree to which they are widely understood, stretched and connected); and

3   incentives and people management (how employee talent is attracted, managed and rewarded).

'Best management practice' occurs when performance monitoring information is routinely collected and analysed, and feedback is given, when the targets that are given are challenging and linked to organizational aims and when those who perform highly are rewarded for their outputs, and low performers are closely managed.

The Bloom and Van Reenen studies have been widely reported and have provided a wide range of studies indicating considerable evidence suggesting that management capability is indeed a key determinant of organizational performance. Their studies have gathered data from 10,000 organizations, a range of sectors and across a number of different nations (including both developed and developing countries), with results highlighting that the UK is relatively weak in a number of ways in comparison with competing nations (UK Commission for Employment and Skills (UKCES), 2014).

Bloom et al. (2012) summarized the key findings from their research:

- There are not only substantial links between variable management practices and organizational performance, but these practices differ across sectors. For example, publicly funded sectors were reported to have worse management practices across the range of sectors studied. In particular: public sector organizations have persistently low performers that are less likely to be moved or retrained, thus providing limited input to organizational productivity; promotion is not usually linked to performance but usually based on organizational tenure, and incentivized practice is weak.

- Among private sector firms, those with professionally recruited (i.e. external and non-family related) CEOs tend to show better management practices, compared with those who are run by their founders or familial descendants (e.g. first-born sons) – which tended to report bad management scores.

- How educated managers and non-managers are is strongly linked to superior management practices. In their initial study, Bloom et al. (2007) reported that the UK has relatively less educated managers.

- Management practices vary between countries. For example, US manufacturing firms score the highest in best managerial practices than any other country, with countries such as Canada, Germany, Japan and Sweden displaying high levels of good management practices. The UK ranked seventh out of twenty countries included in the studies. Developing countries such as Brazil and India were typically less well managed.

Further research has attempted to link management scores to publically available outcome data, and there is now a consistent range of data suggesting strong correlations between management scores and performance, with firms who reported better management practices reporting better performance on a range of variables (Tamkin and Ni Luanaigh 2016). For example, in a health-care setting Bloom et al. (2010) discussed that better management scores were associated with improved heart-attack survival rates, as well as improved outcomes for other kinds of general surgery and hospitals having shorter patient waiting lists. In the education sector, schools who reported better management also displayed higher test scores.

In the sales sector, Bloom and Van Reenen (2012) found that there was a significant relationship between sales per employee and management practices. When better management practices were reported there was improved labour productivity, increased profitability, higher annual sales growth and a reduction in exit (reported through liquidation or bankruptcy).

Tamkin and Ni Luanaigh (2016) also reviewed the evidence regarding the relationship between specific people management practices and organizational performance. In particular high performance working (HPW) emphasizes practices that result in improved performance, and has been defined as, 'a general approach to managing organisations that aims to stimulate more effective employee involvement and commitment to achieve higher levels of performance' (Belt and Giles, 2009: 1,7). Evidence has suggested that when introducing HPW using bundles of practices together significantly increases productivity in comparison to the introduction of one or two practices.

The main areas through which HPW can be divided were identified by Cox et al. (2012) as:[4]

- practices that structure work organization and job design;
- practices ensuring high levels of skills are an input into the production process;

- appraisal and performance management processes, including both formal and informal one-to-one discussions;

- practices that provide opportunities for employees to participate in and/or influence decision-making through direct or indirect methods; and

- practices that provide rewards for performance.

Research findings are beginning to show that the link between HPW and management practices are clear, as they focus on the management of people and embed such workplace practices with the aim to develop and improve employee commitment and involvement. Additionally there is evidence suggesting that HPW practices are related to improved organizational performance. For example, Combs et al. (2006) conducted a meta-analysis of research findings with the aim to answer the question: Do HPW practices matter? The results highlighted that HPW practices do enhance organizational performance and the effects on performance were stronger when measured in systems rather than individual practices. Ogbonnaya et al. (2013) explored both the independent and synergistic of HPW practices for employee attitudes and employee well-being. Their findings indicated that employees in firms who scored highly in their use of HPW and management practices were more likely to display better work-related attitudes in comparison to firms with low adoption of these practices. Those who used more innovative approaches also reported a more satisfied, committed workforce and lower work-related strain. This study also looked at the independent effects of HPW practices on employee attitudinal outcomes, finding that training, performance-related pay, flexible work and supportive management provided positive independent effects for employee job satisfaction, and flexible work and supportive management were also positively related to organizational commitment. The researchers concluded when employees appear to be valued and supported by management they increased levels of employee attachment, displaying positive and beneficial work-related outcomes.

However, how well HPW is adapted into organizations can be shaped by contextual factors. For example, Stone et al. (2012) found that the majority of organizations in their research incrementally adopted HPW practices, and let practices evolve over time, and those who did adopt such practices were aiming to improve performance or thought such practices already matched the management style and culture of the organization.

McBain et al. (2012) provided evidence to suggest a significant link between the way in which employees implemented management development practices and overall implications for organizational performance. Their study, surveying nearing 4,500 managers (including both CEOs and HR managers), found a number of practices particularly associated with high-performance organizations, including: how committed CEOs and senior managers were to management and leadership development, implementing HR practices that reinforce management development (e.g. performance management), and whether there was an alignment between business strategies and the HR strategy (so that managerial skills can develop to drive business results).

In summary, there is now a more robust evidence base to suggest that management practices can have a significant impact for workplace productivity. Organizations with better management tended to report improvements in a number of variables, including sales, profitability and consumer satisfaction ratings. Alongside the development of enhanced methodological rigour to highlight this relationship, there has been a growth in understanding of how people-management practices can also have an impact for organizational performance. HPW research now suggests that when implemented efficiently employees display improved beneficial work-related attitudes, not only improving employee well-being and job satisfaction, but also benefiting organizational performance.

Improved employee performance

The impact that work can have on an employee's well-being has attracted increasing interest in recent years, with well-being at work being recognized as an important factor in determining organizational success (Baptiste, 2008). An employee's physical and mental well-being is a major factor for organizational competitiveness (Bajorek et al., 2014). There is a range of evidence to suggest that employees who are in good health can be up to three times more productive than those with poor health and well-being, they can be more motivated to perform towards organizational goals and they can be more resilient to organizational change (Vaughan-Jones and Barham, 2010).

There is now an increasing and consistent message that the ways in which employees are managed is key to improving workplace well-being and reducing the likelihood of employee sickness absence (Donaldson-Fielder et al., 2013), and there are a number of ways through which this could occur, including: enhancing positive well-being, reducing the causes of stress, modelling healthy behaviours and supporting those who may suffer from health conditions. Black (2008: 59) was very clear about the role of management, when she reported: 'Good management can lead to good health, wellbeing and improved performance. The reverse can be true of bad management. Good health equals good business.'

Researchers have started to focus on management characteristics important for improving employee health and well-being. For example, Vahtera et al. (2000) concluded supportive management styles and low control led to a decreased risk of long spells of sickness absence. Similar findings were reported by Labriola et al. (2006) who, when examining the psychosocial work environment, also found that poor management support and lack of colleague support increased the likelihood of long-term sickness absence. Munir et al. (2011) in a longitudinal study examining management quality and sickness absence, found management quality (defined as the extent to which supervision was provided, development opportunities and job satisfaction were considered to be important, and work planning was provided) was related to long-term sickness absence, good-quality management being associated with reduced absence levels (Donaldson-Fielder et al., 2013). Managers also have a crucial role in return to work. Yarker et al. (2010) found that communication and support during sickness absence, inclusive behaviour on return and proactive support are competencies 'good managers' display.

It is important that employees are able to work in a stress-free environment, and it is a manager's responsibility to provide this. If employees perceive that employers have no regard for their health and well-being, this can negatively affect their motivation, commitment and performance. Ensuring that managers are aware of these issues and have the adequate level of skills to address them can have a large impact in helping staff manage workloads, and reduce absence levels (BIS, 2012).

People-management research has also garnered interest in employee engagement. An accepted definition of employee engagement has not yet been developed, with the 'Engaging for Success' report (MacLeod and Clarke, 2009) including over 50 definitions of employee engagement. A definition of employee engagement widely used was developed by Robinson et al. (2004: 9):

> Engagement is a positive attitude held by the employee towards the organisation and its values. An engaged employee is aware of business context, and works with colleagues to improve performance within the job for the benefit of the organisation. The organisation must work to nurture, maintain and grow engagement, which requires a two-way relationship between the employer and employee.

Evidence is accumulating suggesting that engaged employees can provide businesses with a competitive edge, and that improved employee engagement correlates with improved performance. The MacLeod review (2009) provided a number of business performance benefits that are associated with employee engagement:

- Engaged employees are more loyal to organizations, and are 87 per cent less likely to leave an organization than those who report high disengagement scores. The cost of turnover among disengaged employees can be very expensive (as a result of low productivity and recruitment costs), and estimates have put the cost of replacing a disengaged employee at equal to the average salary.

- Employees who display higher levels of engagement also report less sickness absence (disengaged employees taking 6.19 days on average, in comparison to 2.69 days). The MacLeod review calculated this to be £13.4 billion.

- It is thought that engaged employees have a greater understanding of customer needs: 70 per cent of engaged staff reported having a good understanding of how to meet customer needs, compared to only 17 per cent of non-engaged employees.

Practitioner studies are now providing evidence to suggest how management behaviours can be drivers of employee engagement. Maslach et al. (2001) suggested a number of work practices that can lead to engagement or burnout including: workload, control, recognition and reward, fairness and level of support. As Donaldson-Fielder et al. (2013) wrote, these areas of practice are ones in which management can influence, as they help to determine organizational culture, create perceptions of fairness, and they can vary the level of support and recognition they provide employees. Organizations that reported higher levels of engagement reported increased levels of management development activities (CMI, 2008).

In summary, managers can help organizational performance indirectly through enabling positive staff health and well-being, consequently reducing the amount (and duration) of sickness absence enabling a smoother return to work and having an impact on the level of employee engagement that employees display.

How are managers performing in the UK?

Accumulating literature suggests that management in the UK is not as good as it can be. The CMI (2014) sought to understand just how good management in the UK was, and what could be done to improve future management. The results were sobering:

- The UK lags behind its competitive nations in terms of both productivity and management. Even though the UK remains an attractive location for business, statistics from the ONS (2014b) indicated that output per hour was 21 per cent lower than the average for the rest of the G7 nations, and the cost of this loss of productivity is huge – a report by the CMI (2012) suggesting that poor management can cost UK businesses over £19 billion a year in lost working hours. It was concluded that management practices are a major factor holding the UK back from reaching its full economic potential.

- The CMI showed that although there were a number of world-class businesses operating in the UK, with many examples of excellence, there was also a large evidence base to suggest concerns about the effectiveness of management, and that 'managers are simply not up to the job' (p. 16). Interventions to develop management practices can make a real difference, and effective management development could result in 23 per cent higher organizational performance scores (CMI, 2012).

- Evidence from the Cranfield University School of Management (2013) surveying UK employers found that 64 per cent of employers perceived the lack of UK management skills and development was a major factor in holding back productivity growth. Additionally, 68 per cent of the sample believed these deficiencies prevented their employees from achieving their full potential.

- In term of management 'ethics', the CMI (2014) report highlighted that four-fifths of workers thought that their managers did not provide a good morale example to their employees, arguing this was a 'grave concern' (p. 17) and a key area for transformation if businesses were to reach their full economic potential. The CIPD (2013) also had similar findings, reporting that only 37 per cent of UK employees trusted senior management.

- Management skills gaps and management training is 'too little and too late' (CMI, 2014: 17). Changes are occurring in the UK labour market, and there have been estimates suggesting that between 2012 and 2020 the management workforce would need to grow by 586,000 people. This is additional to the 'replacement demand' created by employees leaving the labour market (retirement has been predicted to lead to the loss of 1,378,000 managers). The UKCES (2013) reported that management vacancies had reached 24,000 and it was calculated that approximately 1.96 million employees will enter management roles over the course of the decade. There are concerns that a large proportion of these managers would not be provided with sufficient training and development for their roles.

- Management positions are becoming harder to fill because of skill shortages; e.g. 57 per cent of cases strategic management skills were lacking (UKCES, 2013).

- Many managers do not have specific management qualifications, and UK competitors spend significantly more on management training than organizations in the UK (CMI, 2014). In the UK only 34 per cent of organizations provided management training.

- Of managers already employed, the top five skills most lacking include: strategic management skills (46 per cent); planning and organizational skills (44 per cent); team-working skills (38 per cent); problem-solving skills (35 per cent); and oral communication skills (33 per cent) (UKCES, 2013).

- Oral evidence provided to the CMI (2014) by Ruth Ambrose (Director of Legal AMEC) indicated that it was not that the UK lacked management talent, but the limited access to training, a lack of focus at the early stages of a manager's career and less consideration given to career-path development across industries was where the UK was failing. Other written submissions highlighted that managers were only likely to receive four days of training per year, and there was unlikely to be access to much more when their career started. Research published in the *Harvard Business Reviews* reported that managers first received training at the age of 42, often about 10 years after they took on their first supervisory role.

- The UKCES (2013) found that more than one-third of organizations did not provide any management training in the previous year, and when managers do receive training they may not have the opportunity to implement what they have learnt effectively; consequently a lot of management training is wasted.

- The CMI report suggested that one of the main consequences of the last economic recession was a focus on short-term goals and priorities for 'survival', and management development was not considered to be a priority. If the development of managers is left to current managers, then there is a risk that underperformance will continue.

- Certain sectors have more difficulties in the provision of management training. SMEs have particular issues, with cost especially being a barrier to training, thus they try to take advantage of other lower-cost development routes. Other factors related to SME training were a limited availability of suitable training and taking time out of work to attend training. This is another concern for future management development, especially with the current growth of SMEs in the private sector. With this lack of training comes the limited ability to see where improvements and change can be made. The training and development of SME managers was highlighted as an important factor for management development for UK productivity.

This summary paints a bleak picture of management practices in the UK. Thus, there is a need to have a closer look behind management theory, and what a 'good manager' looks like to see how they can be developed.

The employment relationship and 'good management'

How an employee experiences work depends on the critical role of management in an organization, as Drucker (2002) argued that productivity of individuals depends not only on the environment in which they are placed, but how they are managed and motivated. Therefore the employment relationship between the manager and the employee is important, and one way this can be viewed is through the psychological contract.

There has been a lot of development around the concept of the psychological contract, but the idea can originally be traced back to the work of Argyris and social exchange theory, which has been described as one of the most influential paradigms for understanding workplace behaviour (Cropanzano and Mitchell,

2005). Social exchanges involve a set of interactions between two parties, which in turn generate obligations (these actions are contingent on the actions of the other person), and these interactions have the potential to result in high-quality relationships (Cropanzano and Mitchell, 2005). These exchanges come in two broad categories: economic (characterized by both parties fulfilling specific obligations of a formal contract, typically short term and usually involving the exchange of concrete resources; Rupp and Cropanzano, 2002); and social (based upon unspecified obligations with the nature of the return left to the discretion of the respective party, is viewed as a longer-term relationship, necessitating trust). Social exchange theorists described the employment relationship as a form of an exchange relationship; for example in exchange for organizational benefits such as wages, positive work conditions and perceived organizational support, employees should display loyalty and effort towards the organizational goals and outcomes (Rhoades and Eisenbeger, 2002). When employees perceive fair treatment by an organization's employers, they respond with increased organizational citizenship behaviour, commitment and fewer turnover intentions, in comparison with those perceived to be unfairly treated (Rupp and Cropanzano, 2002).

Social exchange theory has been used as a framework for exploring the employee–organization relationship, including the development of the psychological contract. The psychological contract between an employer and employee can be defined as 'the perceptions of both parties to the employment relationship – organization and individual – of the reciprocal promises and obligations implied in that relationship' (Guest and Conway, 2002: 22). The psychological contract specifies what the organization and the individual employee are expected to give and receive from each other in this exchange relationship, and it is the perceived discrepancy between what has been promised and what is received that provides the basis upon what each side will reciprocate in the employment relationship.

From understanding this, it can be easy to recognize why the psychological contract has been used as a lens through which organizational and individual workplace behaviours, outcomes and attitudes have been explained. A psychological contract can specify how employees define a deal, and whether or not the deal has been honoured or fulfilled (McLean Parks et al., 1998), and can also allow for any exploration regarding how deals change over time (Guest, 2004). However, different representatives of an organization may have different messages regarding their expectations and obligations in their psychological contract, and consequently an employee's perceived contract with an organization can be unclear (Herriot et al., 1997).

Understanding the state of the psychological contract is therefore important for managers, and the level of communication at the developing stages of the psychological contract will lead to fewer misunderstandings regarding its content (Herriot and Pemberton, 1997). Thus when determining what is important for management practices, communicating the psychological contract may be just as important as balancing its contents (Guest and Conway, 2002). HR managers who reported more extensive use of communication have reported clearer and less breached organizational contracts and promises, as well as a fairer exchange and more positive effects of policies and practices on employee attitudes and behaviours (Guest and Conway, 2002).

One of the constructs of the psychological contract in terms of explaining employment relationship outcomes has been contract breach (Conway et al., 2011), which occurs when one partner in the employment relationship perceives another to have failed to fulfil promised obligations (Robinson and Rousseau, 1994). Rousseau (1989) argued that contract breach was a defining feature of the psychological contract, and once a promise had been broken it was difficult to repair. A violation of the psychological contract is the extreme affective or emotional reaction that may accompany breaches (Conway and Briner, 2005). Management consequences if contract breaches have occurred (or perceived to have occurred by employees) can reduce negative organizational behaviours, such as reduced organizational commitment, or an increase in intention to quit. Maintaining a positive psychological contract is a core task of managers, and if they are sensitive to the consequences of contract breach, it leads us to question why this still occurs.

Guest (2004) highlighted a number of factors that could affect the viability of 'traditional employment relations', one being the increasing flexibility and fragmentation of the workforce, including the introduction of different patterns of working (e.g. sub-contracting, working from home, various patterns of working hours), which can provide increased challenges for management in attempting to co-ordinate workplace activities, as well as ensuring a psychological contract based on trust. It could be that different individuals perceive their psychological contract differently, and that idiosyncratic deals are negotiated when an employee joins an organization or in the subsequent months. These will differ from standard deals usually applied to large groups of employees and could reflect legislated employment rights or those determined under a collective agreement (Guest, 2004). The notion of the idiosyncratic deal is that it allows for traditional employment relationship deals as found in the standard deal, but can be more informal and flexible based on the individual situation. Although Guest (2004) argued that the idea of idiosyncratic deals is becoming more important for organizations, he also noted a number of consequences for management:

- They can provide management with a greater challenge of managing complexity, as the resulting range and types of idiosyncratic deals that can be developed could result in a greater opportunity for contract breach and violation (and the resulting negative implications for organizational behaviour).

- There could be an increased risk of perceived unfairness from other employees regarding the idiosyncratic nature of another employee's deal.

- There are issues related to trust (an important component of the psychological contract), and what may appear as a sensible agreement for one employee could be reflected as favouritism.

- The climate in which these deals are developed may have an important influence on whether these deals are developed and what the personal and organizational outcomes of these deals may be.

The management of the psychological contract was termed as a core task for organizations to people-build, rather than people-use, in a climate characterized by trust (Schalk and Rousseau, 2001). Therefore, it can be argued that one of the main roles for managers when developing an employee relationship is the communication of expectations, so that the psychological contract can be more effective, reducing opportunities for contract breach and a greater likelihood to produce positive organizational outcomes. Alongside this improved communication will come fairness and trust. When a psychological contract is more explicit, levels of fairness and trust reported by employees and effective communication reduced perceived breaches and were associated with better employee-related outcomes (Guest and Conway, 2002).

So what can understanding the role of that the psychological contract mean for determining what makes a 'good manager'? It can be argued that having a greater understanding of the importance of people management is critical for what makes a good manager. BIS (2012) reported that good managers communicate with clarity, they review and guide performance (thus can report if expectations are being met, and provide feedback on performance), offer praise and identify where current and future skills are required.

The CMI (2014) reported a number of traits that managers should have to be effective that support the concept of the psychological contract. These include:

- Managers need to take responsibility for the morale and sense of purpose of each person reporting to them, developing a style that is collaborative, open and fair. Thus, developing an employment relationship based on trust where employers and employees are able to discuss employment needs and training, and have difficult but honest conversations about performance, in a way that will not lead to contract breach.

- Having the ability to communicate effectively was also seen as important – managers are not just about developing strategies and giving instructions, but they have to communicate in ways that continue to engage employees. In this way ensuring that their communication is clear, and work distribution is perceived to be fair across all employees, and appropriate feedback about performance is communicated will help to ensure co-operative performance.

- Managers need to be collaborative, supportive, show concern and care for staff, show willingness to work towards the interests of the team and show support for career development. This is very similar to the idea of 'people management' highlighted by BIS (2012), but clearly emphasizes the two-way relationship between managers and employees, and the importance of the employment relationship built upon fairness and trust.

In summary, the psychological contract can be viewed as an analytical lens through which the management of the employment relationship can be viewed. There is now a growing body of literature showing that both the nature of the exchanges between managers and employees, and whether they have been perceived to have been fulfilled have implications for organizational outcomes and productivity. The framework can be used then to highlight the role of people management, especially the roles of communication, trust and fairness to be essential skills that managers should display if positive organizational outcomes are to be achieved.

First line management

Line managers in organizations play an important role in the management of psychological contracts, especially in ensuring and maintaining levels of organizational productivity. Line managers are managers to whom individual teams report directly and who have responsibility to a higher level of management for those employees or teams, and as a result they have a key role in achieving core business objectives (Gilbert et al., 2011). The line manager has been referred to as being a critical factor in an employee's overall experience of work, and as a result of their direct supervisory responsibility they are important in how organizational policies and practices influence their attitudes and behaviours (Bowen and Ostroff, 2004). Line managers can be vital in making the difference between low-performing and high-performing organizations (Hutchinson, 2008). In the *Engaging for Success* report (MacLeod and Clarke, 2009), Dame Carol Black said:

> If I could wave a magic wand, the one thing I would do is to improve the relationship between line managers and employees ... The nature and characteristics of the jobs that employees are required to do in term of satisfaction, reward and esteem and a degree of control in the task are vitally important to them. The line manager has a key role. (p. 31)

Line-management responsibilities have expanded beyond their traditional supervisory role (McConville and Holden, 1999; Hales, 2005; Purcell and Hutchinson, 2007), and they now have an increased role in the implementation and delivery of HR practices. Line managers are now expected to be involved in recruitment and selection decisions, providing coaching and guidance, conducting performance appraisals, dealing with any problems within the workforce, and being aware of any health and well-being issues that could be affecting employees (Hutchinson, 2008) – all this on top of their role that they were additionally recruited to fulfil.

In their report for the CIPD, Hutchinson and Purcell (2007) noted that there was an understanding that line managers play an increasingly important role in people management, but little detail was known with regards to what line managers actually do in practice, and what behaviours and competencies are needed to perform the roles. Their research was undertaken in six organizations from a variety of sectors, and the main results included:

- All line managers discussed their increasing role in people-management areas, and this had been taken on without relinquishing any duties from their 'old roles'. As a result, line managers had an important influence in the employee's attitudes and behaviours, with one of the managers quoted as saying that they 'bring policies to life' (p. 4).

- Perceptions about line-management behaviours, including: communication about organizational change, employee voice and fair treatment were most important in explaining differences in employee job motivation, satisfaction and discretion.

- Reward management can have a profound impact on an employee's behaviour (both those who do and do not receive it), and how this is implemented by line managers can be of primary importance. In terms of extrinsic rewards (usually transactional financial rewards, e.g. salary, determining reward-related pay or employee bonuses), the research found line managers were unable to use these as rewards without approval from managers higher up in the organizational system. In contrast, line managers reported that intrinsic rewards such as enabling job enjoyment and the ability to provide more fulfilling work were more up to their discretion and easier to implement.

- Line managers were seen to be more involved with a number of learning and development activities, both formal and informal. Specifically, they had a large role in identifying and agreeing employee training needs, something that is usually conducted during the employee's performance appraisal. Line managers may also be involved in the delivery of training in a number of methods, for example on and off the job training, sharing knowledge and providing structured courses. Some line managers voiced frustrations in this regard, as if training needs were identified, then access to employees could be limited due to financial constraints beyond the line manager's means.

- Line managers may also be involved in less formal learning and development practices that can still be considered as fundamental to employee productivity. Examples included: induction activities (organizing a guide or buddy to advise a new employee, or arrange work shadowing); providing access to challenging work or becoming a member of a project team; job rotation (a line manager would be able to ensure that individuals can contribute to other work, teams or departments); and organizing career development.

If line managers are considered to be important for organizational performance and the enactment of HR policies, how are they perceived to be doing? The answer to this question in general is, not as good as they could be. Recent employee outlook statistics published by the CIPD (2016) showed areas where line managers were perceived as performing well, and where there is need for development. Overall, 79 per cent of the employees surveyed reported that they at least have a line manager/supervisor who they could report to as part of their job. This highlights that 21 per cent of employees perceive they have no line manager, and consequently may not be receiving the employment, professional and personal support they require for their role.

In terms of how satisfied employees are with their managers, those in the public sector were found to be more satisfied than employees in the private sector. Areas where the most positive perceptions of line managers were reported included: line managers are likely to be very well/fairly well committed to their organization (70 per cent), treat their employees fairly well (70 per cent) and make clear what is expected of their employees (64 per cent). In terms of employee support and well-being, 63 per cent of employees reported that their line managers are supportive if they have a problem, 62 per cent responded that line managers listened to their suggestions and 60 per cent of employees felt their line managers tell them when they are doing a good job (CIPD, 2016). However, problems with line-manager behaviours were reported in terms of some of their performance-management duties. For example, line managers are fairly poor or very poor at coaching employees on the job (31 per cent), keeping employees in touch with what is going on in the organization (25 per cent), discussing training and development needs (23 per cent) and acting as a role model to the organization (23 per cent). This can have negative implications for employee engagement and motivation and organizational productivity, if employees are not being encouraged or developed to the best of their potential. There is also some evidence to suggest that employee turnover can be affected by line-management behaviour, providing support to the adage that 'employees join an organization, but leave a manager'.[6]

There is evidence that some line managers have reported tension and limited willingness and awareness to undertake the additional HR responsibilities (Renwick and MacNeil, 2002; Hutchinson and Purcell, 2010). Hutchinson and Tailby (2012) highlighted that despite the changes reported in line-management roles, 85 per cent felt that they had clarity about what their roles meant, with 83 per cent understanding what was expected of them as line managers. Additionally, 77 per cent understood the importance of their role and how they contributed to the organization's strategy and productivity. Less positively, 67 per cent thought they managed people well, with 61 per cent of line managers reporting they felt they gave enough emphasis to the people-management side of their role. Worryingly, however, only 35 per cent of line managers reported that they met all the demands of their role. This finding provides support to academics and practitioners who have discussed that the devolvement of HR activities to line management occurs in addition to the previous roles that line managers were undertaking, thereby significantly increasing their workload. As a result it must be asked, now that line managers have these added responsibilities for people management to undertake, are they prepared to take these roles, or are there barriers to their efficiency?

Research has raised a number of concerns about the effectiveness of line managers, with three issues of concern: line managers' lack of skills and knowledge about the roles they are to undertake; competing priorities and work overload; and a lack of commitment to people management (Hutchinson and Purcell, 2007). Barber et al. (1999) argued that given the value that line managers have in influencing the experiences of the employees they manage, how organizations adequately prepare, support and invest in their line managers so that they are able to deliver the people management aspects of their role is of increasing importance. A common theme throughout line-management research is that line managers lack the skills and competencies needed to complete the performance-management aspect of their job, and that it is necessary for them to acquire new skills to competently achieve this role.

What is worrying is that little is being done by organizations to improve the training that line managers clearly need. For example, in CIPD's (2014b) Learning and Development survey, nearly 40 per cent of organizations reported inadequate training, or a lack of training for their line managers, and this is having an impact on line-management capability. Additionally, 26 per cent of organizations had not prioritized line-management training. In the 2016 CIPD employee outlook survey line-management training was one of the top three priorities of leadership development for 50 per cent of organizations, to equip line managers to improve people-management performance – once again highlighting that not enough priority has been given to this. Finally, in an HR Outlook report (CIPD, 2017c) one in six HR professionals reported that line managers received neither formal nor informal tailored support when they were required to undertake their new HR responsibilities. It was found that 60 per cent of organizations did provide some form of tailored support, and

44 per cent received formal training, even though the later training is of most importance. These limitations to skill development, learning and training could therefore be having a negative impact not only on the productivity of those who they manage, but also the health and well-being of employees, having indirect consequences for organizational productivity. There is still work for organizations to adequately train and develop line managers, and improve recruitment practices for deciding which employees become line managers.

The level of training and development that line managers receive can have an impact on how managers rate their own performance and well-being, and the performance of their team. Unsurprisingly, line managers who have more access to training are more likely to have higher well-being scores and perform at higher levels. As line managers are usually recruited to the position as a result of their performance in the more technical aspects of their role, rather than their people-management skills, the need for training and development in these areas becomes increasingly clear. Training line managers and prospective line managers in ways that would help them to cope with the 'stretching' of their workloads, time management and planning will be of use to fulfil their duties (ILM).

FRANCES O'GRADY

A COMMON CRITICISM OF BRITISH management is lack of people-management skills or lack of focus on managing employee relations – too often people get promoted into management because they are good at their job and no thought is given to their ability to manage people or teams. What's more managers, who often determine the training and development that is made available to staff, can be placed under substantial pressure to deliver short-term gains, which limit the extent to which they can focus on wider medium-term productivity improvements. Many managers are required to deliver team performance to meet overall organizational targets with little leeway to improve staff competences.

Line managers in the public sector commented that HR functions were increasingly dominating their day-to-day work, and there was a growing reluctance to take on any extra responsibilities that detracted them from fulfilling their 'original duties', especially if they were being measured against these outcomes (Harris et al., 2002). In addition to the increased workload, there was a perception of reduced resources to undertake this work, and line managers described being 'dumped upon'. HR functions that require performance management and evaluation are time consuming and often reduce opportunities for investing time in quality personal interactions with staff, which is considered necessary for gaining high trust manager–employee relationships (Harris, 2001).

Worryingly the CIPD (2013) reported that only 61 per cent of employees agreed that their line managers were trustworthy and 53 per cent said that line managers would be the first person they approached for support or advice on a work issue. This indicates that there is an apparent struggle for line managers to balance the need of the organization with the needs of individual employees. Additionally, the survey reported that 27 per cent of line managers faced conflicts of interest every day when trying to balance strategic priorities alongside people management.

The ability of line managers to cope with stress and the management of their workload is an important part for their own well-being and their overall success as managers (ILM). Managers felt 63 per cent of managers were able to cope with the stress of their workload (which, however, indicates that a substantial amount cannot), but they were less able to cope with the size and pressure of their workload (56 per cent). This is an important finding due to research indicating a correlation between the stress levels of direct reports and their line managers, and the resulting implications for performance and well-being. Equipping managers with the skills to cope with the stress of their increased workload is essential to improving the level of performance and well-being in the future.

A further reason for barriers to good line management in organizations related to difficulties that organizations have in recruiting graduates with the right skills to become line managers in the first place (BIS, 2012). This is specifically a problem for smaller firms who have reported difficulties in both attracting and retaining graduate talent as graduates prefer to work in larger organizations. Organizations with under 50 employees are less likely to have a graduate recruitment scheme, or a talent management programme, and have to recruit managers externally. The limited internal management challenges have also been viewed as a block to organizational growth in medium-sized businesses.

There are many ways through which line management and management practices in general could and should be improved if organizations are to reach their full economic potential. The CMI (2014) and BIS (2012) have provided a range of top tips for improving organizational management, including:

- Recognizing that good management matters. Organizations must recognize that how employees are managed and how much they are engaged is crucial to the success of the business. The evidence above has suggested that management is difficult and can go wrong easily, and so the more organizations dedicate time to developing good managers, the better.

- Good working practices should be implemented as a business strategy throughout the organization, and not solely as a framework for management. Organizations need to develop effective recruitment practices, appropriate skills and development training, practices to engage employees, and to ensure that employees have the skills that are needed to be applied in organizations.

- Recruitment of line managers should not solely be based on their technical competencies, but also on the basis of their personal attitudes and capabilities.

- In addition to the above, it is necessary to provide training, support and mentoring to line managers, as it is not enough to just expect them to pick up the necessary skills on the job. All new line managers need to be prepared with the people-management skills that may be new to their role.

- Line managers should receive appropriate line-management training within the first 12 months of promotion into their role (if not received previously), through a management training qualification.

- There needs to be clarity about what good management skills and behaviours look like – managers need to be clear, have an appreciation for the effort and contribution employees make, treat employees as individuals, make sure work is organized effectively and ensure that all employees are supported to do their role. Thus the good skills that line managers need are: recognition, autonomy, empowerment, reviewing and guiding, feedback and reward/praise.

- Effective management does not just need to occur at the line-management level, but it needs to run throughout the organization. Consequently it is important to audit for management capability and plans are needed to address any skills deficits. This needs to be assessed regularly at both an individual and organizational level, and where any issues are noted change or development of managers needs to occur. To do this, organizations need to have the practical tools available to conduct these assessments and skills evaluations (or know where this support is available to them). Such tools include 360-degree feedback, e-learning and mentoring schemes.

In summary, line managers have been defined as an important role in the management cog, especially as they are key in implementing HR policies on the line, and for developing the psychological contracts with employees to engage and motivate employees. Line management can be challenging as a result of the people-management aspect to their roles that they have to undertake on top of their original duties, and many have reported not receiving the adequate training or development necessary to undertake this role. Line managers must be given the recognition and support they need and deserve to ensure those they manage are as productive and efficient as possible.

What management challenges do we have in the future?

So what about the management needs of the future? In recent years the term VUCA (volatile, uncertain, complex and ambiguous) has been bounded around to suggest that this is what the future is going to be – and if this prediction is correct, how will managers have to adapt to ensure their effectiveness, and to help maintain, or even improve organizational productivity?

A number of future challenges have been identified by the literature and these revolve around:

- The workforce is ageing and becoming more intergenerational. Organizational management will need to focus on how to retain and engage an ageing workforce when, at the same time, new generations are entering the workforce who may require different managerial needs.

- Technology is continuously developing, and may become more important in organizations than it is already today. Technology is also changing traditional methods of working – so what skills will managers need to adapt to this? Additionally, social media is becoming ever more progressive – will managers need to be more aware of the different methods through which information or ideas can be exchanged?

- The workforce is becoming more diverse, both in terms of gender representation and the integration of different cultures. We have yet to see what Brexit will do for the UK, but will managers have to use different skills to manage the different needs of the diverse workforce?

Amongst all of this change, as Tamkin (2016) commented, the ability to adapt and to retain talent will become more important for organizations, and will be a competitive factor for business operations. Management skills and being able to adapt to business models will then be key to compete within global markets and to remain efficient and productive.

ANNE FRANCKE

MANAGEMENT IS CHANGING TO SOMETHING far more flexible and fluid than in the past. We already know that managers who coach are far better than managers who control. This will continue. Work is a state of mind not a location – you can work from everywhere and increasingly people do. So the ability to tightly control the action of those who work for you disappears. Equally, multi-level, rigid hierarchies are no longer necessary or desirable in many organizations. There simply isn't the time for things to cascade up and down a line – and indeed, the ability to keep such aspects confidential is greatly diminished when everything can be videoed and tweeted within seconds.

The trends driving this are technology, and how it shapes attitudes in generations – young people in particular are always on and used to using technology to communicate. Technology also drives collaboration, transparency and ever more change. It shapes what we do as well – we are more into knowledge and less into routine roles which increasingly can be done by robots or computers. Technology also means that you can shape your work around your life. You can take your kids to school, visit your elderly mother, put your kids to bed, and still get all your emails and presentations and phone calls done.

Globalization and the immediate impact of knowing about everything everywhere means that we can have much more diverse mind-sets in organizations than previously. Your employee base can be across the street or across the world. They can be flexible and part time or indeed crowdsourced.

The impact of all this on organizations means that rulebooks are no longer valid. The fast pace of change tells us that no one can ever know the answer to everything. So values and ethics become even more important.

The intergenerational workforce

Deloitte (2014) reported that by 2025, Generation Y or 'millennials' (those born in the 1980s and 1990s) will comprise 75 per cent of the global workforce, and will therefore play an important role in shaping the future of management. The CMI (2014) looked at what Generation Y expected from work, finding that they wanted ethical employers, organizations where they have good opportunities for progression, good work–life balance and interesting work. However, dividing the workforce into arbitrary sections depending on date of birth may be helpful for marketeers, but less so for managers. In many ways we would argue that this is what people in the workforce have always wanted and still want now – no matter what generation they are in. Flexibility is also really important to Generation Y, with 45 per cent wanting flexibility over pay, and more that 57 per cent intending to leave their job within one to two years of joining. However, this is matched against their feeling of a strong sense of entitlement, a tendency to be over-confident, having a poor level of self-awareness and low work ethic (Tamkin, 2016). Generation X have more of the fundamental management characteristics; however, it is clear that attracting and retaining young employees is a priority as they are creative, open minded, multi-culturally aware, confident and technologically savvy (CMI, 2014), but they are also the least experienced cohort of managers currently working in the UK.

The challenge of attracting and retaining the young generation is that in the UK we have an ageing workforce, and as a result 22 per cent of graduates recruited to roles are over-qualified for the work they are doing (UKCES,

2014), and so young employees can be trapped in the low-level entry positions. This becomes a management dilemma, as employers are being encouraged to retain the older workforce and attract a younger workforce, and if they fail at both, management talent will be both lost and underdeveloped. In economies with very high employment rates for older workers (e.g. Norway and Japan), and in places where there have been big increases in the ageing workforce in recent years (e.g. Germany) rates of over-qualification have been low. This indicates that good management of this in the future is important for other economies to develop similar practices. It has been predicted that by 2020 there will be up to five generations working alongside each other in the workplace (Tamkin, 2016). Consequently, managers need to have the skills to work with and manage both those potentially significantly older and significantly younger then themselves. A recent report by the Institute of Employment Studies (IES) and The Centre for Ageing Better (2017) found that older employees (those aged 50 and above) and younger employees valued the same things from their work (e.g. making a meaningful contribution, social interaction and opportunities for learning and progression), but that health factors are important in their decisions to remaining at work. This once again emphasizes the important role for the development of people-management skills and ensuring that they are applied effectively.

Technology

We have already looked at how technology is changing the future workplace in Chapter 4. In this section we focus on how technology might change the way we manage. The CMI (2014) reported that in the future of the workplace, technology will be integral to the way that managers both work and manage. If you look around the current workplace it is clear to see that a 'technological revolution' has transformed the way we work – not only physically – but we are able to work globally, across time zones and become more innovative in how, when and where we work. Some have argued that technology has enabled workplaces to work more effectively (although when struggling with video-conferencing we would disagree), but as the UKCES (2014) have acknowledged the advancement of some technology has and could further lead to redundancies, or unemployment for a number of sectors.

The CIPD (2014) reported that 94 per cent of businesses now have internet access, 93 per cent have a broadband connection, and in 2011 81 per cent of companies had a website – this we are sure will only grow if organizations want to remain competitive. However, it is important that all members of staff are engaged in this technological agenda, and it is not just Generation Y that leads this progression.

Technology has not only become integral to the way that we work, but it will become an integral feature in management. Generation Y have a desire for flexible working hours and the development of the internet and smartphone technology has meant that people are able to work more flexibly, and in a variety of geographical locations, so this will be (if not already) a challenge for managers to lead teams and workers who may not all be in the same place but will require the same information (CMI, 2014). Although this increased flexibility and the technology associated with it may become the future of work, it is important to note that there are negatives to this reliance on technology, and some of these have already been reported. For example, 65 per cent of managers reported feeling under pressure to work extra hours (a sense of needing to be 'always on'), and only 13 per cent felt they had good work–life balance. Smartphone technology has been seen as a contributor to being overworked, with employees often checking emails outside of work.[7] This can lead to unhealthy work practices that can have negative implications for the health and well-being of staff which, as previously seen, can lead to reduced productivity. There have been some attempts by organizations to reduce this; for example Volkswagen took steps to improve the work–life balance of their staff by turning off BlackBerry email after work hours, as a result of complaints from staff that their work and home lives were becoming blurred,[8] whilst France has introduced the right to disconnect from work emails after 6 p.m. to re-install a sense of work–life balance.[9] However, it could be argued that if there is a good employment relationship and a supportive work culture, employees should not even feel the need to use or connect to work emails after their working hours.

Managers in the future will have to develop a deeper understanding of using big data that can be captured, which can be used to lead people more effectively (CMI, 2014). For example, in the future there will be tools that can gauge employee engagement from staff email and staff social media accounts, and this data can then be used to manage performance. Additionally, by monitoring the social media use of potential and current recruits, managers can assess the stability and emotional stability of staff, and predict the likelihood of staff turnover. The UKCES (2014) rightly acknowledged that this does lead to ethical concerns regarding data storage and data management.

But this also asks questions about what skills managers will need. Ironically, it will not be technological skills (although having the capability to use computer devices would be helpful) but people-management skills. Managers will always be needed, communication is still going to be important (even though the means through which messages are passed may differ), and managers will have to learn how to use emotional intelligence, sympathy and develop that emotional relationship, even when the employee may not be in the same 'work space' as them. Managers must learn to trust their reports to avoid the use of micro-management (ILM, 2013), which could mean an adjustment in their expectations of what a 'good outcome' is – measured by actual task performance and not the hours worked doing it.

Workplace diversification

It has been predicted that not only will diversity be a feature of the workplace of the future but it will be an imperative. A number of studies have suggested that the role of globalization will continue to develop and have an impact on the make-up of the workforce. The CIPD (2014) discussed how since 2004 there was a vast increase in the 'in-migration' of people from Central and Eastern Europe, and this was especially seen in certain sectors (e.g. agriculture). However, with the recent Brexit vote, there is increased uncertainty regarding how this will have an impact on both those coming into the UK to work, and those from abroad who already work here. This will obviously have to be handled sensitively by managers – and communication of both national and organizational policies will be key in such situations. Studies by both the CIPD (2014) and Leeds University (as cited in the CMI, 2014 report) have predicted that the proportion of black, Asian and other ethnic minorities will increase. The 2001 census reported at that time they comprised 8 per cent of the UK population, and it is predicted to rise to 20 per cent by 2051. Asia, in particular, is now producing more science and engineering graduates than the US and Europe combined, and it has been argued that this talent will be essential for enabling the future prosperity of the manufacturing industry (Homkes, 2014). For future managers, this means there is a greater need to develop cross-cultural awareness with and between employees, to have an understanding of cultural sensitivities, and how they interact with employees. Additionally there may be a need for managers to develop a shared understanding of the company values, especially if diversification also leads to having offices and groups of staff in different countries.

A Working Futures report by the UKCES (2013) estimated that by 2020 women are expected to take up 56 per cent of the net increase in jobs in the UK. It has been argued that women are an untapped resource and that currently their potential is not being fully realized. Legislative measures such as maternity leave and return-to-work policies have improved the number of women currently employed by organizations, but there is still a considerable gender pay gap. For example, 10 November 2016 was Equal Pay Day, the day where female employees were effectively working for free due to the 13.9 per cent gender pay gap for full-time workers. This is not just a pay or equality issue, but it can have a substantial impact on organizational productivity (for example, companies with the most women on the board of directors significantly and consistently outperform those with no representation[10]). Organizations both now and in the future must tackle this pay gap if they wish to both retain and attract diversity. Thus managers of the future will need to be successful in recruiting and retaining a diverse workforce, ensuring that all talent is recognized, and enabling all employees to work to the best of their ability. Managers must be aware of creating a culture where inclusion and diversity is second nature, and thus once again, there needs to be awareness and sensitivity to changes in the work environment and recognize the role they have in people development.

Finally, in terms of workplace diversity, attention needs to be paid to the changes of skills in the workforce. Young people suffered disproportionately in the 2008 recession, and have also been left behind in the job recovery (Bajorek et al., 2016). The large proportion of young people who are NEET (not in education, employment and training) will also be at an employment disadvantage as the UK economy is shifting towards recruiting employees with higher skill levels, thus in the future there may be increasing competition for entry requirement roles. Young people are now often over-qualified for the roles they are in, and may not make use of the skills they have. Employees unable to make use of their skills and qualifications are less likely to feel engaged or motivated towards the aims, values and missions of an organization, thus creating both challenges for employers to find the right jobs for all, and for managers to manage the development of the workforce, so that work can remain challenging and young people can feel they are valued in organizations. The CMI (2014) reported that the skills of managers in 2020 to deal with the challenges of sustainability and diversity will include being agile, authentic and talented, and having people-management skills that include good communication, collaboration and creativity. Once again this indicates that people management will continue to be of critical importance to show that diversity is not just an organizational policy, but a way of thinking.

Conclusions

Even though the debate about what management should be defined as, and how it differs to other concepts such as leadership, has not been concluded (and is likely to continue into the future), the evidence is clear that management matters. Management has been shown to be influential for organizational productivity, the health and well-being of employees and how engaged the workforce is. However, we also know that the workforce is changing, and both psychological contracts and traditional legal contracts are also changing, and thus more focus needs to be placed on the role of management to ensure that organizational development can keep up with external changes.

For us, it seems that what managers of the future need is very similar to what managers need now – the development of people management skills. Managers both now and in the future must ensure that their core people-management practices are successfully implemented, and applied in the workforce. With this development, they will be able to effectively ensure that employee skills are easily adapted to changes in the workforce to provide the competitive edge that organizations will need to remain successful. Managers will need to successfully build and maintain that employee relationship, ensuring that two-way communication and trust is experienced, and be seen to encourage and support employees to produce their best, but also highlight their opportunities for development. Organizations must begin to realize the importance of people management and adopt training and development programmes that mean they have strategic management skills that fit the long-term aims of an organization.

To have the managers that we need for the future, action needs to start now. Organizations should be focusing on attracting, appointing and especially retaining employees who they believe have the skills to be good managers, but importantly they need to ensure that the skills are developed and managers are provided with the support they need to do their job effectively.

Management is not easy – and it doesn't look it will get easier in the future – but providing managers with the skills to help them will be a massive start.

6

The future health of the workforce

One of the paradoxes of technological and scientific advancement is that life expectancy is increasing but that we spend a greater proportion of our lives living with chronic health conditions. In many Western economies, life expectancy is now increasing by five hours per day,[1] largely as a result of dramatic improvements in health care and treatment. Yet, by 2030, over 40 per cent of our working-age populations will be living with at least one chronic health condition.

For governments, other public authorities, social insurance systems, employers and individuals, this represents an irresistible tide that now has to be managed because it cannot be prevented. Coupled with the ageing of our populations and our dependence on a shrinking proportion of younger people to support the ageing and retired population, the impact on health care and other resources, on work productivity, on patterns of consumption, on inequality and on social exclusion are likely to be more significant than we can currently comprehend. In this chapter, we will focus only on the health of our working-age population, although the wider demographic shifts that form part of the landscape of change cannot be easily ignored.

The growing burden of ill health among modern workers

In 2013, 555,000 EU citizens of working age died of non-communicable diseases such as heart disease, cancer and strokes (OECD, 2016a). A large proportion of this disease burden and mortality can be attributed to what public health specialists call 'modifiable health risks' – primarily linked to health behaviours such as smoking, obesity, sedentary lifestyles and excessive alcohol consumption. The economic impact of these deaths is striking. They are the equivalent to 3.4 million potentially productive years of life across the EU and €115 billion in potential economic loss (about 0.8 per cent of EU GDP).

But mortality is still not the main concern when we look at chronic illness among working-age people. Morbidity has a far bigger impact on labour-market outcomes because chronic conditions increase absence from work, increase so-called 'presenteeism' and work productivity loss and also cause millions of workers to leave the labour market prematurely.

Workers with chronic illnesses also have lower employment rates. Among EU workers aged between 50 and 59 years old, chronic illness – especially where people are living with more than one condition (known as co-morbidity) – employment rates can be dramatically reduced. For example, among those with two or more co-morbid conditions the employment rate is only 52 per cent. This pattern is broadly the same whichever condition is examined, including smoking, obesity and excessive alcohol consumption.

Chronic conditions are also associated with higher rates of sickness absence. Figure 6.1 shows OECD analysis of data from across the EU showing that, among 50–59-year-old workers, the number of sick days taken in a year increases steadily in most countries as the number of chronic illnesses multiply.

This can obviously have an effect at the level of the economy but also for individual employers and businesses who are understandably keen to maximize

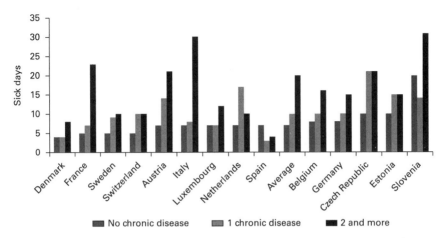

FIGURE 6.1 *Sick days among 50–59-year-old employed people with chronic conditions.*
Source: OECD (2016c).

the productive capacity of their workforce. There is impact here too for individuals – in the USA we know that men with chronic conditions work 6 per cent fewer hours and earn 6 per cent less that men with no chronic conditions. Among women with chronic conditions a similar reduction in working time reduces earnings by 9 per cent (OECD, 2016c).

The financial consequences of this morbidity among working people is considerable. In the US labour market musculoskeletal disorders (MSDs) account for 29 per cent of all days lost to illness and account for over \$575 billion in lost productivity (2.9 per cent of GDP). For every 100 employees, MSDs cost US employers \$103k annually (Summers et al., 2015). In the EU, 44 million workers have MSDs attributable to their work at an annual cost of €240 billion each year (Bevan et al., 2009), a number likely to be larger when co-morbidities are taken into account.

A very common co-morbidity is depression, especially among those living with a physical illness that may involve chronic pain or fatigue or that might be fluctuating in nature. Co-morbid mental illness increases health-care costs by up to 45 per cent (Naylor et al., 2012) and increases the risk of longer periods of absence from work, accounting for an additional seven days of sick leave per year – more than having two or more chronic conditions.

Finally, chronic illness also leads to premature exit from the labour market either through unemployment or early retirement. According to OECD analysis of data among EU workers, 16 per cent of men (and 13 per cent of women) with chronic conditions leave work early because of chronic illness (OECD, 2016c). The biggest cause is long-term mental health problems – for example, severe depression more than doubles the odds of a labour-market exit (OECD, 2016c). These patterns are common across many developed economies (see, for example, analysis from Australia by Schofield et al., 2015). The picture that emerges is, to some extent, a 'perfect storm' involving several substantial forces:

- an ageing workforce;

- longer working lives and later retirement resulting from problems with pension funding;

- a growing burden of chronic ill health in the working age population.

Together, these forces will affect the ability of national economies, health-care systems and businesses to harness the productive capacity of the workforce and to maintain a high quality of life and maximize independent living among those whose functional and cognitive capacity are impaired. In this chapter we will look in more detail at the implications for employers and policy-makers, and the impact that both can make to mitigate the risks of ill health in the workforce and take steps to make improvements in health and well-being.

The business case: why employers want a healthy workforce

On balance, a healthy workforce is – compared with an unhealthy one – more likely to be alert, vital, energetic, agile, resourceful, resilient, innovative, collaborative, motivated, engaged, loyal, in attendance and productive. These are all attributes that employers certainly look for when they recruit staff. They also hope that their management practices, organizational cultures and leadership styles will be able to build upon and marshal these resources in ways that help the organization meet its objectives, fend off and outperform the competition, and create value that helps sustain business success. From this perspective, taking steps to optimize the health of the workforce seems one of the most logical priorities that CEOs of labour and knowledge-intensive organizations will have.

Of course, the degree to which businesses value and invest in the health of their employees is, in many ways, a good test of the oft-quoted rhetorical statement that 'people are our most valuable resource'. There is an obvious parallel to be drawn with an organization's willingness to devote energy and resources to maintaining and repairing plant and machinery, or business-critical information technology (IT) systems, or a website that is vulnerable to hacking and its willingness to ensure that employees are physically and psychologically ready to perform at their best. For many organizations, however, this is a weak parallel because a broken or vulnerable IT system will almost always take priority over a workforce that is susceptible to work-related stress or work-limiting chronic back pain. Unless the employer, as is the case in the US, has a substantial health-care bill to pay, spending on workforce health interventions is all too often one of the lowest budgetary priorities for many organizations. But why might this be? There are several reasons:

- A significant proportion of employers still fail to see why – aside from their legal duty of care – the health of their employees is any of their business. Many of these organizations argue that it is not their role to interfere in what is essentially a private affair. They are of the view that, if employees want to indulge in unhealthy behaviours outside working time (for example, smoking tobacco, drinking excessive alcohol, taking no exercise or even taking too much exercise) then they should be allowed to do so without interference from their employer. If this leads to high levels of sickness absence or poor performance, they reason, then the employee can eventually be 'managed out'. In support of this position, these employers will argue that most of the illness that leads to sickness absence from work has its roots outside work. For example, colds, infections, depression caused by financial or relationship problems, chronic illnesses or child-care issues are seen as entirely the business of the employee or the health-care system and, as such, they are expected to leave these problems at the factory gate or office door.

- Even if an employer recognizes that there may be short-term economic advantages to minimizing ill health and sickness absence, many still struggle to pull together a business rationale for investment in workplace interventions to convince finance directors that there is a genuine and identifiable return on investment (ROI) to be had from them which will find itself onto the balance sheet.

- The arguments for investing in health-related employee benefits, as part of the wider remuneration package, often have more resonance and economic credibility for senior executives than the 'productivity' argument. Offering dental cover, income protection insurance, subsidized gym membership and the social 'glue' of fun runs and pedometer challenges makes much more sense as elements of a recruitment, engagement and retention strategy than interventions that improve cardio-vascular health, psychological well-being or sustained rehabilitation back into work after a health scare. While there are many health-related remuneration 'benefits' that employers are happy to offer to mainly senior staff whose scarcity in the labour market gives them bargaining power, this is only rarely where there is either the more elevated health risk or the clinical need.

- There is no shortage of advice about the ways that employers can take action to improve the well-being of their employees – and the volume of advice has grown substantially – but the big challenge is the relatively weak evidence that any of these interventions makes sufficient sustained difference to justify their use. Senior managers asking for proof that improvements in physical and mental health can be achieved in ways that will bring about measurable improvements in attendance, productivity and performance are all too often disappointed with the answers they get. Of course, some regard the moral argument that promoting well-being is part of an employer's responsibility as sufficiently persuasive, but for many this is insufficient.

The health of employees is a major factor in an organization's competitiveness. Employees in good health can be up to three times as productive as those in poor health; they can experience fewer motivational problems; they are more resilient to change; and they are more likely to be engaged with the business's priorities (Vaughan-Jones and Barham, 2010). In the 2008 Black review it was calculated that improved workplace health could generate the UK government cost savings of over £60 billion, the equivalent of nearly two-thirds of the National Health Service (NHS) budget for England. Among the relatively small number of organizations that have successfully undertaken impact and economic evaluations of their health and well-being programmes, most have identified the financial benefits. They have found a causal link between programme costs and intermediate financial benefits with a favourable return on investment of between 1:2 and 1:3 not uncommon. They have also monitored the change in the key financial variables before and after programme implementation (Global Corporate Challenge, 2013). A review of 55 organizations in the UK that had implemented a variety of health and well-being interventions found that 45 per cent experienced a reduction in days lost through sickness absence with an average reduction of 30–40 per cent. The same review also found improvements in staff turnover, employee satisfaction and a decrease in accidents and injuries reported (PwC, 2008).

The reasons why employers invest in workplace health are often wider than just reducing the costs of sickness absence. In some cases, health-promotion activity can be motivated by no more than a desire to comply with health and safety requirements or the need for the business to discharge its legal duty of care. For many businesses, there is a strong ethical or moral case for investing in workforce health; that is they feel strongly that is the right thing to do (Vaughan-Jones and Barham, 2010). Others invest through 'enlightened self-interest' – being able to demonstrate an array of workplace health interventions to prospective and current employees supports the development of a distinctive employer 'brand' and may contribute to improved employee engagement. According to a world-wide survey involving 378 organizations (Global Corporate Challenge, 2013), the main reasons for employers developing wellness strategies were: improving employee health (69 per cent), improving work engagement (68 per cent), reducing sickness absence (36 per cent) and increasing productivity (27 per cent).

Cooper and Bevan (2014) provide a range of methodological reasons as to why evaluations of workplace health and well-being programmes can be difficult and why caution should be expressed when reviewing evaluation evidence. For example, using programme uptake or participation as a measure of success does not necessarily equate to behaviour change or lead to a reduction in sickness absence. In fact, it may be the case that those least in need of the well-being scheme are the ones who participate most frequently. This suggests that a more thorough evaluation of who participates in health and well-being programmes is required, and uptake should be only one source of evidence for evaluation. Evaluations may also include an attribution error, where if outputs are only restricted to a limited range of explanatory variables, it then becomes difficult to be able to draw definitive conclusions about cause and effect. Additionally, even if changes are reported in employee behaviour, there is still difficulty in determining whether the changes would have occurred without the use or implementation of the health and well-being scheme. Cooper and Bevan (2014) also mention the 'time-lag' effect, which calls into question what the time difference should be between the introduction of a health and well-being programme and any measurable behavioural change. Even if a health and well-being programme evaluation has shown success in changing employee behaviours, studies are rarely longitudinal, and therefore there are very few cases of sustained behavioural change, which as Cooper and Bevan (2014) argue is what is needed to lead to direct tangible bottom-line outcome benefits. They conclude that the evidence of 'success' of workplace health and well-being initiatives is still relatively patchy, and therefore as engaging in practices to promote employee well-being is important organizationally, individually and economically, organizations may have to implement them in 'good faith'.

Interventions to improve workforce health: what works?

It is clear that there are a number of health conditions that have their roots in ageing and in what are frequently characterized as being related to 'lifestyle'. In many cases, therefore, employers are faced with the challenge of managing the consequences of health conditions that their employees have developed outside of the workplace and bring to work. In addition, there are health conditions, illnesses and injuries that can be attributed to their work, where action by employers (usually framed by regulations that set out the legal obligations of employers and their 'duty of care') can both prevent and mitigate the risks of exposure to hazards, dangerous substances and other health risks.

In terms of workplace interventions, therefore, there will need to be a match between the causes of ill health and the employer responses that can have most impact. Inevitably, this impact can be high (e.g. reducing exposure to hazardous or carcinogenic substances at work) or, on the other hand, less direct (e.g. helping employees manage distress caused by divorce, bereavement or financial difficulties).

Looking at the interventions that employers are currently implementing, the most common include:

- flexible working and access to part-time working;

- Employee Assistance Programmes (EAPs);

- subsidized gym membership;

- health eating initiatives;

- support for increased physical activity (fun runs, pedometer challenges);

- stress-management programmes;

- access to occupational health support;

- training for line managers in mental illness symptoms and referral.

Research looking at which interventions are most effective is, in general terms, disappointingly inconclusive. In part, this is because the challenges of constructing a well-designed study in real-world settings are hard to overcome. In addition, some interventions are not firmly based on a systematic needs or risk assessment (e.g. are healthy eating initiatives designed to resolve diet-related ill-health problems that manifest themselves in sickness absence and productivity loss?). Also, many interventions are not set up to host an evaluation of their impact other than to measure rates of participation or satisfaction.

A systematic review conducted in the UK by Hillage et al. (2015) looked at well-designed studies of workplace health interventions from across the English-speaking world. The conclusion of the review was that very few

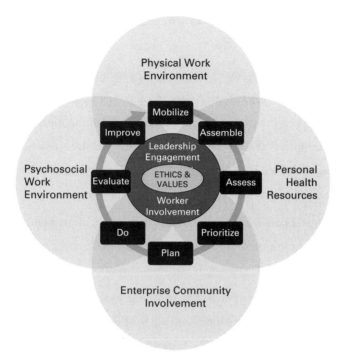

FIGURE 6.2 *The WHO healthy workplaces framework and model.*
Source: World Health Organization (2010).

specific interventions could be shown to be effective. Nonetheless, there was more evidence that organizations that had invested in upskilling line managers, imaginative job design and a supportive culture most often experienced the most positive health outcomes among employees.

Recognizing this, the World Health Organization (WHO) has developed a helpful model to guide employers in the development of a holistic approach to thinking about workforce health and setting priorities for action. The model appears in Figure 6.2.

The merit of the model is that is recognizes that health challenges faced by employees can originate in a number of environments and it prompts employers to:

- take into account risks both to physical health and mental health, and in doing so, recognize that there are aspects of both physical and psychosocial risk over which employers exercise at least some control;

- recognize that employees are not homogeneous and that individual differences are important in determining the impact of health problems on job performance and functional limitations – this means, for example, that employees may have different stress reactions to the same workplace challenges (e.g. tight deadlines or conflicting demands) based on the resources those individuals bring to their jobs;

- emphasize participative approaches to framing, implementing and evaluating workplace health interventions, while ensuring that the organization shows strong leadership commitment to them;

- adopt a systematic approach to planning, executing, measuring and monitoring workplace interventions to allow informed decisions to be made about the effectiveness of each.

At one level, it may be disappointing to find that the evidence for commonly used interventions is weak. However, the evidence also shows that the timing of an intervention may be a more critical aspect of some interventions than their precise nature. For example, early referral of an employee to appropriate medical or occupational health support may make the biggest difference to that employee's chances of remaining in or returning successfully to work. Indeed, studies show (Bevan, 2015) that early intervention for people with MSDs can:

- reduce sick leave and lost work productivity among workers with MSDs by more than 50 per cent – early intervention is commonly more cost effective than 'usual care';

- reduce health-care costs by up to two-thirds;

- reduce disability benefits costs by up to 80 per cent;

- reduce the risk of permanent work disability and job loss by up to 50 per cent;

- reduce the risk of developing a co-morbid mental illness;

- deliver societal benefits by supporting people with work-limiting chronic conditions to optimize their functional capacity and remain active at work and maintain economic independence.

Prioritizing early intervention also means being able to deliver at least some elements of vocational rehabilitation, which can also involve risk assessment and prevention. This means that, in most cases, a solid and joined-up approach to workplace health that has early intervention, job redesign and vocational rehabilitation at its core may be better than any single intervention, no matter how eye-catching or well-branded.

'Good work': the ultimate workforce health intervention?

The idea that work might fulfil a human and psychological need (beyond the need for income) has a long history. This concept is now increasingly part of the analysis that tells us that meaning and purpose at work can be an important way of engaging employees and connecting them to the wider aims of their employer in a way that unlocks their motivation and commitment (Parker and Bevan, 2011). Although considerable attention is paid to clinical or public health-related interventions at work that can help promote physical and psychological well-being, perhaps the most sustained impact on health at work can be achieved by paying more systemic attention to the intrinsic quality of the work we give people to do. By this is meant a range of factors that affect:

- the amount of control, autonomy, variety and discretion workers have;

- the balance between the effort they expend and the rewards they feel they get for their efforts;

- the amount of positive social interaction, social capital and social support provided by their working environment;

- the extent to which workers feel the way they are managed and decisions are made is fair and just;

- the extent to which employees feel able to use their skills fully in their work and have opportunities to learn new things at work;

- the extent to which work offers security;

- the extent to which employees feel they have a 'voice' at work.

One of the things that distinguishes this list is its non-medical nature. Yet we know that organizations that experience low levels of sickness absence, high retention and high morale and engagement tend to be those whose culture and management practices attach high priority to these factors. Arguably, much of the current discussion about 'good work' and job quality can be traced back to classical works of moral philosophy. For example, Immanuel Kant (1997: 154) noted that: 'If a man has done much he is more contented after his labours than if he had done nothing whatever; for by work he has set his powers in motion.' In other words, work has the power to animate us. What makes work so humanly important is that, through it, life can take on a wider purpose. In Kant's terms, we have an *existential* need for work, even though the choices we make about work may be constrained by our position in a labour market and the enlightenment of our leaders in the workplace. These ideas were certainly not mainstream in the early days of industrialization. Henry Ford, according to this account, was not a proponent. At Ford's River Rouge plant in Michigan in the 1930s and 1940s, David Collinson (2002: 276) reports the following incident:

In 1940 John Gallo was sacked because he was 'caught in the act of smiling', after having committed an earlier breach of 'laughing with the other fellows', and 'slowing down the line maybe half a minute'. This tight managerial discipline reflected the overall philosophy of Henry Ford, who stated that 'When we are at work we ought to be at work. When we are at play we ought to be at play. There is no use trying to mix the two.'

However, by the 1960s the Quality of Working Life (QWL) movement was beginning to influence the design of industrial processes and work organization to take into account the need for employees to derive satisfaction and fulfilment from their work. In 1975 Albert Cherns summarized some of the assumptions of the QWL approach as follows:

1 Autonomy is preferable to dependence.

2 High levels of skill are preferable to low.

3 Learning is good.

4 A high degree of self-investment in work is good, provided that the work itself and the work situation offer opportunities for growth and self-realization.

The QWL movement was subsequently at the centre of an expansion of research by industrial and organizational psychologists, sociologists and economists to examine whether work that was organized and designed with these 'high involvement' principles in mind delivered improvements in job satisfaction and productivity. As developed Western economies in the subsequent decades grew their service industries (often at the expense of manufacturing), expanded access to higher education and became more recognizably 'knowledge-based', there was also a growing realization among most employers that employee 'engagement' in – and commitment to – their work were becoming core to the 'psychological contract' and strong drivers of organizational performance. Despite the enlightenment journey that we have witnessed since Henry Ford, however, awareness of the connection between 'good work' and employee health has taken longer to establish.

Job quality and health outcomes

With an ageing workforce a major feature of many modern economies that will continue well into the future, and with young workers now likely to have to work for 50 years before they can retire, it is no surprise that the health of working-age people has become a challenge that is attracting considerable interest from policymakers and employers. Dame Carol Black's 2008 review estimated that poor workforce health costs the UK about £100 billion a year and we currently lose in excess of 130 million working days a year to sickness absence, with significant economic and social costs. It is easy to blame this phenomenon on a 'sick note' culture, where malingering employees feel free to take time off as and when they choose, but this can ignore that over 40 per cent of the workforce takes no absence at all as well as several underlying problems that may be driving high levels of increasingly long-term absence among the remainder. Employer responses have traditionally focused on improving attendance management through better information systems, return-to-work interviews and increasing senior management attention on the problem. All of this is sensible and necessary but all too often treats the symptoms rather than the causes.

When we start to think about what some of these causes might be it is clear that, in some cases, we might have been guilty of over-medicalizing the problem – especially if we ignore the complex connections between job quality and health that are now becoming much clearer. In 2006 the Department of Work and Pensions published a landmark review by Gordon Waddell and Kim Burton. It asked a deceptively simple question: 'Is work good for your health and well-being?' After detailed scrutiny of the available evidence the review set out very clearly that work and health were closely linked, and not just in terms defined by conventional 'health and safety' or worklessness frames of reference. The diagram in Figure 6.3 illustrates the core relationships.

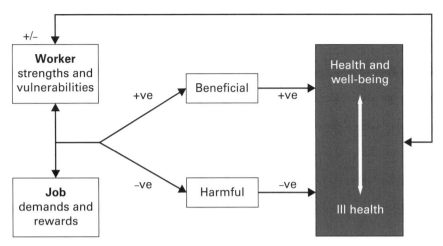

FIGURE 6.3 *Work and health: interactions can lead to differing consequences.*
Source: Waddell and Burton (2006).

Importantly, the authors were clear that there were a number 'provisos' that needed to be thought about when considering the implications of their findings:

The provisos are that account must be taken of the social context, the nature and quality of work, and the fact that a minority of people may experience contrary effects. Jobs should be safe and should also be accommodating for sickness and disability.

WADDELL AND BURTON, 2006: 38

The year 2006 also saw another major contribution to the evidence base, this time from the disciplines of public health and epidemiology. The publication of *Status Syndrome: How Your Place on the Social Gradient Directly Affects Your Health* by Professor Sir Michael Marmot presented compelling evidence that workers in lower-status jobs enjoy worse health and lower life expectancy than workers in higher-status jobs. This is described by Marmot as the 'social gradient' in health. The argument can be summarized quite simply. Workers in lower-status jobs are exposed to more stressors than their more highly paid and highly qualified colleagues which, in turn, increase the risk of mental illness, gastro-intestinal conditions and coronary heart disease (CHD). Figure 6.4,

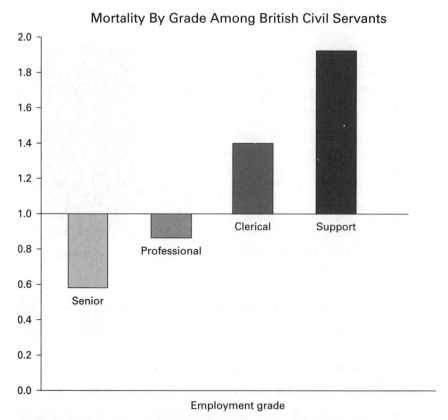

FIGURE 6.4 *Job status and mortality rates in UK civil servants.*
Source: Institute of Health Equity (2010).

drawn from a large study among UK civil servants, illustrates the link between grade and mortality rates, indicating that higher-status employees have lower mortality rates than those in lower-status roles.

Prompted to examine why such a clear relationship between status and mortality existed, Marmot and his team looked at a number of characteristics of both the employees and jobs to see if a more precise set of indicators could shed light on the link between work and health outcomes. In Figure 6.5 we can see data from the same civil-service population that shows a clear correlation between the amount of job control reported by employees and the incidence of coronary heart disease – again with low control associated with poorer health outcomes.

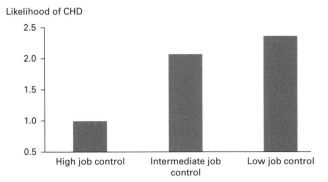

FIGURE 6.5 *Job control and heart disease in UK civil servants.*
Source: Institute of Health Equity (2010).

A significant conclusion from the Whitehall II study is that, contrary to the popular misconception, the security guard in the entrance lobby is a more likely heart attack victim than the archetypal highly stressed senior manager in the C-suite. Of course, workers in these lower-status jobs are more likely to be affected by other negative social factors such as poor housing or unalleviated caring responsibilities. However, studies that have controlled for these elements point strongly to the significance for health of imaginative work organization, fulfilling job design and empowering organizational culture. Marmot and his colleagues at the Institute of Health Equity (IHE, 2010) have also more recently demonstrated that differences in job quality also explain some of the widening in health inequality in the UK. In addition, the evidence establishes very clearly that work is a social determinant of health, leading Marmot to call for improved access to fair workplaces and good work. As the 2010 'Fair Society, Healthy Lives' research identifies:

a large 'unused' potential for developing and expanding 'good' working conditions exists in all advanced and rapidly developing economies where the benefits of implementing 'good' work include medium-term and long-term increases in return on investment, enhanced productivity, health and commitment of workers, and reduced costs related to sickness absence and work compensation claims.

SIEGRIST et al., 2010

Interest in job quality has also intensified as awareness of the burden of mental ill health in the UK workforce has grown. This has forced policymakers, employers and clinicians to recognize that the psychosocial work environment can have damaging as well as therapeutic effects (OECD, 2015). Indeed, the psychosocial quality of work has received attention from those researching the impact of welfare policies aimed at encouraging the unemployed to find work, with evidence from both the UK and Australia suggesting that the health impact of jobs of poor psychosocial job quality may be equal to, or worse than, being unemployed (Butterworth et al., 2013; Bevan, 2014).

It is perhaps inevitable that, during a period of elevated unemployment as in the recent recession, focusing attention on job quality rather than quantity will be seen as aspirational or even naïve. Nonetheless, the data shows that job quality can be adversely affected in a downturn, especially when employers are faced with labour surpluses. Results from the Skills and Employment Survey (SES) illustrate this effect. As well as an increase in fear over employment loss, many employees also expressed high levels of fear over employment status loss – with 51 per cent of employees in the 2012 SES reporting fear of at least one of the following aspects of employment status change: less say over their work, less use of skills, less pay and less interesting work (Gallie et al., 2013). One-third of employees in the 2012 SES were also concerned over at least one aspect of unfair treatment at work – further threatening job quality – including dismissal, discrimination and victimization from management (Felstead et al., 2013). Overall, between 2000 and 2012, there was a rise in levels of anxiety experienced by employees and a decline in job-related well-being (as measured by levels of enthusiasm and contentment) between 2001 and 2012 – see Figure 6.6.

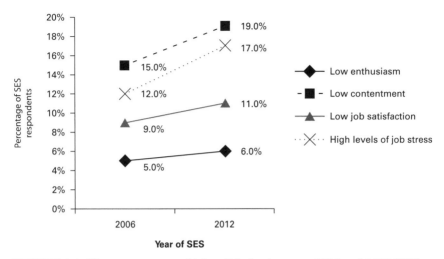

FIGURE 6.6 *Changes to reported job well-being between 2006 and 2012 (UK).*
Source: Graph developed based on Skills and Employment Survey (SES) data from Green et al. (2013).

Whilst the recession may not be entirely responsible for the increased threats to job quality and job-related well-being, controlling for factors that typically change during times of recession (including work effort, job security, work organization) the recession was at least partly responsible for the overall decline in employees' job-related well-being (Green et al., 2013).

On the international stage, however, the UK seems to fare better than several other countries on many aspects of job quality. The OECD has developed a framework to measure and assess the quality of jobs that considers three objective and measurable dimensions, including earnings quality (capturing the extent to which earnings contribute to workers' well-being in terms of *average earnings* and their *distribution* across the workforce), labour-market security (capturing those aspects of economic security related to the risks of job loss and its economic cost for workers) and the quality of the working environment (capturing non-economic aspects of jobs including the nature and content of the work performed, working-time arrangements and workplace relationships) measured as the incidence of job strain characterized

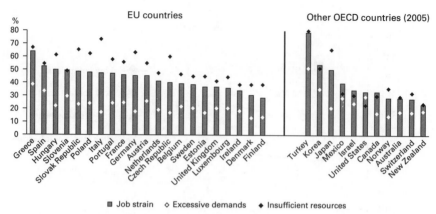

FIGURE 6.7 *OECD measures of job strain, 2015.*
Source: OECD (2016d).

as *high job demands* with *low job resources*. Figure 6.7 illustrates the scores on the job strain dimensions, for 2015, across a number of OECD countries.

The fact that international and domestic bodies such as the OECD, the ILO, the European Foundation, Eurostat, the Office for National Statistics and the Department for Work and Pensions (DWP) are now routinely collecting and reporting data on job quality is a sign that policymakers recognize that 'good work' is an important part of the policy 'mix' if we value outcomes such as productivity and well-being.

Good work and health: future directions?

Since John Gallo lost his job for being 'caught in the act of smiling' in 1940, we have witnessed a revolution in the way we think about the role work plays in people's lives and how we need to manage people at work. It is vital to remember that work is a social act as well as an economic one. Workplaces are where we seek fulfilment, social connectivity, a sense of purpose, opportunities for personal growth and a sense of identity. In addition, as well as the basic expectation that work should not cause us physical or emotional harm, it is now reasonable to expect that – as far as possible – work should be good for our health and well-being. Of course, we need more data and practical evidence about which interventions work best and have most sustained positive impact. But we also need other changes to both policy and practice to embed the notion that it is only good work that is good for our health. Some of these changes are summarized below:

1 Government sponsored 'back-to-work' programmes need to take more explicit account of job quality in their commissioning, targets and tariffs. Poor quality work only adds to the risk of such programmes becoming 'revolving door' schemes where work remains precarious, casualized, contingent and psychosocially harmful.

2 More countries should embrace the principles of the Scandinavian 'workability' model with more enthusiasm. As our workforce ages and experiences more chronic illness, approaches that help redesign work around the capabilities and strengths of the individual worker will help vocational rehabilitation, job retention, productivity and engagement.

3 Businesses need to recognize that most of the active ingredients of staff engagement that they are now accustomed to measuring and reporting are co-terminus with employee well-being because they focus on job quality. This means that workplace well-being programmes that focus on fruit and Pilates alone, ignoring job quality, will not be effective.

4 Some of the components of 'good work' are challenging to the conventions and mores of UK managerial culture. However, in a knowledge-based economy with a much more highly educated and multi-generational workforce, employers who resist the need that employees have for a voice in the way the organization is run, to be trusted by (and to trust) their leaders, for transparency in the way decisions are made and for consent to the way the organization does business, are likely to lag behind in both performance and competitiveness.

5   In the instances where employers get this spectacularly right or
    spectacularly wrong the common feature is the skill, awareness,
    capability and attitude of line managers. For some, the idea of good
    work is common sense and is instinctively woven into the way they
    manage, coach and support their staff. Unsurprisingly, these managers
    experience less sickness absence, voluntary turnover, poor
    performance or dysfunctional team behaviour than those managers for
    whom good work represents weakness, anarchy and a challenge to the
    managerial prerogative and the 'command and control' style from
    which they derive so much comfort.

Good work is far from being a clinical intervention. It is a modern and
enlightened approach to organizing work, designing jobs and engaging
employees that needs to inform – even more than it does today – the way that
policymakers, employers, managers, unions, health-care professionals and
employees themselves think about the way that work can benefit the health
and well-being of nations.

What should policymakers do?

Over the past decade, progress has been made to further our understanding
that work is important for our health, and that it is not just health and safety
that should be the focus of the workplace, but that the psychosocial work
environment should also be considered to support and promote healthier
lifestyles (Bajorek et al., 2014). 'Working Together for a Healthier Tomorrow'
(Black, 2008) was a catalyst to encourage policymakers, employers and
practitioners into action to consider health and well-being initiatives at work.
However, the area of adopting evidence-based initiatives to improve workplace
well-being, remains an area where employer investment and engagement is
patchy (Bajorek et al., 2014); consequently this is an arena where government

policymakers, and other stakeholders need to come together to improve workplace outcomes for the employee, the employer and wider society.

So why should the government be encouraging employers to do more? There are a number of reasons why this might be the case. The recent ONS sickness absence[2] data report shows that in 2016 an estimated 137.3 million working days were lost due to sickness or injury, with musculoskeletal conditions (30.8 million days) and mental illness (15.8 million days) being among the top health problems experienced by those in the workplace. This lost productivity can undermine the performance of their employer, and if not adequately addressed by the NHS, then their absence may become long-term. Thus, greater investment in early prevention, signalling and treatment, even if work may not be the primary cause of employee ill health makes good business sense.

Second, the workplace is an under-utilized space for delivering public health and well-being measures (many of us spend a majority of our day at work), and interventions to improve our health (e.g. education, health and well-being risk-assessments, exercise and healthy eating promotions, smoking cessation programmes, just to name a few). If there was investment in such practices at work, this could reduce the level of sickness absence experienced by employers and also reduce the knock-on burden on our public health systems. Thus, not only will there be a private benefit for businesses, there is also public benefit for the wider society.

However, Bramley-Harker et al. (2006) argued that although this does look like an obvious area for to government to encourage employer investment, the situation is indeed more problematic. Benefits of interventions implemented to improve workplace health and well-being go beyond those for just the employers themselves. For example, the individual and their families will benefit from improved health and reduced caring responsibilities; the NHS could have lower health-care costs, the DWP could benefit through lower welfare costs and the HM Treasury may have higher income tax receipts. It then becomes a hard business case to make for some employers, especially if the costs of the interventions are high, and they may not be the main beneficiaries. As Bramley-Harker et al. (2006) concluded, it could be rational for employers to under-invest in workforce health.

This is of course not a helpful conclusion for those of us who advocate the importance for employers to invest in health and well-being initiatives, and argue that there is a compelling business case for them to do so. Vaughan-Jones and Barham (2010) highlighted that employees with good health and well-being is a major factor for the competitiveness of the workplace as they are more productive, motivated and engaged with business priorities. For organizations who have undertaken financial evaluations of health and well-being interventions, benefits have been realized. For example, PwC (2008) reviewed 55 organizations who had implemented a number of health and well-being initiatives and found a reduction in days lost to sickness absence, with an average reduction of 30–40 per cent. It must be noted that the emphasis for implementing health and well-being interventions should not solely be focused on reducing sickness absence, or a desire to comply with health and safety requirements, but many organizations have a strong sense that it is the right thing to do, or may even show to prospective employees that they are willing to invest in their employees, and this may then contribute to developing employee engagement.

The Work Foundation's report (Bajorek et al., 2014) discussed a number of organizational barriers to the implementation of health and well-being interventions, and a range of policy options for improving workforce health. It was argued that barriers to workplace interventions could occur at three stages: the planning stage, the implementation stage and how they are evaluated and managed.

The planning stage

Although there is evidence to suggest that building a business case in critical (Robertson and Cooper, 2010), this can be difficult to do because there are both direct and indirect costs and less tangible benefits are harder to measure.

A common barrier is a lack of employee interest, especially from employees considered to be more high-risk, and there is often a lack of consultation with employees when designing health and well-being programmes.

If the board and senior managers do not consider health and well-being important to invest in, then however strong the business case, there will still be difficulties in implementation.

Health and well-being interventions may not be successfully implemented as there is not a culture of taking health and well-being at work seriously.

Lack of both funding and physical resources can be barriers to intervention implementation.

The implementation stage

Lack of effective communication about health and well-being programmes limits management and employee engagement with them. Using multiple communication methods is recommended, alongside the development of a communication strategy.

Health and well-being interventions need to be co-ordinated with members of the organization, who are able to respond to queries and provide the necessary information.

Evaluation and continued monitoring stage

Evaluation of health and well-being programmes can be very difficult, and if organizations fail to evaluate initiatives, or do not capture all the benefits they provide, then making the business case for further interventions or development of the schemes will be difficult.

There are a number of measures that policymakers should consider if employers are to be encouraged or incentivized to both promote and improve the health and well-being of their workforce. The basic policy goals should be continuing to encourage those employers who are already undertaking health and well-being interventions to continue to do so, and for those who currently are not doing anything, to begin to undertake a few simple initiatives. Importantly, if the analysis by Bramley-Harker et al. (2006) is correct, and the benefits of implementing workplace well-being initiatives are spread across a number of stakeholders, there is a need to co-produce initiatives with a number of stakeholders, including the government.

The Work Foundation recommended that the government must do more to actively promote the issue of health and well-being at work, so that the issues are considered in the mainstream policy debate and are clearly understood by employers. To help with this, it was also recommended that advice regarding what health and well-being interventions are important, effective and evidence-based should be updated and more proactive. For example, there should be a review of both the content and use of the HSE stress management-standards, and a more active promotion of the National Institute for Health and Clinical Excellence (NICE) well-being guidelines and Public Health England (PHE) public health guidelines.

At the same time, to help organizations more economically, the report recommended that the government should review the feasibility of using targeted fiscal incentives to redress market failures and encourage more employers to act and invest in workplace interventions. However, these should first be piloted for feasibility so that there is a clear understanding how this could be implemented.

Finally, The Work Foundation recommended that the government should consider reforming procedures for procurement processes, so that considerations for workplace safety, health and well-being are included when deciding on what suppliers to use.

Health and well-being in small businesses

Many of the arguments noted above have been based on large organizations, however SMEs now represent a large proportion of UK workplaces. McEnhill and Steadman (2015) reported that in 2015 over 99 per cent of all UK private sector businesses were SMEs, and they employ 15.6 million people, which accounts for 60 per cent of those employed in the private sector and approximately half of the entire UK workforce. It is therefore important that the health and well-being of employees in SMEs are considered, as their health is crucial to UK productivity. But, SMEs do provide a complex challenge when developing and implementing workplace health and well-being initiatives because they are made up of a range of businesses (both in the work they do, and their size). As McEnhill and Steadman (2015) argue, what works for one SME may not necessarily work for another, and their ability to provide support for employee health and well-being will often be mostly influenced by their size and the time and availability of resources (both human and financial) that are available to them.

Understanding and measuring employee health in SMEs is difficult to do, but evidence suggests that they are more likely to report lower levels and shorter durations of sickness absence than larger employers (CIPD, 2015). However, the majority of SMEs do not collect sickness absence data, and rarely belong to professional bodies where such data is collated and reported, so there are limitations to the extent that larger-scale survey data represent the health and well-being of the SME workforce. Steadman et al. (2015) reported that employees in larger organizations are more likely to report stress than those in SMEs (and as reported stress and mental illness is one of the leading causes of sickness absence). However, those in SMEs may experience different stressors than employees in larger organizations, including work overload, job insecurity and poor career progression (Lai et al., 2015). Stress may lead to presenteeism, and Chua et al. (2004) provided evidence to suggest that presenteeism is a particular issue for organizations that are family run, as a result of the high levels of job demands asked of them and the long hours they are asked to work. However, having said this, McEnhill and Steadman (2015) argued that smaller firms are likely to generate positive work environments, often reporting finding their role and work more rewarding and feeling fairly treated and trusted by their managers.

The health and well-being of SMEs must still be taken into consideration, especially in terms of how this is managed. The average day-to-day pressures of running an SME could leave very little time (either strategically or reactively) to consider employee health and well-being. Thus while they may understand that there is a moral and ethical imperative to look at employee well-being, making a business case of its importance may be less clear. When the term 'business case' is discussed, immediate thoughts turn to financial implications, but there is very little, if any, evidence of costs associated as a result of poor health and well-being for SMEs (HSE, 2013). However, it would be expected that the costs of any absence in terms of reduced productivity, and the potential for reduced client satisfaction, may be felt harder than larger employers, as there are fewer staff members to cover for absent colleagues, thus the productivity gained for supporting and maintaining good health and well-being in SMEs could make the stronger business case.

McEnhill and Steadman (2015) considered how well typical health and well-being interventions and activities applied to SMEs, and what barriers SMEs face when accessing current health and well-being practices. Examples are discussed below.

Sickness absence management policies help to monitor employee absence, but SMEs are less likely to have written policies than larger organizations, and absence may be dealt with using a less formal approach.

In larger organizations interventions such as occupational health (OH) services or Employee Assistance Programmes (EAPs) are often commonplace. However, SMEs are much less likely to offer this support to employees, as a result of either financial (i.e. paying for certain services on a continuous basis may be viewed as an unreasonable cost) or knowledge limitations.

Office adjustments to help employees with a health condition or disability to remain in work are a legal requirement, and Steadman et al. (2015) reported that employees in SMEs were more likely to indicate that workplace adjustments had been made, but factors such as leadership attitudes or levels of support in SMEs could lead to variations in the levels of support provided.

Training can be effective in ensuring that understanding the importance of employee health and well-being is known so that interventions can be implemented effectively. However, taking time for the training may be difficult for SME managers, and they may not receive the economy of scales that larger organizations achieve. Additionally, there is little knowledge about the efficacy of certain interventions and their training for the SME context.

For government policy initiatives such as Fit for Work and Access to Work, little evidence is available for how adaptable they are and how they have been used in the SME context, in addition to the limited awareness of the schemes among SME owners, and the working population at large.

As a result of the lack of alternative services, or access to OH, the NHS is a key provider of services for SMEs, with EEF/Jelf (2015) reporting that one-third of the SME sector that responded to their survey relied on the NHS exclusively for treatment and rehabilitation services. This could have implications for both waiting for treatment, and the flexibility needed for time off for the treatment. There are also concerns as to the extent that general practitioners (GPs) are able to refer individuals to the appropriate support necessary.

Central to this issue is that SMEs are seemingly unaware of the support that is available, and this is compounded by the lack of locally based or industry-based networks where good practice can be shared. This is also partnered with a lack of understanding that still exists about the understanding of workforce health and well-being and especially when messages may not be tailored towards the business needs of SMEs. The advice given to SMEs can appear to be fragmented and confusing, with a limited understanding where individuals can go to get respected, reliable and relevant advice.

The authors also developed a range of recommendations for policymakers that could be implemented to help both understand the extent of health and well-being issues in the SME context and how this can be improved. It has been argued that a more strategic approach is needed; importantly, developing a co-ordinated cross-government department narrative that highlights the business, economic and human case for engaging the SME context to support staff health and well-being. Stronger messages are needed from government departments such as the Department for Business, Energy and Industrial Stategy (BEIS), the DWP and PHE who could provide more SME business focused information, and interventions specifically amended for SMEs need to be properly evaluated. Recommendations were also focused around the development and delivery of training resources and support from the government, including greater investment in training for SME managers about employee health and well-being, provision of OH similar to the system in Scotland and Wales to be evaluated and the Health and Work Joint Unit to review models of local partnerships to enhance the support given. Finally, the authors recommended the government create better communication pathways to access advice and support, including a one-stop portal for SME health and well-being, and recommending better channels of communication and SME relationships to share best practice.

Young people with health conditions entering work

For many young people the transition from education to employment is relatively smooth (especially if they are healthy, and have the relevant skills and work experience). However, for others the pathway is less easy, and if a young person has a chronic condition, then achieving their desired labour outcome is increasingly challenging (Bajorek et al., 2016). Maslow et al. (2011) reported that young people with chronic conditions are more likely to have fewer qualifications, are more likely to be unemployed, and if employed more likely to earn less than their healthy counterparts. Bajorek et al. (2016) argued that as early experiences of the labour market can shape future opportunities, then there are clear policy implications to help young people with chronic conditions make the transition from education to employment.

The UKCES (2013) highlighted that young people in general suffered disproportionately in the labour market following the 2008 financial crisis, and that they have also been left behind in the recovery. In 2014, the ONS estimated that 955,000 young people were not in education, employment or training (NEET), and with characteristics of NEETs including lower levels of career exploration skills and self-awareness, not enjoying school, likely to have left school without obtaining any or minimal qualifications, these young people will continue to struggle to gain employment as there is now a tendency to rely on skills, and young people are having to compete with more experienced and mature workers for entry level positions. Young people with chronic conditions are over-represented among those who are NEET (UKCES, 2012).

Bajorek et al. (2016) argued that differences in employment outcomes across all stages of an individual's life between those with chronic conditions and their healthy counterparts suggest that early disadvantages can have a long-term cumulative effect. Challenges that young people with chronic conditions face at school (e.g. poor attendance as a result of medical issues, stigma and poor illness management) can have an impact on obtaining qualifications, or reaching their full educational potential, which could increase their likelihood of experiencing unemployment in later years (Bevan et al., 2013). Young people with chronic conditions have also been reported to have concerns about being screened out of the recruitment process as a result of the stigma related to those with chronic conditions (Bevan, 2013), and the recruitment process itself can create barriers (e.g. performance in stressful face-to-face conditions may be affected by symptoms of their condition).

However, we know that work is good for an individual's well-being, so helping young people with chronic conditions get into work will improve both their mental and physical health outcomes (especially if it is good work), and will also reduce the life-course ill-effects of unemployment. Bajorek et al. (2016) recognized that there are a range of national initiatives intended to make the transition from education to employment smooth, and while these also have flaws for young people in general, it was argued that young people with chronic conditions will face additional barriers, and so it is important that these universal services work best for them. These services include the following.

Careers guidance

There is a range of research available showing the critical importance that impartial career guidance can have for aiding the transition between education and employment. Careers advice helps young people understand what options are available to them, what subjects they may specifically have to study and what skills are needed to help them reach their career goals. Two main sources for careers guidance are available: careers advice provided in schools and the National Careers Service (NCS).

There have been a number of changes to careers advice provided in schools, and as a result, provision has often been described as variable, often being inconsistent and fragmented. Many schools do not have the trained staff to provide the necessary guidance, and collaboration with employers is rare. Although statutory guidance for careers advice was introduced by the Department for Education in 2015, it is still unclear as to whether this has improved the provision of careers advice, especially as no additional funding has been supplied to enact the necessary changes.

In relation to the NCS, this service offers a range of professional support and information about training, education and work for young people aged over 13 to adults. Support is predominantly website based, although face-to-face advice is given to those aged 19 and above. Extra support (having access to up to three face-to-face meetings with an advisor) can be provided to young people with disabilities. However, the NCS is under-promoted to students, and despite the provision of advice being more extensive to those with disabilities in comparison to those without, the lack of provision earlier in the transition stage and the limited flexibility in service provision still constitute a number of barriers to young people with chronic conditions.

Finally, a generic weakness in careers advice is the lack of specialist occupation health-service provision, which limits the opportunities for conversations regarding the particular challenges in the workplace that individuals with chronic conditions can encounter.

Work experience

Young people who have had the opportunity for work experience are more likely to have better labour-market outcomes, as employers are increasingly demanding that young people have some experience of the skills required for the workplace. There is a special requirement for young people to display 'employability skills', such as teamwork and communication. For young people with chronic conditions work experience can also provide that opportunity to understand how they can manage their conditions in the workplace, and what adaptations may be needed.

The government launched a 16–19 study programme in 2013, with work experience forming an integral part of this, as a short period of time to test out vocational ideas either connected to further studies or employment options, vocational experience, or an extended model of work experience. However, there are disparities between schools in the nature of work experience provision (e.g. tasters of work provided to only informing students when university open days are). Young people with chronic conditions are often excluded from arrangements made by schools, as these are usually focused on those who are closest to the labour market, and because employers are either unable or unwilling to make adjustments to the workplace for them. Schools may also lack the appropriate understanding of the nature of the conditions to assist in work experience placements, and consequently, there are increasingly limited opportunities for young people with chronic conditions, which could hinder their longer-term career expectations.

Vocational education

Vocational education includes schemes such as apprenticeships, traineeships and internships, and these can be useful routes from education to employment.

In the 2015 Queen's Speech it was announced that the government had set a target to create three million new apprenticeships by 2020, and later that year details of an apprenticeship levy to help fund these was also announced. Although there is evidence to suggest that apprenticeship completion rates for young people with learning disabilities and physical disabilities is positive, those with mental health or behavioural problems do not seem to have fared as well. There are also no current plans to evaluate how widely the three million apprenticeships will be used by young people with chronic conditions, or whether the structure of the apprentices themselves will be a barrier.

Traineeships are education and training programmes with work experience, available for young people aged between 18 and 24. However, as with apprenticeships, there is little data currently available to understand what the outcomes of traineeships are for young people with chronic conditions, although overall trainees have rated the experience positively.

A supported internship is a programme specifically aimed for young people between 16 and 24 who have a statement of special educational needs, a learning disability assessment or an EHC, who plan to enter employment, but may require additional help to achieve this. They help young people by ensuring they have the specific skills needed for the workplace, by receiving higher levels of support than provided in traineeships or apprenticeships. Although there is evidence indicating positive results for supported internship programmes, there is little evidence available suggesting whether this is a suitable intervention for young people with chronic conditions.

Health-related transition services

Young people with certain chronic conditions may benefit from personalized or specialist support that will help to address the specific barriers they experience when attempting to make the transition into the labour market. There are a number of health-focused services that have been seen to have an important role in supporting these transitions.

Education, Health and Care (EHC) plans were introduced in 2014, and look at the needs of the individual in those three areas, focusing especially on what the individual wants to achieve, and aims to identify the support that the young person may need to achieve this. These plans are available to those not able to be met by special educational needs and disabilities (SEND) services provided in educational settings. EHC plans are reviewed once a year, and everyone who is involved in supporting the young person discusses their progression and whether the needs of the young person have changed. What remains unclear within these plans is how special educational needs and disabilities are defined and whether this includes young people with long-term chronic conditions. Additionally, when the young person makes the transition into university or into employment the EHC plans are no longer valid, or are replaced by another scheme, and so support and reviews regarding what extra services the individual may need are no longer discussed – a missed opportunity for helping young people when they need it.

Child and Adolescent Mental Health Services (CAMHS) are NHS services that are focused on offering young people with emotional, behavioural or mental health difficulties assessments and treatment. The service consists of multi-disciplinary teams consisting of psychologists, nurses, occupational therapists, psychiatrists, social workers, support workers and substance misuse workers. The service usually works with children and young people until the age of 18, and when they reach this age they will make the transition to Adult Mental Health Services (AMHS). However, access to CAMHS is patchy, and there have been many reported concerns regarding the level of funding that the service is receiving. This is concerning as inadequate funding reduces the opportunity for dedicated support, and young people will not be able to access the dedicated services that they may require. Additionally, the transition to AMHS is not always easy, and young people may fall out of the service at this point resulting in an increased likelihood of falling out of education and employment opportunities.

Early Intervention in Psychosis (EIP) services provide holistic support for young people and adults aged between 14 and 35, to help people recover from their first episode of psychosis. A team would comprise, among other health professionals, social workers and support workers, and the team focuses primarily on recovery with a specific emphasis on personal empowerment, social development and vocational outcomes. Some services include an integrated employment support – Individual Placement Support (IPS) – an evidence based model of employment support which evidence suggests has helped people with severe mental health conditions enter paid employment. EIP has been seen to have positive effects for the young people using the service, by improving employment outcomes in comparison to individuals who access standard mental health care. However, the services may be subject to major funding cuts, meaning that they may struggle to continue to provide and maintain the high levels of care they currently provide. Also, access to care is not equal across the country, and thus young people who may benefit from these services may face delays in accessing the care they need.

Physical and mental illness among young entrants to the labour market can, as we have seen, have a cumulative life-course impact which can mean that educational, career and life potential may not be fully realized. As most people face the prospect of working until they are 70 before they can retire on a state pension in tomorrow's labour market, it will be important that those with health problems are no more systematically disadvantaged than necessary.

Workforce health: future prospects

By some calculations, something approaching 40 per cent of the UK workforce will have at least one chronic illness by 2030. Similar proportions are expected in other developed economies. The bulk of the health burden among working-age people (see Figure 6.8) will continue to be shared between mental illnesses and musculoskeletal disorders (MSDs), though other conditions such as cancer, asthma and chronic obstructive pulmonary disorder (COPD) also play their part in impairing the full productive capacity of the future workforce.

While not all of these illnesses will always be work-limiting, some impact on functional and cognitive capacity, social inclusion, premature withdrawal from the labour market and labour productivity is inevitable. This represents a challenge not just for health-care systems across the world, but it also threatens to increase the burden on social welfare and social insurance schemes (including workers' compensation schemes), as well as on employers, individuals and their families.

All of this has to be seen against the background of a number of familiar demographic trends that will affect the world of work in the coming decades – ageing, longer working lives and a growing burden of chronic illness in the working-age population. As remaining life expectancy at age 65 for men and

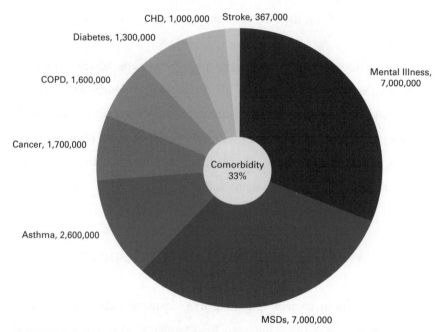

FIGURE 6.8 *Long-term health conditions in the UK workforce by 2030.*
Source: Vaughan-Jones and Barham (2010).

women in most of Western Europe now exceeds 25 years, it will be inevitable that we will have many more older people remaining in work. Another factor that is of increasing concern to policymakers is the stubborn health inequality gap between rich and poor. This is not just a high-level public health challenge because, as Marmot and colleagues have demonstrated on many occasions, work is a social determinant of health and divisions and the 'social gradient' in health in the wider labour market can be perpetuated by widening gaps in status and income.

Figure 6.9 illustrates the interconnectedness of all of these trends and pressures, suggesting that the benefits of improving workforce health can accrue to stakeholders as diverse as employers and health-care professionals.

It would be easy to couch this problem purely in terms of its impact on the national finances (welfare spend, tax revenue forgone, etc.), but Australian data looking at a similar set of challenges estimates that the biggest financial impact

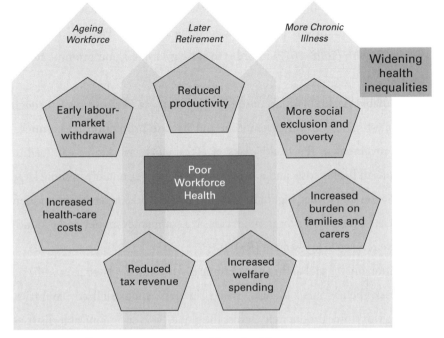

FIGURE 6.9 *Future pressures on workforce health.*

is always likely to fall on individuals and their families. It is common to find that workers with long-term illnesses are the primary income-earners in their household and, as a result, any health-related threat to their job security or to their ability to continue to retain work can have serious consequences.

Poor health is not just a threat to the global economy but to employers too. The new role for business in the area of health promotion both within and beyond their organizational boundaries is building. In September 2015 the UN adopted good health and well-being in its sustainable development agenda.[3] The global business community is recognizing a vested interest in ensuring that the health and wealth outcomes across global populations are improved.[4] Within this there is increasing public acceptance that health and well-being at work can have profound impacts on individuals, communities, organizations and societies. With over half of the working population spending the majority of their time at work, the WHO has identified the workplace as a target setting for health promotion, forming a *Global Plan of Action on Workers' Health (2008–2017)* in order to raise awareness and promote health at work.[5]

Modifiable health risks are also showing signs of improvement through workplace-financed health promotion and disease-prevention programmes. An improvement in the health risks of a company's workforce can lead to reductions in health costs and a handful of case studies, notably in some large Anglo-Saxon employers, highlight that preventive worksite health-promotion and disease-prevention programmes can save companies money and produce a positive return on investment (ROI).

Additionally the global threat of chronic disease, often related to modifiable health-risk behaviours, is also rising in less industrialized countries, affecting workforce productivity across the globe. Non-communicable diseases (NCDs) such as heart diseases, stroke, cancers, diabetes and chronic kidney disease, are amassing prevalence in low- and middle-income countries (LMICs).

It is no surprise therefore that effective investment in workplace health and well-being is playing an increasingly central role to save some employers more in terms of health-care spend, and lost productivity due to absenteeism and presenteeism. It has the combined benefit of improving population and corporate health and well-being outcomes at a country, regional and global level. One of the challenges for the future is to involve large employers with well-resourced workplace health facilities to play a wider part in supporting community-based public health initiatives.

A clearer partnership and understanding between private companies, their supply chains and government regulation and incentives is required to create mutually beneficial, universal and integrated approaches to population health and social impact. The global challenge and scale of these efforts is only now emerging and it is time to highlight the positive social impact, as well as corporate returns, of these programmes. It now looks quite possible that some workplaces of the future will be playing as much of a role in providing population health screening and delivering public health interventions for local communities, suppliers and family members of employees as traditional workplace health promotion and occupational health support for employees.

7

The future of pay and reward: the triumph of faith over evidence?

Employee pay and reward is such a fundamental part of the landscape of work that it has become an arena within which philosophy is debated, pitched battles and power struggles are fought out, and symbols of organizational culture and values are fashioned. Everyone has a view about pay, whether evidence-based or not. They know with an impressive certainty how to use pay to motivate people, why pay should – or should not – be linked to performance, how incentives drive behaviour, what market rates should be and how to make the way we pay employees demonstrably fair, proportionate and equitable. The financial compensation we get for our labours is also a very tangible way our absolute and relative 'value' to the economy, if not society more generally, is determined. It also unlocks or constrains our ability to afford the basic needs of modern life (food, housing and transport) or the ability to buy discretionary goods such as holidays, fashion and luxuries.

From an employer perspective, pay represents one of the biggest operating costs, if not the largest cost of all. This means there is a financial imperative to get the most from every dollar, pound or euro of pay-bill costs in terms of productivity and performance and to avoid these costs spiralling out of control. Reward management is akin to a form of balancing act. During periods of low inflation or recession the focus on pay-bill control intensifies and, in extreme circumstances, pay-bill costs are reduced by cutting posts. During a boom or if inflation is rising there is also pressure to increase pay – either to reflect the cost of living or to share in the success of the business.

Such is the complexity of some pay and reward systems that it can be easy to be drawn into a series of tactical adjustments to who gets paid what and why. If a high-flier who threatens to leave gets a pay rise to keep them, will this undermine the integrity of the grading structure and lead to others trying the same approach to get a pay increase? Can an organization justify paying discretionary bonuses to key staff without there being transparency over the criteria being used? Should an employee who is not performing because they have had been off work through illness have their pay held back or even reduced?

To avoid pay and rewards becoming fatally corrupted or any veneer of consistency or fairness being eroded irreparably, it is important that reward 'strategy' provides a clear set of principles, values and rules that allow senior managers, line managers, employees and, if present, trade unions to understand what the pay system is for, how it is expected to support the organization meet its strategic goals and how its application aligns with and supports other HR policies and practices.

Sadly, this tension between 'strategy' and 'tactics' in reward management is rarely resolved satisfactorily. In part, this is because too much is expected of pay and rewards where – in practice – good-quality line management, clear and inspirational senior leadership, excellent and inclusive communication and well-executed change management can often do the job better. Yet, as organizations face the challenges of global markets, the proliferation if ICT and more diverse, knowledge-rich and more demanding workforces in the twenty-first century, the pressure to make sure that pay systems are strategic, performance-focused and agile will grow.

The retreat from collectivism

The institutional landscape for setting pay has changed hugely in the UK with the decline of collective bargaining. Some estimates suggest that up to 80 per cent of workers in 1980 had their pay determined to some degree by collective bargaining compared with around 30 per cent today (Visser, 2013). The latest estimates for the UK by the Department for Business (BIS) for 2013 show that only 15 per cent of employees in the private sector say they are covered by a collective agreement, compared with 60 per cent in the public sector (ONS, 2014a). Trade-union membership has also declined sharply, from about 50 per cent of the workforce in 1983 to 25 per cent in 2013, according to the OECD.

The decline in union membership in the UK was exceptionally large but it has also been part of an OECD-wide decline, with trade-union density across the OECD falling from 33 per cent in 1983 to 17 per cent in 2013 (OECD, 2013b). Only a handful of countries have bucked the trend. The UK's relative ranking has changed very little – in 1983 it ranked joint 12th and in 2013 it also ranked 12th out of the 23 OECD economies for which we have comparative information for both years. Union membership remains higher in the UK than in Germany, France, the US and Japan.

The story has been different on collective bargaining coverage. Overall, the decline in collective bargaining coverage across the OECD has been modest, falling from 70 per cent to 62 per cent of the workforce between 1990 and 2009 (OECD, 2012). We can identify three broad trends. First, there have been significant long-term declines in collective bargaining coverage in the Anglo-Saxon economies, including the UK. Second, there has been little change across most European economies, although some such as Germany have seen some decline over the past decade. This is mainly because in these labour markets collective bargaining coverage is legally supported. Third, there has been a decline across most of Eastern Europe as part of the shift away from Communist-era institutions.

The changes in membership density and collective bargaining coverage since the 1980s are shown in the charts for the G7 economies in Figure 7.1.

The reasons for the fall in union membership across most OECD economies are complex, but are related to changes in the structure of economies away from manufacturing towards services and towards smaller workplaces, with unions unable to break out of their established strongholds. Globalization is also seen as making it harder for unions to exert influence, with an increased threat that unionized jobs will be offshored or undercut by cheaper producers elsewhere. In some countries – notably in the UK and Eastern Europe – extensive privatization programmes have also contributed. Some commentators have put more emphasis on differences in the legislative and political environment, contrasting for example the different fortunes of unions in closely related economies such as the US and Canada and between the UK and Ireland (Freeman, 1998). As we saw in

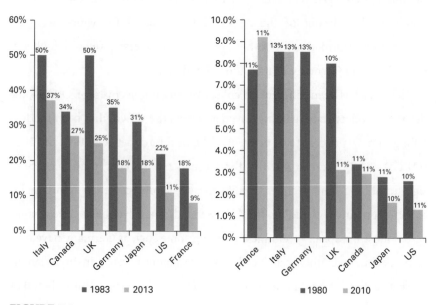

FIGURE 7.1

Source:

Chapter 2, significant shares of the labour market are regulated by professional standards which may have helped raise wages in the absence of unions.

Some have detected a generational shift, with the younger generation's greater emphasis on individualist solutions and a preference for membership of different organizations with other values (it is sometimes said that the collective membership of heritage and environmental organizations is now much greater than trade unions). However, it is hard to separate this out from changes in the occupational and industrial structure of the economy, as a result of which most young people outside of the public sector will typically enter non-unionized workplaces. Moreover, it is important to distinguish between a genuine generational shift so that young people entering the labour market in, say, 2014 have a significantly different view of work and the merits of collective bargaining and the value of union membership than similar young people entering similar workplaces in 1984; and views that change in each generation as people get older, so that for example the *insurance principle* of union membership may become more attractive to older workers.

What most evidence does suggest is that there is an association between trade-union strength and wage inequality at the national level and that unions have a sword of justice effect – so that gaps in pay between men and women and black and white workers tend to be less in organized workplaces (Metcalf, 2005). An OECD review (OECD, 1997), now dated, concluded: 'many of the statistical results show little in the way of significant statistical relationships between measures of economic performance and certain indices of bargaining systems with the major exception of earnings inequality'. A more recent assessment (Wright and Brown, 2014) has concluded:

Over the past 30 years, British unions have been marginalised from economic policymaking. Union membership and collective bargaining coverage have fallen dramatically, and the sometimes negative economic impact of unions at the workplace level has disappeared. While strong unions were once key contributors to macroeconomic problems such as high inflation, the weakening of organised labour has created other economic problems for policymakers in Britain, such as rising inequality.

The structure of pay

As we discussed in Chapter 2, the UK labour market showed unprecedented flexibility in wages over the crash of 2008–2010. According to the 2011 Workplace Employment Relations Survey (WERS) just under 40 per cent of private-sector organizations used wage freezes and cuts as a response to the recession, as did over 60 per cent of public-sector organizations (Stationery Office, 2012). The reasons for this greater wage flexibility are not well understood – it may simply reflect a long-term change in bargaining power between labour and capital in the workplace in a labour market where the potential costs to the individual of becoming unemployed have increased. It is also easier for some people to sustain falling real wages when inflation is relatively low.

There is a persistent belief that a bigger share of wages is now dependent on variable elements, including traditional forms such as overtime and shift payments and the more novel approaches such as performance-related pay. For some people these elements are a very important part of the total wage package. Yet the statistics are not consistent over time, but the underlying trend is clear. Overall, these variable elements account for a relatively small share of pay which has not changed significantly over time (ONS, 2014c). Indeed, since the mid-2000s the share of pay accounted for by these variable elements has fallen. In 2014 overtime payments accounted for 2.7 per cent of full-time average earnings, shift payments 1 per cent and incentive payments 1.2 per cent. It may be that the greater flexibility of pay at the macro-level has made variable pay less relevant to employers.

Pay and reward challenges

In this chapter we take a look at some of the most common and contentious pay and reward challenges and choices facing organizations today and in the future. We will assess the evidence for or against some of the approaches to paying employees that are in common use and explore the steps that can be taken to help pay and reward systems over the next few decades become more closely aligned to HR and business strategy. We begin by looking at the main components of pay and reward systems (from grading structures to flexible benefits) and then look at six big questions that organizations need to address if they are to get their systems 'fit for purpose' for the future. These questions are:

1   How good is pay at motivating high performance?

2   How closely should performance management and rewards be linked?

3   Has executive compensation undermined trust in the integrity of reward systems?

4   Does wide pay dispersion matter and will more transparency help?

5   Is 'Total Reward' the answer?

6   Is a new 'collectivism' in reward emerging?

In answering these questions, this chapter will also look at the evidence of 'what works' in the field of pay and reward. As others have observed (Kessler, 2007), reward management is the area of human-resource management where the gap between rhetoric and reality is at its widest and very clear evidence is frequently ignored in favour of 'gut instinct' or 'common sense'. One chapter in one book among many does not have the power to reverse this, but it is hoped that some of the arguments that follow will help some organizations to simplify and ground their practice in evidence rather than dogma.

Core components of reward

In the interests of clarifying terminology and setting the context for what follows in this chapter, it is important to establish the core components of reward. In Figure 7.2 the positioning of reward strategy relative to business and HR strategy is identified.

Here, the assumption is made that the business strategy of an organization leads to choices being made about the wider approach to human-resource management (including skills, training and development, workforce planning, work organization, job design, leadership and culture) which needs to be implemented in order to support the core goals of the business. In turn, the approach to pay and reward that is adopted should – in theory at least – be aligned to both business and HR strategy.

Within the ambit of pay and rewards, it is common to differentiate three main elements – base pay, variable pay and benefits.

'Base' or 'basic' pay'

An important characteristic of basic pay is that it is almost always driven by the post or job that the organization wishes to be done rather than the

FIGURE 7.2 *Aligning business, HR and reward strategy.*

attributes, talents or performance of the post holder. In setting the value of a post, an employer may wish to take account of some or all of the following:

- the value of this post in the marketplace – this market may be local, regional, national or international, or it may be occupational;

- the value of this post relative to other posts in the organization;

- the extent to which the organization has a system or hierarchy of posts within which post-holders may move or progress;

- the extent to which the organization wishes (or is required) to review basic pay in relation to the 'cost of living'.

There are three approaches to basic pay that employers are using to help them manage remuneration:

Job evaluation is a mechanism through which the requirements of posts within an organization are assessed against a number of dimensions (e.g. job knowledge required, degree of financial accountability). These assessments result in a ranking of posts according to their relative 'size' or value to the organization. This ranking may also result in the design of a grading system to order posts of related size. Job evaluation is frequently used to 'benchmark' jobs with those in other organizations, helping the employer maintain a position in the marketplace.

The main advantage of job evaluation is that it imposes a logical order on the ranking and positioning of posts within an organization. In addition, it allows more objective 'benchmarking' with competitors and offers some protection against claims of unfairness – job evaluation can make pay structures more objective and 'transparent'. The key issue with job evaluation is the amount of time and effort it takes to design, administer and maintain. In addition, it can reinforce the notion of hierarchy, job levels and status when the organization is seeking to flatten its structures. To this extent, job evaluation can be too rigid in times of change. Another problem with job evaluation is that individuals and their managers can be tempted to 'bend the rules' to re-grade posts. In systems that equate management accountability with job size, it is not uncommon to find attempts to inflate the size of a job through 'empire-building'. This can be made worse if managers fail to understand the distinction between the demands of the post and the attributes of the post holder.

Broadbanding is a way of reducing the number of narrow grades in a pay structure into a smaller number of wider bands. It is based on the view that narrow ranges cannot reward people who have reached their range maximum but who are still performing well (even though no promotion opportunities exist for them). Broader-banded structures are intended to provide greater flexibility to reward the acquisition of wider skills and competencies without needing to promote the post holder in every case. On the positive side, broadbanding can enhance opportunities for flexibility by drawing the boundaries between jobs less narrowly. It can be a useful tool in changing working practices to allow greater multi-skilling and cross-functional working. In addition, it can serve to help simplify previously complex pay systems. However, broadbanding is not without its disadvantages. The first problem with broadbanding is that many employers fail to implement it fully. Rather, they combine large numbers of grades into ostensibly broader bands, but continue to manage the structure as if nothing had changed. Another problem can be cost – broad bands can provide some posts with unexpected new 'headroom' with no apparent brakes on progression.

Job families are a development of both job evaluation and broadbanding. They allow an organization to cluster jobs into groups where there is apparent functional synergy. For example, in a manufacturing business it is possible to categorize the majority of posts into the following four 'families':

- the 'buying' job family – all posts associated with purchasing raw materials and components;

- the 'making' job family – all posts whose primary purpose is manufacturing;

- the 'selling' job family – all posts involved in selling finished products;

- the 'support' job family – all posts performing a support role.

The attractions of such arrangements is that pay levels can be linked more explicitly to external comparators and that they can more readily reflect the career paths that individuals follow and aspire to and the distinctive labour markets from which the employer recruits (and to which it loses people).

Variable pay

Variable pay is an 'umbrella' term that encompasses a range of approaches to distributing pay which 'varies' according to the contribution or skills of an individual or team. Unlike basic pay, variable pay is allocated to individuals or teams, and is usually intended to incentivize or reward contribution over and above the core requirements of the post. In many organizations, this has come to mean that a proportion of the pay bill is allocated on a discretionary basis, often with line-manager involvement. Variable pay can take the form of bonuses (usually not pensionable or consolidated into basic pay) or other awards such as increments, which move the employee through a grading structure by increasing their basis pay. The main forms of variable pay are summarized below.

Performance-related pay

Performance-related pay (PRP) is a generic term for a variety of approaches to awarding discretionary payments to individual employees on the basis of their contribution. Among the most common approaches include pay awards for meeting work objectives or targets, for demonstrating work-related competences or a combination of the two. As noted above, awards can be given as non-consolidated bonuses or as consolidated progression within a pay structure. The pros and cons of PRP are discussed later on in this chapter.

Competency-based pay

Strictly speaking, competency-based pay is no more than a specific form of PRP. It has started to be identified separately in recent years mostly as it represents a product area that reward consultancies have been keen to promote. In essence, it involves linking individual merit payments to the acquisition and performance of a range of competencies. Most often, an organization will develop 'core' competencies that it feels all its staff should have, together with some technical or functionally specific competencies. Employees will be assessed against a pre-agreed competency 'profile', and a payment will be made dependent on performance against this profile.

Skill-based pay

This approach to pay rewards the jobholder for acquiring accredited, job-related skills. It is based on the principle that job groups can be broken down into skill modules and levels, and that the more of these blocks of skill the jobholder has, the more competent and flexible they will be. From an employer perspective, skill-based pay offers the opportunity to broaden the range of skills and tasks that employees can perform. In particular, employers have seen it as a way of challenging the traditional craft or technician job boundaries and moving towards greater multi-skilling. Trade unions have seen advantages in skill-based pay because it offers employees the opportunity to enhance their skills and, thereby, their market value. In addition, skill-based pay relies far less on subjective judgement by managers and is therefore favoured over other forms of variable pay.

Team pay

This is any form of payment or bonus based on the performance or output of a team of employees. In some instances, individual performance may be taken into account (e.g. poor performers may be excluded). The payments may be made after a fixed period (as a reward) but they are most commonly offered as an incentive linked to targets or measures at the beginning of a period.

Benefits

Once base pay is determined and any share in variable pay is allocated the other main component of pay and reward systems is benefits. These can be core benefits, including those defined by regulation (e.g. paid holiday, sick pay, basic pension) all of which might be enhanced by the employer at their discretion. Voluntary benefits are 'perks' that the employee opts into and pays for (often at a reduced rate), such as health insurance, gym membership and child-care vouchers.

Flexible benefits schemes give employees the option to access their benefits according to their own preferences. Many employers are concerned that employees do not perceive the real 'value' of their benefits package – often taking it for granted. They are also concerned to ensure that employees receive benefits that will have most impact on recruitment, motivation and retention. Offering more flexible access to benefits (e.g. being able to get the cash value of a car, being able to trade in annual leave, forgoing pension rights in favour of cash) is seen as a way of both making their total value more explicit and offering them in a manner that is valued by employees. This approach offers the chance for employees to tailor their benefits to their own needs. They can help in attracting and retaining employees, and they help make explicit the value of an employee's total remuneration package. The main disadvantage of these schemes is that the costs associated with setting up and administering them can be substantial, especially as the evidence of employee demand for flexibility is very thin on the ground. The highest demand tends to be among senior managers, with little interest among employees at lower levels.

Recognition schemes allow local managers to provide immediate (usually non-financial) rewards to individuals or teams who have contributed 'above and beyond' their core job. Some organizations provide line managers with a small budget which they are encouraged to use during the year to take their team out for a meal if they meet a difficult target, or to buy shop vouchers for an individual who has stayed late for a week to meet a deadline. Others have explicit guidelines (even a hierarchy) prescribing the kinds of recognition awards that can be given for certain types of contribution. Most still emphasize the need for line managers to say 'thank you' occasionally. There are several advantages to recognition schemes. First, they are immediate, and therefore can be very motivational. Second, they are inexpensive – those who use them claim that they can yield results far beyond their direct cost as they have significant symbolic value. Third, they can focus employee behaviour on added-value activities such as customer service, on generating and implementing innovations in working practices. Fourth, they can emphasize that the role of the line manager is to motivate and empower his or her employees.

Some of the downsides to recognition schemes are usually as a result of poor design and management. Recognition awards can be seen as patronizing, especially if employees feel they are not paid enough. They can be perceived to be unfair, especially if managers are seen to reward their 'favourites'. If they are awarded only to those in high-profile or glamorous jobs, they can demotivate those quietly working away in support roles.

Overall, the core components of pay and reward are designed to do different things and should be straightforward to both design and execute. However, a big challenge faced by many organizations is that, even if the design of a pay and reward system is elegant, its execution is rarely so. For the remainder of this chapter, therefore, we will take a look at a number of contemporary challenges facing organizations as they seek to execute the delivery of reward, and highlight some of the future challenges (or opportunities) that they need to tackle if they are to get pay and reward to play a full part of motivating and retaining talent.

How good is pay at motivating high performance?

Despite extensive research and debate, since the early 1990s in particular, organizations seem no closer to exploiting the link between pay practices and employee performance. Compensation and benefits executives face increasing pressure from top management to cut reward costs, limit growth in total rewards spending and ultimately increase the return on investment from payroll spend. Many organizations have over the years turned increasingly to pay for performance as a strategic reward lever only, it would seem, to find disappointment and frustration. Whilst data from the Corporate Leadership Council (2002) suggests that more than 70 per cent of organizations use at least one broad-based variable pay plan to drive or reward employee performance, a separate study by Hewitt Associates showed that only 17 per cent believed them to have been 'very successful'.

It has to be recognized, of course, that many senior figures in business and in government have a firm and genuinely held set of beliefs and convictions about the inherent fairness, natural justice and effectiveness of performance-related pay. These beliefs are frequently based on a number of assumptions about individual motivation, the effort–reward relationship and managerial capability. Chief among these assumptions are that:

1   Employees will increase their effort or output in order to attain the reward on offer.

2   Employees feel that the rewards on offer to be of sufficient value to them to incentivize extra effort.

3   Employees are confident that the reward will still be on offer at the end of the period during which their individual performance is being measured.

4   Organizations are able to establish and use clear and transparent measures of performance for all relevant employees, and apply these measures consistently.

5   Individual, rather than collective, contribution is the primary driver of organizational performance (even in organizations where there is a strong emphasis on team-working).

6   Line managers have the time, commitment and competence to explain and administer PRP effectively, transparently and consistently (and see the importance of doing so).

7   Any performance improvement brought about by PRP is sustainable over time.

8   PRP will deliver sufficiently large pay increases to motivate and incentivize employees, even during periods of low inflation.

Performance: the definition problem

If we are to analyse the link between pay and performance we must start by posing the question: 'Are we clear about what we mean by performance and the factors that drive it?' This is a subject that has spawned a whole genre of literature on its own and whilst the central purpose of this chapter would not be served by a lengthy regurgitation of the academic and practical debate here, it is nevertheless essential that the conceptual and operational difficulties in defining and measuring this construct are summarized as it is evident that many organizations are still trying to find their way out of this maze and are therefore disappointed when introducing money into the equation drives unexpected and unwelcome outcomes.

On the face of it, it may mean that job performance is a relatively straightforward concept. Job performance is how well people perform their jobs, and it is as simple as that. However, the truth is that job performance is one of those concepts that becomes more complex and problematic the more you think about it. Some influential thinking in this area was introduced by Campbell et al. (1993). Campbell and colleagues made the important distinction between performance and the results of performance or, as we more typically describe this today, between inputs and outputs. For them, 'performance' was clearly the former – behaviour that is relative to goal completion – and as such clearly distinguishable from both effectiveness and productivity. Their taxonomy of performance components (including job-specific task proficiency, demonstrating effort, facilitating peer performance) is therefore much more behaviourally focused than outcome defined. The view that performance is actually behaviour rather than outputs or results has been challenging to the historic and collective psyche of many organizations, which has resulted in an opaque and confusing mix of definitions and practices. As Williams (2002) observes, the term 'performance' tends to be used in everyday practice in a loose way that embraces both outputs and behaviour, but if organizations are not entirely clear on what they are defining as performance, how can they be sure of what they are rewarding with their base and variable pay mechanisms?

The behavioural notion of performance gets more confusing still when the concept of organizational citizenship is introduced into the mix. Borman and Motowidlo (1993) distinguish between task performance (i.e. activities that contribute to the technical core of the organization) and contextual performance (which supports the broader, but arguably no less important, social/psychological environment of the organization). These behaviours (e.g. volunteering for extra work, helping others, protecting the organization, developing oneself) have also been referred to as organizational spontaneity (George and Brief, 1992) or 'extra role behaviours' (Van Dyne et al., 1995). It is too easy to dismiss such behaviours as peripheral or 'nice to have' as the shift in emphasis towards quality and customer satisfaction may mean that, for many jobs, they are explicitly related to successful performance outcomes. Research (MacKenzie et al., 1991, 1993; Motowidlo and Schmit, 1999) has also shown how line managers place emphasis on such behavioural inputs when making performance evaluations.

Regrettably the concept of performance as behaviour has also been overcomplicated by the use and misuse of competencies. Here, also, is another definition problem. Whilst for many, such as Woodruffe (1992), competencies are synonymous with behaviour, others adhere to the work of the McBer consultancy as described by Boyatzis (1982), who take a more outcome-based approach to performance influenced by what people *are*, not what they do. In other words, competencies here are not behaviours that are therefore performance in themselves but are rather personal characteristics – traits, motives, self-concepts – that determine or cause performance.

Little wonder, therefore, that confusion abounds in a way that exhausts the limited attention span of hard-pressed business managers. Instead of simplifying the issue, every development seems to make matters more complex and opaque. And yet it is a fog that needs to be lifted. Issues of inputs versus outputs, performance means versus performance ends, behaviours or traits are central to the issue of defining what an organization wants and needs from its employees. It can be hard to escape the conclusion that spending vast sums of money on pay and incentive schemes without such clarity may be a gamble that risks waste and disappointment.

Economic theory and PRP

PRP has long been an important idea for economists. At its heart is the principal–agent problem, which defines the employment relationship and the role of pay in the way it operates. In short, it is argued that the modern employment relationship does not naturally align the interests of principal (employer) and agent (employee). The principal's interest is that the worker works as hard, efficiently and responsively as possible, in order to maximize profit and improve outcomes. The agent, on the other hand, will aim to minimize the effort they expend in order to reach the basic standards required to receive pay. From this perspective, PRP is often regarded as a mechanism designed to better align the interests of principal and agent. The agent is incentivized to maximize their outputs – and consequently organizational outcomes – by tying a proportion of their remuneration to their performance. In theory, PRP will therefore encourage effort and offset the 'shirking' behaviour that might otherwise be expected from employees (Goodman and Turner, 2009: 4). It will also offer the employer cost flexibility, allowing them to reduce the pay bill in cases of poor performance.

It is important to outline the assumptions that underpin this logic, which are based on expectancy theory and reinforcement theory. The logic of expectancy theory is that expenditure of an individual's effort will be determined by their expectations that an outcome will be attained, and the degree of value placed on this outcome by the individual (Porter and Lawler, 1968). Reinforcement then operates when the intended effort elicits the desired outcome. In the case of PRP, employees will be expected to work harder if they value monetary rewards and believe that these will result from their increased efforts. This idea originated with Taylor's 'piece rate' system, which offered different wage rates to workers depending on their efficiency (Reilly, 2003). If workers are primarily motivated by the money they earn, then an economic perspective will argue that this is the best incentive to ensure they maximize their efforts. However, the system also has to consider issues of equity. Rewards need to be perceived to reflect employees' efforts. Moreover, if the reward is either too small or something the employee does not consider important, then it will fail to motivate the employee to increase their efforts.

In many studies, however, the underlying foundations of these standard economic theories have been called into question. For example, in a notable study on timber workers in North America, Locke and Latham (1990) found that the employees involved could also be motivated by the setting of clear goals and feedback on performance, without any financial reward being provided. It was argued that this was due to the fact that the workers both trusted their managers and viewed their goals as reasonable. In cases where PRP has not operated along the lines the theoretical logic would suggest, some studies have suggested that financial motivations may not be of particular importance to the employees, or that PRP has created divisive effects between co-workers (Perry et al., 2009: 43–4). Conflicting evidence has thus created significant debate around PRP and its potential effectiveness.

Motivation, pay and performance

Whatever position one takes on whether performance is outcomes or competencies or whether competencies are behaviours or traits, it is evident that there is something more here to successful task completion than just capability or proficiency.

For Campbell et al. (1993) motivation was one of the three 'performance determinants' (alongside declarative and procedural knowledge), whilst in the McBer model motives and mental attitudes are captured under the overall heading of competency. Boxall and Purcell (2003) make the role of motivation even more explicit in their 'AMO' model in which performance is defined as a function of ability + motivation + opportunity. Again, whilst a detailed analysis of the different theories of how motivation works would not be helpful, an overview is necessary before we can ask the question: 'So what impact does money have on these different perspectives?'

Unlike performance, motivation is a construct that is relatively easy to define. One of the most widely used definitions, possibly because of its simplicity, is offered by Jones (1955) who saw motivation as 'how behaviour gets started, sustained, stopped and what subjective reaction is present while all this is going on'.

Herzberg's (1968) motivational-hygiene (two-factor) theory postulates that there are two groups of influences that affect motivation. The first are *motivators* which involve achievement, advancement, recognition and autonomy. Motivators represent sources of satisfaction for employees. The second group of factors was named hygiene factors and include salary, work environment and company policy. These represent a possible source of dissatisfaction. The presence of motivators improves performance and generates a motivated and satisfied workforce. However, their absence does not cause dissatisfaction. Hygiene factors, when present, create an acceptable work environment without increasing individual dissatisfaction. What is important to note, however, is that the absence of hygiene factors causes job dissatisfaction. Salary for Herzberg was a hygiene factor. Thus the need for money was a necessary condition in order to avoid dissatisfaction but was not sufficient to generate job satisfaction and motivation. Money, then, is a motivator to the extent that it stops dissatisfaction but its power extends only to fending off negative feelings rather than encouraging positive ones. Therefore, if people are fairly and equitably paid in line with market forces they will simply be not dissatisfied and, even if generously paid, will not experience greater motivation.

Questions over the methodological rigour employed by Herzberg to arrive at this model have challenged its validity but not diluted its popularity. Perhaps the most important and lasting element of its legacy is the distinction between intrinsic and extrinsic motivation. Intrinsic motivation comes, literally, from within doing something – it is part of its very nature of being. Therefore, the sense of enjoyment, achievement, autonomy and so on that Herzberg refers to as motivators are intrinsic. Extrinsic motivators, conversely, come from the outside and are likely to include the hygiene factors that Herzberg details as such things like pay, workplace environment and holidays. The distinction is important therefore when considering the role of pay in motivation. Here, pay only works as a motivator to do things we find less appealing, possibly stressful and frequently boring. This presents organizations with an interesting choice: spend increasing sums of money to motivate people to do unappealing and/or boring work or save money by instead making work more appealing and rewarding, thereby raising more powerful levels of intrinsic motivation. To quote Herzberg again: 'If you want people to do a good job, give them a good job to do.'

This choice is given an extra twist by the work of Deci et al. (1999) who contends that intrinsic and extrinsic sources of motivation are not mutually exclusive. They argue that the use of expected financial incentives such as salary, awards, prizes and bonuses *reduces* intrinsic motivation for the task and therefore decreases performance for individuals who are intrinsically motivated. External incentives such as money act as demotivators for work as they reward task completion and pay little attention to the reward gained from the task itself. Intrinsically motivated people will draw their motivation to work from the inherent properties of the task and the goal of completing it well. Rewarding such individuals for task completion will have the effect of demotivating them for other tasks that do not have rewards attached to them. This expectancy factor is illustrated by Furnham (2005) in his example of a house owner trying to move children playing outside further away by paying them to continue. Over time the payment is reduced until it is withdrawn altogether, whereupon the children state that they are not going to play there for nothing and stomp off in disgust! As we will see later, the evidence for this counter-intuitive way of thinking about money and motivation is mixed. It does, however, raise the very real question of whether organizations have lost sight about the power of intrinsic motivation inherent within their activities and have locked themselves onto a narrow and never ending treadmill of applying more and more extrinsic rewards for increasingly marginal and ever diminishing returns.

The differing nature of individual rewards also plays a role in the expectancy theory (Vroom, 1964; Porter and Lawler, 1965), arguably the most empirically tested and validated process theory of motivation. There are two types of expectancy at play here. The first is the extent to which individuals perceive that additional effort will lead to successful task performance. The second is that successful task performance will lead or be instrumental in obtaining 'rewards'. The greater the perceived value of the reward in question, the greater the motivation. Therefore, if we believe that extra effort will lead to task success *and* that task success will bring valued rewards, we will be motivated to act. Money in this model will only motivate as long as it is an outcome that has perceived value for individuals. Again, we will look at the evidence later but it is easy, as many organizations do, to overplay the value of money as a perceived reward and underplay the latent functions of work highlighted by Jahoda (1982) and/or the issue of work centrally to many people's lives, where matters of self-image and self-esteem are far more powerful motivators than pay and benefits.

Finally, it would not be appropriate to close this section without revisiting the work of Locke and Latham and the motivational power of goal setting. One of the most robust research findings in the behavioural sciences field is that goal setting has a beneficial effect on motivation and performance. As long as certain criteria can be fulfilled, goal setting leads to an increase in the intensity and persistence of effort which, if mediated by ability, leads to an improvement in performance. The criteria that studies of goal setting typically reveal as being necessary to release this motivational impetus are:

- Specific goals lead to higher performance than general 'do your best' goals.
- Difficult goals lead to higher performance than easy goals.

- Goals must be accepted by the individual as fair and reasonable.

- There must be an element of commitment or ownership of the individual.

Accepting the work of Locke and Latham dictates a mind shift in the value and nature of goal setting. In this world, objectives are not *just* about making sure that everyone is pointed in the right direction or that everyone can be held accountable for what they do or even that the reward 'cake' can be shared equitably in light of relative contribution. They are instead an instrument of motivation and higher achievement. Studies by Locke et al. (1968, 1980) and Locke (1968) suggest that monetary rewards may enhance the motivational nature of goal setting by affecting the degree of goal commitment but again this presupposes that money is what is valued most here.

Important as it is to revisit the basic concepts around constructs such as 'performance' and 'motivation', we need to return to the central issue here of what this tells us about whether pay is a good lever of performance or not. Can financial incentives really drive discretionary effort and productivity or are organizations barking up the wrong tree here?

Unsurprisingly, the evidence presents rather a mixed picture, which in itself helps to explain why this whole issue seems often to be a perennial debate that goes round and round in circles without any definitive resolution. So, what salient points can we pull out of the debate for analysis here?

The first observation we can make with some certainty is that there is sufficient hard evidence to refute the position, which has always seemed counter-intuitive in any event, that money is absolutely not a motivator in the workplace. Whilst work psychology textbooks often choose to steer clear of the whole money issue, to the lay person, particularly the manager who finds it difficult to motivate his/her staff, it is a critical and powerful tool. Furnham (1996) has commented on this power, highlighting that there is little doubt that people work harder when paid by results as opposed to the time they have put in. Other studies have shown the effect of incentive plans on reducing absenteeism. A British study of six factories where payment by results had been introduced without any other changes found an increase in output of 60 per cent (Davison et al., 1958) whilst a meta-analysis of 330 American intervention programmes found that introducing financial incentives had the greatest effect across a wide range of motivational levers – training, work design and so on (Guzzo et al., 1985). In their work, Locke et al. (1980) found that incentives increased worker performance by a median of 30 per cent. Other, more recent, large-scale meta-analyses by Eisenberger and Cameron (1996) and Jenkins et al. (1998) concluded that financial incentives are related to performance *quantity* and challenged the work of Deci (1971) in arguing that the 'negative effects of reward on task interest and creativity have attained the status of myth, taken for granted despite considerable evidence that the conditions producing these effects are limited and easily remedied'.

So what of the counter-arguments that see money as a flawed motivator of improved performance? One of the fiercest critics of the use of money as a motivational tool is Kohn (1993) who challenges some of the statistical analysis in the Guzzo et al. (1985) study and contends that rewards do not create a lasting commitment – at best they merely, and temporarily, change what we do. Money is a poor motivator for Kohn because:

1   Rewards *punish*. Rewards are a manipulative tool, in the same way as threats. To say, 'do this and I will give you this' is as good as saying 'do this or this will happen'. A promised reward that is not received is psychologically as bad as a punishment.

2   Rewards *rupture relations*. High performance often requires teamwork. If a group of workers are chasing the same incentive then they will be in a state of competition that creates a divisive win–lose climate.

3   Rewards *ignore reason*. If a company is not performing, to simply offer a financial incentive to bolster performance ignores the many possible

root causes. If the only tool in the box is a hammer, then everything gets made to look like a nail.

4   Rewards *deter risk taking.* When money is at stake, individuals are far more likely to take the easy, tried and tested option which may suboptimize the desired outcome.

5   Rewards *undermine interest.* The enjoyment of a task is a far more powerful influence than any incentive can be (intrinsic vs extrinsic again). Like Deci, Kohn argues that the more financial incentive is pushed into the faces of workers, the more this will be their only reason for continuing the task.

Other organizational psychologist 'heavyweights' lend support to Kohn's position. In his 'six dangerous myths about pay', Jeffrey Pfeffer (1998) argues that individual incentive pay undermines performance by eroding teamwork, creating short-termism and inculcating a belief that pay is not related to performance at all but instead to having the 'right' relationships and an ingratiating personality. Myth number 6 also attacks the belief that people work for money for leading organizations to confuse bribery with loyalty and commitment. Furnham (2005) also argues that money is a poor motivator because, amongst other things, the effects of money quickly wear off and that it is not the absolute amount of money you receive that is important but how much it is relative to your immediate social comparison group. Pay someone inequitably and you have a *very* demotivated individual. Pay them equitably but you still need to do many more things at work to achieve a contented and productive individual.

More empirically based evidence about the inadequacy of PRP schemes is offered by Thompson (1993) who examined the attitudes of nearly 1,000 employees in three organizations (county council, food retailer, building society) operating individual based PRP systems. The results of the first analysis clearly showed that the benefits most often claimed for PRP were not met in practice. First, PRP did not serve to motivate (even those with high performance ratings) and may have done more to demotivate employees. Second, there was little evidence to suggest that PRP could help to retain high performers and no evidence to point to poor performers seeking to leave the organizations. Third, employees were negative or broadly neutral on its impact on organizational culture even in schemes that had been in operation for three or more years. Lastly, employees were unclear as to whether PRP rewards fairly (neither agreeing nor disagreeing). However, high performers were likely to perceive it to be more fair than low-rated performers.

Another systematic study of PRP in practice (across two government departments, two NHS Trust hospitals and primary and secondary school head teachers) was conducted by Marsden and French (1998). This showed that whilst there was evidence that a majority of staff in two of the case study organizations were working harder as a result of PRP this was achieved at a cost of creating distrust of line management and of souring employee relations.

Finally, reference to a large-scale quantitative analysis by the Corporate Leadership Council (2002) is illuminating. In their survey of more than 17,000 employees and managers across 50-plus organizations they found that:

- Employee commitment is the central driver of employee performance and pay satisfaction is a poor predictor of such commitment.

- Employee perception of pay fairness was a 25 times stronger predictor of employee commitment than pay satisfaction.

- Pay *process* fairness is the most important element of overall pay fairness.

- Every 10 per cent improvement in process fairness perception increases employee commitment levels by 5 per cent, leading to a 2 per cent increase in discretionary effort.

Despite this challenging evidence, in some parts of the world there has been considerable enthusiasm among governments for the use of PRP among public-sector employees, based on the desire to drive up individual and collective efficiency and performance. As we will see, these attempts have had distinctly mixed results.

PRP in the public sector

The use of individual PRP in the UK public sector was first introduced as part of formal pay policy in the 1980s. Although it has taken several forms (from appraisal-driven pay and skill-based progression to team-based bonuses) and has only been used comprehensively in parts of the public sector (e.g. the Civil Service), its use has been based on a number of principles. First, that an element of public servants' rewards should contain a 'contingent' element that reflected their individual performances. Second, that this contingent element should be used to motivate, incentivize and reward higher performance. Third, that the value of this 'contingent' element would be variable in line with affordability criteria. Fourth, that using performance-related rewards to differentiate between higher-level performers and poor performers would promote feelings of distributive justice in the workforce and lead those whose performance was poor to strive for improved performance ratings. However, the use of PRP in the public sector has always been controversial. Many public-sector trade unions and some academics have argued that PRP is a mechanism borrowed from the commercial sector that is inappropriate in an environment where an 'ethos' of public service rather than the so-called 'profit motive' dominates the culture. In addition, others have argued that the use of PRP was always intended by government to individualize the employment relationship in the public sector as part of an explicit attempt to undermine the role of trade unions in collective approaches to pay bargaining. Other, more operational, concerns about the use of PRP have included its potential to reinforce the gender pay gap and adverse outcomes for women, the motivational impact of very low or zero awards in periods of low inflation or economic austerity and whether the direct, indirect and displacement costs of administering these schemes can be justified in terms of the performance 'premium' they generate.

For some time, the use of PRP was largely restricted to the private sector, where it was demonstrated to be effective in roles where individual effort and contribution are more easily measurable, such as sales or production. For example, the classic study by Lazear (2000) showed the effectiveness of piece rates – the simplest form of PRP – in raising individual worker output in the Safelight Glass Corporation during the 1990s. However, the rise of New Public Management theories during the 1980s opened a new discussion about its potential applicability in the public sector. These theories were based on the idea that performance in the public sector was being held back due to an absence of the incentives and management practices that drove organizations working for profit. The way to improve public-sector performance was thus to simulate some of these features of private-sector management practice (Bajorek and Bevan, 2015).

The economic theories outlined earlier have also been developed and applied to common concerns for public-sector managers. For example, existing ways of setting public-sector pay rates, based on experience, time-served or qualification levels, may not always identify and reward the best performers. In education, for example, while teacher effectiveness plays a significant role in pupil performance, effectiveness cannot be predicted from easily observable characteristics (Woessman, 2011: 404). The characteristics frequently used to set teachers' pay rates, such as experience or acquisition of higher qualifications, have only a low power in predicting teacher effectiveness (Goodman and Turner, 2009; Leigh, 2013). It is argued that this creates limited direct incentives for teachers to improve their performance. This is also compounded by the fact that the nature of many public-sector contracts makes it difficult to remove poor performers (Figlio and Kenny, 2007). From this perspective, PRP is seen to be useful both for its motivation and selection effects. If effective teachers are hard to identify using recognizable characteristics, offering an element of PRP should better attract and retain those who perform well in post (Leigh, 2013: 1–2). It may also induce a 'clearing effect', by which poor performers are encouraged to leave the profession.

There are other issues affecting the public sector which PRP may also help to address. For example, the scale of public-sector organizations and the nature of their work means that many employees operate in a setting in which the majority of their actions and inputs are not directly visible to their managers (Neal, 2011: 1). Its use can therefore lead to an increase in oversight and accountability. PRP schemes can also steer and direct the focus of employees, which may help to clarify to employees how best to fulfil their responsibilities where a job involves numerous tasks or its nature is broadly defined (Goodman and Turner, 2009: 4).

PRP has therefore been seen as an answer to what classical economic theory would view as some of the fundamental challenges facing the public sector: that it lacks the clear links between performance and pay that can be used to drive improvements in profit-seeking organizations.

Performance management and pay

Performance management (PM) has, for several decades, been a feature of the way many large organizations have sought to improve their effectiveness. At its core, PM is a way of aligning the goals of the organization with the annual objectives of individual employees so that everyone knows what is expected of them and so that managers can support and even reward good performance. While the approaches that these organizations have taken to PM often share common features, one of its more elusive characteristics has been that it is never implemented the same way twice. This has made generalization about the true nature and effectiveness of PM something of a thankless preoccupation among HR academics and practitioners.

In some ways, the heterogeneity of PM in practice is a hopeful sign. Each organization has differing business goals, structures, cultures and processes, suggesting that a prescriptive, 'best practice' model of PM would be more than likely to fail. The debate over PM typifies the alternative thrust towards the notion of 'best fit': that overarching HR-led processes need to be driven by business needs, and shaped by the need for internal integration with existing systems and processes (Bevan, 2014). To work well, PM needs to become a natural part of the way the organization and its managers operate, rather than a paper-based, bureaucratic system that is widely resented because it is seen as interrupting 'real' work.

There is a consensus that PM needs to be 'owned' by line managers as a mainstream tool that forms part of the fabric of the way they manage, motivate and monitor their teams. Yet, too often, PM is seen as an HR-led process that consumes time and energy for little discernible benefit. Additionally, if PM is used to deliver individual performance pay, it can become the focus of tension and anxiety, or even feelings of inequity or resentment wildly out of proportion compared to the amount of cash on offer – especially during a time of low inflation and austerity. Handled badly, PM can become a binary, HR-administered, annual verdict on each employee's contribution. Handled well, PM can be a way of co-producing excellent performance in a supportive and developmental climate where collaboration and a drive for continuous improvement are shared between managers and their direct reports. In practice, the effectiveness and utility of PM tends to be as much about its implementation as its design. And therein lies the real challenge.

Private- and public-sector organizations where PM is part of the managerial landscape are today faced with using PM to drive ever higher levels of performance from employees who, on average, are disengaged from their work, are experiencing higher than normal anxiety about the security of their jobs and who have been subject to lower than trend real wages. Despite the rhetoric from some CEOs about the importance of an engaged workforce, or a workforce that is 'mindful' and psychologically healthy, PM processes are where the often relentless demand for increased productivity and output meet (or conflict with?) the need among many employees for varied, challenging and rewarding work where they have a voice and feel valued. Sometimes the results are not pretty, with a growing concern that PM is being increasingly used as a blunt instrument.

We should, perhaps, start with setting out the purpose and characteristics of performance management as it is articulated in the management literature. This is, frankly, easier said than done because there are so many variations in definition. Figure 7.3 sets out a simple representation of what we might call the 'performance management cycle'.

An important point to make here is that almost every definition reflects the important idea that PM is intended to go significantly beyond the annual appraisal interview that managers have with their direct reports. As Aguinis et al. (2011) suggest in their paper entitled 'Why we hate performance

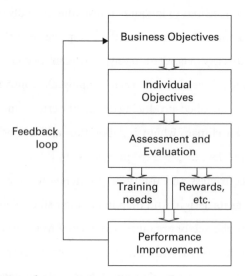

FIGURE 7.3 *Basic performance management cycle.*
Source: Bevan (2014).

management – and why we should love it': 'Despite its importance, performance management is not living up to its promise in most organizations. A major reason for this is that most performance management systems focus almost exclusively on performance appraisal' (p. 507).

The distinguishing difference is that PM attempts to locate the setting of individual objects – and the assessment of progress against these objectives – in the wider context of the organization's goals. This is intended to provide a clear 'line of sight' for the employee which helps them understand where their job fits into the grand scheme of things and how the efforts they make contribute to the greater good. Another important element is that there should be some evaluation (through a feedback loop) of the extent to which performance at individual level has improved and whether this translates into tangible improvements in overall business performance. In general, there is nothing inherent in the concept of PM that prescribes that financial rewards should play a part in either incentivizing high performance or acknowledging it once it has happened. Indeed, there is often a rather polarized debate among academics and some practitioners about whether PRP has to be a central component of PM or whether its use has a toxic and distorting effect and that PM should just focus on setting goals, giving feedback and meeting development needs. A recent review of the evidence looking at the effectiveness of PRP in the public sector (Ray et al., 2014) suggests that there are many practical factors that undermine the impact that PRP can have on performance.

In many ways the model set out in Figure 7.3 is an 'ideal' description of the main elements of PM. As with any management process, there can be big differences between design and implementation. Some of the common issues that arise are summarized below:

Line managers: as a rule, organizations should avoid designing an approach to PM that is beyond the capability of its line managers to manage effectively.

In organizations where PM works well, the common factor has been high-quality line management. This is supported by good training, clear role definition and accountabilities, minimal paperwork and a deceptively simple 'line of sight', for all staff, between business goals and individual objectives. However, in some organizations managers see their primary role as being about *managing upwards*. On occasions, this emphasis can leave the *managing downwards* part of their role somewhat of a poor relation and managers can see PM as a bureaucratic system with which HR makes them comply.

A 'good' PM system by itself should comprise a robust set of processes that good managers will use well to motivate, involve and direct the efforts of staff. It should also provide a good vehicle for feedback and discussion of training and development needs. PM, however, cannot drive performance improvement by itself. Clarity of purpose, leadership and involvement have to come first – PM is then a useful tool. A key challenge for any organization is to encourage line managers to see PM as part of their natural, or 'mainstream', approach to directing and motivating performance improvements among staff. In the final analysis, line managers should be *advocates* of PM, not *apologists* for it.

Integration: PM rarely works if it is just seen as a 'system'. It is not a mechanical set of procedures that can be managed in a linear and sequential manner. PM has to be a set of 'processes' that the organization, its managers and its staff embrace and integrate into the way they do business. PM must not, therefore, be episodic in nature. It must be continuous. It must not allow managers to hide behind paperwork. PM must have clear and organic links with a range of other management processes such as development, learning, progression and advancement, competencies, team-working and communication. If the only conversation an employee ever has about their goals and performance is in an annual appraisal meeting, PM is not working.

Outcomes of performance review: if PM ever becomes dominated by pay, many of its wider benefits to the organization can become twice as difficult to achieve. In these circumstances, PM becomes indistinguishable from PRP in the eyes of staff, and PM becomes a 'lightning rod' for a swathe of other staff concerns. Clarity and balance in the outcomes of performance review on the 'reward or develop' axis is essential, therefore.

Simplicity: it is common for organizations to give their approaches to PM multiple objectives. This can result in the risk that none are fully satisfied in the attempt to satisfy them all. A serious consequence of 'overloading' can be that staff faith in either the procedural or distributive justice of PM can be severely (or terminally) undermined. This can result in the worst of both worlds: a time-consuming, costly and cumbersome PM process that actually *reduces* employee motivation to perform. Some attempts to implement or redesign PM have tried hard to de-bureaucratize it, opting for minimum paperwork and maximum flexibility. It is important to be able to demonstrate fairness and consistency (especially if there is a pay link) while putting more emphasis on the importance of the process and less on the rules of the system.

Inputs and outputs: defining the 'what' of objective-setting is easier than defining the 'how'. Some managers will respond positively to being asked to set 'how' objectives, while others will avoid doing so unless forced to. When we talk about inputs, it is important to be clear whether we are talking about how the job is done or about more general behaviours

The contracting principle: many organizations have a very top-down driven model of objective-setting. This is good for business alignment but can leave little scope for individual adjustment or for the employee to feel they have 'co-produced' their objectives. This makes it hard to get ownership, can make a mockery of any notion of a performance 'contract' and leaves limited scope for addressing personal issues (including 'how' objectives).

To be more specific, the list below represents the list of objectives being used to define and measure the effectiveness of performance management in a large public-sector organization where the Work Foundation was providing advice:

- 'Links personal objectives to business objectives which maintain a focus on outcomes such as service delivery and the needs of the customer'
- 'Encourages people to seek and accept responsibility'
- 'Rewards excellence and motivates the best'
- 'Encourages continuous improvement'
- 'Helps to confront poor performance and differentiate between staff on the basis of performance'

So, if the design and implementation of performance management is so vulnerable to imperfect execution, is there any hope that it can ever work effectively enough to justify the costs involved in using it?

Forced distribution

One facet of some contemporary reward-oriented performance-management systems that is the subject of fierce debate and discussion is the 'forced distribution' (Bevan, 2014). Many organizations are grappling with a number of problems when it comes to translating performance 'scores' to individual performance-related pay. Here is a common scenario:

AN ORGANIZATION HAS A PERFORMANCE management process where individuals' performance against their objectives is assessed in a joint, annual meeting with their immediate boss. This often involves a mix of self-assessment and boss-subordinate assessment. In this case, the employee receives a 'box marking' or overall rating on a 1–5 scale, where 1 is 'exceptional performance', 3 is 'performance at the required standard' and 5 is 'below the expected standard'. The ratings are translated to performance pay awards, which, in this case, represent consolidated pay progression up a salary range.

Recently the organization has become concerned that some managers are artificially 'inflating' the ratings they are giving their staff to the point where they judge that far too many staff are receiving Box 1 or 2 ratings than is merited. They believe that this is for a combination of reasons:

- *Many managers find it hard to confront poor performers or to disappoint those staff who are 'only' box 3 performers.*
- *Managers are using the performance pay process to compensate those staff who they view as being poorly paid.*
- *Managers are distorting their ratings to reward those who are most at risk of leaving.*

To combat this problem, the organization issues guidance to managers which provides a set of 'indicative' ranges which are intended to support them as the engage in the performance review process. The guidance suggests that, across the organization as a whole, the distribution of ratings might look as follows:

Box 1	*10%*
Box 2	*25%*
Box 3	*40%*
Box 4	*15%*
Box 5	*10%*

The organization is careful to stress that these indicative ranges are not quotas, nor do they represent any form of 'forced distribution'.

There are several interesting points about this scenario:

- There are a number of aspects of managerial behaviour that can severely distort the way such rating schemes are used. It is questionable whether tinkering with the mechanics of the scheme, without addressing the more deep-seated behavioural issues among managers, will make much real difference.

- Rating people against a set of performance objectives employs an 'absolute' assessment of their contribution. However, using indicative ranges, quotas or forced distribution systems pushes managers to make 'relative' assessments of their staff – often as part of a 'moderation' process with other managers that can often resemble crude 'horse-trading'. Thus, they are really beginning to make ranking decisions (i.e. placing staff in rank order) to ensure that the profile of scores in their team or department broadly fits the indicative ranges.

- The consequence of this can be that an individual may score a Box 2 when assessed against their objectives but be given a Box 3 rating because there are already 'too many' Box 2 performers in the team. This can be confusing for everyone and demotivating for those staff who get 'moderated' down to a lower rating. Essentially, they can work earnestly towards their objectives all year in the expectation that, if they meet or exceed them, they will be assessed and rewarded appropriately. However, imposing a ranking mechanism means that two people who are equally effective in meeting their objectives can receive different ratings and performance pay.

- Of course, the impulse to curb rating inflation is understandable. Rating inflation, for example, tends to disadvantage the best performers. Paradoxically, if there is a fixed amount or performance pay to distribute, the more Box 1 scores that are allocated reduces the value of a Box 1 pay award.

- However, imposing (despite the weasel words) a de facto quota system is a messy way of dealing with the problem. If an organization wishes to influence the distribution of performance pay awards, then the purest (and most honest) way of doing this is through a transparent ranking process. Over the years several private-sector firms and, in the public sector, the Senior Civil Service, have adopted this approach.

- None of these solutions score well on equality of opportunity criteria as relative assessment will often rely on different (and more subjective) performance criteria than those used to arrive at the absolute scores. Thus, an individual may be judged a Box 2 performer against their objectives, but lose out to another Box 2 performer because their internal reputation or behaviour may be felt to be inferior.

- The real danger of becoming embroiled in the technical debates about rating, ranking and quotas is that is can drain the capacity of performance management to be a powerful vehicle for feedback, motivation and, yes, performance improvement.

For many managers and employees, these characteristics are all too often the most visible manifestation of the performance-management process. If performance management is used as no more than a narrow vehicle for the delivery of variable pay, organizations should be prepared for performance management to struggle in the delivery of its wider developmental objectives. The clumsy implementation of 'forced distribution' systems is, perhaps, one of the most obvious examples of how the many wider benefits of a well-designed and executed PM system can be eroded. As Ed Lawler – one of the great writers on reward strategy – explains in an article entitled 'The folly of forced ranking' (Lawler, 2002), it can be a way of snatching defeat from the jaws of victory.

Because employee performance patterns in organizations often do not follow a normal distribution, identifying poor performers using a forced ranking system is fraught with difficulties. First, a very real danger exists that some satisfactory employees will be misidentified as poor performers. For example, some divisions, departments, or teams are always better staffed than others. In those areas, individuals who are satisfactory or even outstanding performers on a company-wide basis may be judged to be underperformers just because they happen to be among a group of very good employees. The right thing to do is to strengthen weak areas where there are a large number of poor performers by replacing them, rather than removing 'the worst of the best' from areas dominated by high performers. Most forced distribution systems do not produce this result because every area, regardless of the quality of its employees and its performance, is required to make the same percentage of cuts.

While some of the examples of forced distribution and the way it has been implemented are extreme and, in some cases, shocking, the wider point that needs to be considered is whether performance management should have pay consequences at all. If PM can be configured as a continuous process of dialogue and review between line manager and direct report – rather than a high-stakes, set-piece annual assessment process – then it can become a strongly developmental and supportive process that may stand more chance of improving performance. This does not mean that the dialogue will not, on occasion, need to be difficult and uncomfortable if performance is not up to scratch or if challenging feedback needs to be given. However, reducing the potential richness of a high-touch PM process to a simple rating and a 'pass–fail' pay award seems a waste of precious managerial time and effort if all it achieves is an increase in fear and insecurity.

Executive pay

There has always been something inherently grubby about aspects of the executive pay debate. Many of us are happy to accept that the responsibility of running a big business should be handsomely compensated. But, by contrast, many are also left with an uncomfortable feeling – especially in the light of recent history – that too many top executives are being rewarded for greed or failure. Or both.

Sometimes it is hard to disentangle the executive pay debate from a wider concern over growing income inequality in the population as a whole, especially in the UK and the US. This is because some of the executive pay figures seem so eye-wateringly high to most people. As Lawrence Mishel notes in an Economic Policy Institute paper (Mishel, 2006): 'An average CEO earns more before lunchtime on the very first day of work in the year than a minimum wage worker earns all year.' But it is also because many executives have several disparate and – to many – complex components to their reward packages so that if they are forced either by the market or by regulation to restrain one element they seem to be able to 'make hay' with another. So, if basic pay is kept low, then bonuses or stock options can appear to rise to compensate. In the US, where sustained (though not stellar) economic growth began two years or so before the UK emerged from recession, 95 per cent of the income gains of growth have gone to the top 1 per cent of the population in the first three years of the recovery (Saez, 2012). This has fuelled a feeling that, while ordinary mortals endured a decline in real wages, job loss, underemployment and job insecurity, those in the 'C Suite' were still doing pretty well.

Indeed, the average pay package of a CEO in the Standard and Poor top 500 companies in 2012 was $13.7 million and the average rise in compensation for CEOs of the Russell 3,000 (which represents about 98 per cent of all public US companies) was 8.5 per cent. For the Russell 1,000 (measuring the top 1,000 companies) it was 15.5 per cent. Within these figures, base pay, bonuses and other forms of compensation were largely unchanged in 2012 but the driver of some of the double-digit increases in total packages experienced by some CEOs came from the exercise of large blocks of stock options and the vesting of outsized restricted stock grants.

As GMI Ratings, a pay survey company, said in a recent report looking at top pay in the US, 'while stock options are intended to align the interests of senior executives with shareholders, the unintended consequence of these grants is often windfall profits that come from small share-price increases' (GMI Ratings, 2013).

Of course, in the UK this is not a new debate either. Back in 1995, Sir Richard Greenbury – the then Chairman of Marks & Spencer – conducted a review that called for greater disclosure of executive remuneration. Sir Richard also concluded that incentives for top executives should be more explicitly and transparently linked to the performance of the company. Given that so many of these executives, in turn, imposed performance-related pay on their employees, they clearly believed in the principle, at least. Since the Greenbury Report (Greenbury, 1995), we have seen the setting up of remuneration committees on plc boards and the publication of details of directors' base pay, bonuses, pension contributions and shareholdings in the annual report and accounts of all plcs. We have also seen a handful of notable and well-orchestrated shareholder revolts against what were regarded as excessive pay increases or bonuses. More recently, in his post-crash review of corporate governance in banks and other financial institutions, Sir David Walker (2009) recommended a series of additional changes to remuneration practices:

- the alignment of compensation and its risks to be made the responsibility of remuneration committees;

- greater transparency in the process for setting levels of executive pay;

- clearer rules for the deferral of incentive payments;

- more explicit performance criteria in defining 'long-term' profitability.

These recommendations and eight key principles on executive remuneration were enacted in an updated code for UK banks and building societies that became effective from January 2010.

Despite all this, and depending on whose figures you believe, the average basic pay of a FTSE 100 executive has increased by 92 per cent in the last ten years or so, excluding bonuses (Bevan, 2013). The pay ratio between the average FTSE 100 CEO and the average UK worker has risen from 45:1 in 1998 to 185:1 at the latest estimate (Hildyard, 2013). One hour of an FTSE chief executive's earnings would be enough to move a low-paid employee from the National Minimum Wage to the National Living Wage level for a year (Farmer et al., 2013).

For Will Hutton – who carried out a review of 'fair pay' in the public sector for the UK government (Hutton, 2011) – a key issue here is proportionality rather than equity. Hutton argued, in a development of themes set out by Hurka (2003), that 'due desert for discretionary effort' should play a big part in setting executive compensation and concluded that a fixed ratio between the top and bottom (or median) of a pay range would not solve the problem because it risked becoming a target or a 'norm' that would inflate rather than control top pay. In doing so Hutton, not for the first time, rejected Plato who believed the income of the highest in society should never be more than four times that of the lowest – but then he might have thought differently if he'd had access to stock options![1]

In reality, we are caught in a fairness paradox – most of us probably agree that those who contribute most should profit from their labours, but we also deeply resent any hint that these rewards are in any way out of proportion to their efforts. This is an age-old problem. But most recently the so-called credit crunch has revealed that, in some financial institutions, executives pursued business strategies – such as seeking to make a killing in the market for obscure financially engineered products – precisely because they represent an apparently low-risk route to obscenely high bonuses. As Richard Lambert, former Director-General of the CBI, said: 'For the first time in history officers of a company can become seriously rich without risking any of their own money. Their rewards are so beyond those of ordinary people that they risk being seen as aliens from another galaxy' (Lambert, 2010).

This concern about a 'snout in the trough' approach to remuneration has prompted a new wave of revulsion. It also marks a milestone in the history of executive pay. It represents an opportunity to act decisively which, according to campaign groups like the High Pay Centre, must be grasped.

Testing some assertions in the executive pay debate

Because the debate about the pros and cons of high relative pay for top executives is so emotionally charged and febrile, it sometimes feels as if rational analysis is beyond our reach. At its worst, it seems like one side is being forced to defend the indefensible and the other desperately wants to punish what it regards as outrageous and uncontrolled excess. The result is that the quality of the debate becomes poorer and the mud-slinging more intense. There are many aspects of the executive pay landscape that get the parties on either side agitated; for example, whether there is a global market for CEOs that justifies high pay or whether CEO rewards need to reflect the high risks they bear, or if they have an indispensable role to drive competitiveness (see Hildyard, 2013) which merits high-value compensation packages.

One of the common concerns over executive compensation is that reward packages do not always reflect company performance or, even worse, keep going up even when company performance is in decline. There are, of course, issues of principle at stake here as well as technical arguments about how performance should be measured, the role of long-term incentives and the balance between basic pay and bonuses. In the current climate it can be enough, in some cases, for there to be a perception of a disconnect to trigger scrutiny and even the voluntary forgoing of a bonus by a CEO in the public eye (see, for example, the recent example of Sam Laidlaw at British Gas in the UK who agreed not to take his bonus during the debate over energy prices). So, what does the evidence tell us?

The slightly unsatisfactory answer is, of course, 'it depends'. More specifically, it depends on the measures of performance that are used, the time period over which the measures are made and the component of the reward package being examined. Several, mainly US-based, studies over the last two decades have shown that increases in executive pay are only weakly correlated with the performance of the companies they run (Bebchuk and Fried, 2004). Perhaps the most notable was the research carried out by Jensen and Murphy (1990) which showed that CEO earnings and shareholder value were barely related. Analysis carried out by Paul Gregg and colleagues at Bristol University has highlighted the disconnect between executive pay and company performance in the UK. Gregg et al. (2005) tracked the performance of 415 firms who appeared in the FTSE 350 between 1994 and 2002 (the post-Greenbury and pre-credit crunch years). They found that the significant increases in rewards bore virtually no relation to the performance of the company, as measured by shareholder return. These results mirror those of numerous studies conducted by respected economists. Indeed, many show that executive remuneration rises even when firms are in terminal decline. In 2001, executive pay went up 12 per cent, while the value of the companies they ran fell by 16 per cent. In the same year, profits rose by 5 per cent and bonuses increased by 34 per cent.

However, research from Kingston University (Farmer et al., 2010) shows that many studies fail to account accurately for the lag between pay-outs from chief executive bonus plans and pay-outs from long-term incentive (LTI) plans. Once these lags are factored in, they are in fact strongly related to relative shareholder performance. The link between reward and performance in this context is often far from scientific. It must also be recognized that the balance of base pay, bonuses and share options varies considerably over time and between countries in an attempt to align executive rewards with the goals and priorities of the business – though often with only limited success (Hutton and Bevan, 2005).

There are still too many cases where the credibility gap between executive rewards and business performance is too wide. This is often brought out still further when the value of the exit packages of departing executives is revealed, raising concerns about a 'rewards for failure' culture which also undermines the argument that CEOs and others need to have high rewards to compensate them for the extra risks they take in a volatile global labour market.

Did 'fat cat' pay cause the financial crisis?

In the aftermath of the credit crunch there was not much doubt in many people's minds that excessive executive pay, and especially the perverse incentive effect of poorly calibrated bonuses, were partly to blame. As Adair Turner, then of the Financial Services Authority (FSA), declared, 'There is a strong prima facie case that inappropriate incentive structures played a role in encouraging behaviour which contributed to the financial crisis' (Turner, 2009).

Despite this, a more recent analysis (Gregg et al., 2012) suggests that it is unlikely that incentive structures could be held responsible for inducing bank executives to focus on short-term results. In addition, work by Conyon et al. (2011) shows that the role of compensation in promoting excessive risk-taking prior to the crisis was dwarfed by the roles of loose monetary policy, the housing 'bubble' and poorly regulated financial innovation. Similarly, Beltratti and Stulz (2010), in an international study of the performance of banks during the financial crisis, found that it was the fragility of banks' balance sheets and, in particular, their reliance on short-term capital market funding that explained a much higher proportion of their poor performance than compensation systems alone. Looking at the features of executive pay reward packages, Fahlenbrach and Stulz (2011) suggest that perverse incentives are dampened if the interests of executives and shareholders are aligned through executives' ownership of company stock. They found no evidence that banks with CEOs whose incentives were poorly aligned with the interests of their shareholders performed worse during the crisis.

This is not to say that perverse incentives were not at work in other parts of financial sector organizations in the run-up to the credit crunch. Looking at the impact of incentive pay among bank staff in Chicago whose job it was to make loans to small businesses, Agarwal and Wang (2009) found that the bank lost money by switching to incentive pay because while it led to a 47 per cent increase in the loan approval rate it also led to a 24 per cent increase in the default rate. Essentially, these loan officers were approving more risky loans because of the incentive pay scheme. If we scale this up to so-called 'casino banking' we can begin to understand the potential damage that a carelessly calibrated incentive arrangement can do.

Pay dispersion

The connections between leaders and the led really matter in modern organizations. The financial crisis has challenged the sometimes fragile bond of trust between senior executives and many of their employees because – in many organizations – there has been a transfer of risk from the business to the employee. Alongside this has been a growing suspicion that top managers are protected from job insecurity and the pressure to do more with less that most employees have faced. In a survey conducted by The Work Foundation for the Good Work Commission (Parker and Bevan, 2011) fewer than 40 per cent of employees believed that their senior bosses acted with integrity and almost half reported that levels of trust between management and staff had declined in their organization.

Of course, the last decade has seen most large organizations investing heavily in measures of employee engagement because they believe that engaged and motivated employees enhance competitive advantage. The difference today is that we are in a period of intense, post-recessionary indignation about top pay and fairness which can, if badly handled, undermine efforts to 'engage' the workforce (Sparrow et al., 2013). Until 'social norms' about rewards are fundamentally altered, and businesses work out that stratospheric pay for their CEOs harms their ability to reconnect with their workforces and with the wider public, the fear is that the CEO pay escalator will ride on ever upwards.

Yet the issue of top pay – and more specifically the spread of pay – has the potential to be the most corrosive aspect of the executive compensation debate. Re-engaging with the workforce as businesses (and the whole economy) struggle to achieve 'escape velocity' from the recession will be hard enough. So what does the evidence tell us about the impact that wide pay dispersion has on employee morale, motivation and engagement?

The performance effect of wide pay dispersion is a disputed topic because theories offer conflicting predictions. One field of research highlights what are believed to be the positive effects of large pay dispersion on firm performance. Here, it is argued, that pay dispersion reflects a 'company's interest in rewarding employees' individual performance' (Gerhart and Rynes, 2003), and the link between pay and performance motivates employees to achieve better performance. Pay dispersion also improves the quality of the workforce by shining a light on unproductive workers (Lazear, 2000). With large pay dispersion, productive employees remain with a firm where they consider themselves to be well paid, while unproductive employees quit because they consider themselves to be underpaid. Collectively, wide pay dispersion is expected to improve firm performance by enhancing workforce quality and soliciting greater work effort from the workforce.

Another stream of research emphasizes the negative effects of pay dispersion on company performance. When pay differentials are too large, lower-paid employees consider their pay to be inequitable and react negatively, for example, by withholding effort. Employees may also view their firm's pay distribution as a zero-sum game and choose not to help colleagues (Pfeffer and Langton, 1993). Collectively, wide pay dispersion is thought to harm firm performance by hurting the quality of employee relationships and incentivizing dysfunctional employee behaviours. Other research has revealed that pay dispersion – or the amount of pay inequality created by an organization's pay structure – may influence organizational performance and individual job attitudes and behaviours, such as job satisfaction, commitment and performance (Bloom and Michel, 2002; Shaw et al., 2002).

Some authors have deconstructed this argument still further (Mahy et al., 2011). Trevor et al. (2012) argue that pay dispersion consists of 'dispersion that is explained by performance (DEP) and dispersion that is unexplained by performance (DUP)'. Using the North American National Hockey League's data, the authors show that DEP is positively associated with team performance, while DUP is not. Thus, pay dispersion positively impacts on organizational performance only to the extent that it reflects individual performance. This introduces the notion of 'consent' into the debate. If the senior team of a business are unambiguously and demonstrably driving forward business success which benefits all employees, their compensation packages – and wide pay dispersion – are more likely to be viewed as proportionate and merited.

Yang et al. (2012) found that pay dispersion was unrelated to organizational commitment but was significantly related to both women's and men's job satisfaction, and women's perceived fairness. These effects were dependent on the individual's position in the pay structure. Specifically, when pay dispersion was high, women who were paid less were more satisfied with their jobs, and more likely to believe that they were treated fairly than their female counterparts who were paid more. For men, receiving high pay relative to others was a more consistent positive predictor of job attitudes.

Although most research looking at pay dispersion looks at the gap between the most highly paid and those at the bottom of the pay structure (and sometimes median pay), other studies have shown that the gap between the most senior executives and the next layer of managerial seniority can also be important in generating a sense of collective purpose. Research by Fredrickson et al. (2010) suggests that a wide gap can undermine trust and can result in the disengagement of an important tier of management.

Pay dispersion in R&D groups has been shown to have important consequences for businesses' ability to generate innovation. More particularly, in the R&D context, large pay differentials among employees create disincentives that preclude innovation (Yanadori and Cui, 2013). The argument is that wide pay dispersion influences the development of company knowledge resources both positively and negatively. Large pay dispersion increases the sum of individual employees' knowledge retained in firms by attracting and retaining high quality R&D workers. However, in the face of wide pay dispersion, employees may be reluctant to share knowledge with others or contribute to company knowledge management systems through a concern that doing so might reduce their knowledge advantages and eventually result in decreases in their pay relative to that of their colleagues. Wide pay differentials may also increase the competitive tension between employees and discourage employee collaboration and co-operation (Pfeffer and Langton, 1993). This erosion of collective effort can be highly detrimental to innovation because the generation of new ideas often involves collaboration among employees.

Although in the context of R&D and knowledge-based firms wide pay dispersion allows firms to attract star researchers, studies have shown that large pay differentials between star and non-star researchers can discourage the latter group's commitment by leading them to feel that their contributions are not adequately valued. Lack of commitment from non-star researchers prevents the firm from capitalizing on star researchers' knowledge for the generation of innovation (Rothaermel and Hess, 2007).

As mentioned earlier, Remcos have an obligation under the combined code on corporate governance to consider the 'wider employment conditions' within a company when setting executive pay. HR should go further. Executive pay should never be isolated from pay in general because differentials are fundamental to the calculus of just reward. In the US, the Securities and Exchange Commission's proposed CEO pay-ratio disclosure rule is causing some consternation among public companies. Perhaps unsurprisingly, only one in ten believes compliance will produce useful information for investors and companies themselves (Towers Watson, 2013).

At the core of this debate is the perceived or actual disconnection between executive compensation and that of the employees they lead and the societies from which executives need consent. The sense of unfairness that any disequilibrium in these relationships prompts can be visceral and can undermine trust in business at a time when we need companies to grow and to create both wealth and good jobs.

Unfortunately, there is no science to proportionality. We judge these issues very subjectively and, while fixed pay ratios or tougher regulatory caps appear attractive, they can be flawed both in design and execution. It may be better to encourage greater transparency and to illuminate the damage that excessive rewards can do to the morale, engagement and innovation that we hope our employees will contribute to business success.

Regulation, especially in the domain of corporate governance, certainly has a role to play but it is unlikely that – by itself – it will bring about the scale of change that many are calling for. As Conyon et al. (2011) remind us:

> Part of the problem is that regulation – even when well-intended – always creates unintended (and usually costly) side-effects. Moreover, regulation is often designed to be punitive rather than constructive, and is inherently driven by politicians more interested in their political agendas rather than creating shareholder value. Ultimately, we conclude that improvements in executive compensation will best emanate through stronger corporate governance, and not through direct government intervention.

The trend towards transparency of pay systems

The significant trend towards greater transparency about pay and pay structures is increasingly being played out in organizations as a way of responding to the concerns about what are regarded by many as disproportionate differences in rewards, and is being used as a mechanism to open the debate about what is appropriate and fair. For many organizations today, it is a new discussion. But for the John Lewis Partnership, the concept has a famously long history and, by common consent, has served them well.

The constitution of the Partnership originally defined the need for both a minimum and a maximum wage in 1900 (Cox, 2010). The maximum wage was then set as whatever was lower of the two calculations: 25 times the wage of a London selling assistant with four children, or £5000 a year, both after tax. The equivalent tax rate in those times was 7.5 per cent compared with 20 per cent today. Today, the formula has shifted slightly and is now expressed as 25 times the *average basic pay* of non-management partners *before tax*. Nonetheless, more than a hundred years on, this same approach is apparent, underpinned by a belief that the gap between top and bottom should be both transparent and reasonable. This belief also informed the UK coalition government's fair-pay review in the public sector in 2011, which examined whether a 20:1 pay dispersion ratio could be implemented across most of the UK public sector (Hutton, 2011). Despite the superficial attractiveness of having fixed pay ratios in public- and even private-sector organizations, Hutton came down on the side of rejecting ratios because he felt that they might drive perverse behaviour. More specifically, he felt that there would be incentives to remove or outsource lower pay grades so that the ceiling for CEO pay would be raised, or that the 20:1 ratio would become a norm or a target for those CEOs whose pay had not yet reached that threshold. Instead Hutton recommended a 'comply or explain' approach to reporting the pay ratio on an annual basis, thereby encouraging more transparency and monitoring of pay dispersion as well as more public debate about whether there is a clear rationale (in terms of both external and internal pay relativities) for widening pay dispersion.

The debate about the appropriateness of an ever-widening gap between CEO pay and that of either the lowest paid or median pay in the same organization continues to occupy airtime and debate in remuneration, shareholder activism and corporate governance circles (High Pay Centre, 2015; Gosling, 2017). There are even a few instances of organizations shifting to the extreme of complete transparency on pay for each individual. Happy Computers, for example, is a small business where Henry Stewart, the founder and Chief Executive, believes that complete pay transparency, including about his own salary, has been an important contributor to staff well-being and productivity as well as loyalty and commitment: 'This not only means people see where they might get to, but also forces us to justify what we are paying people,' says Stewart (Simms, 2006).

Generally, though, the trend in business is more about having transparent pay structures than transparency over individual pay rates. The continued prevalence of job-evaluation systems in larger organizations means that the architecture of the pay system – that is, which jobs sit within which pay ranges – is usually transparent to all employees. It is a method of arriving at both an internal and external view of pay relativities, allowing an organization to compare the demands of jobs and their position in the labour market. It has the added benefit of allowing employees to see how their pay, and therefore their careers, may progress within a transparent structure.

There are still sectors, however, where this is resisted. For example, in some media and publishing companies historically salaries have been settled on an individual and idiosyncratic basis – supported by a culture of secrecy about reward levels. In some instances, disclosure of details of one's pay to a colleague has led to dismissal, disciplinary action or career 'death', although contractual clauses imposing pay secrecy have now been outlawed. However, this opaque approach has proven to be an unsustainable situation in the modern workplace. It leads eventually to a chaotic system, a profound sense of unfairness amongst employees and the employer becoming increasingly vulnerable to challenge on equal pay grounds. So, most of these companies have redesigned and modernized their pay systems, resulting in the creation of bands of pay for different roles, making the structure more visible and decision-making processes more transparent. In 2017 the BBC were compelled by the UK government to publish the pay bands within which almost 100 of its most highly paid presenters sat. It exposed that, in some cases, pay levels for presenters doing apparently similar work had resulted from good negotiation rather than meritocratic analysis. Perhaps more worrying, it revealed very significant gaps between male and female presenters and almost no black or ethnic minority presenters in the higher echelons of pay. This and other cases demonstrate that the shift towards pay transparency that is likely to continue into the future, while uncomfortable for some organizations, is likely to have a detoxifying effect as the rationale for pay system design becomes exposed to scrutiny.

The irony is that we have known for a long time that people often overestimate the pay that others receive, particularly when they are separated from them in the pay scale. So, when salaries are kept secret, there is evidence that people judge the distribution to be more hierarchical than it actually is (Lawler, 1971). Thus, being more transparent about pay structures and systems might demonstrate that things are less unfair than people might think they are.

Ultimately, what matters to people is that both pay levels and the process of determining them are seen to be fair, and that people want clarity about how decisions about pay are made and a sense of justice about the outcome. Yet, fairness is not the same as equity – and interestingly both the left and right of the political spectrum agree about that. The aspiration is to reward people who contribute strongly and to be equally clear about those who do not. As Will Hutton (2010) says: 'Fairness is about both outcomes and processes. Outcomes must be proportional to effort, especially discretionary effort that has plainly made a difference to the enterprise. Salaries, wages and bonuses must reflect due desert.'

This represents a challenge for HR managers. Reward strategy exposes the fact that HR needs to be more than the function that organizes the transactional part of the employee/employer relationship from payroll to dispute resolution, important as both are. HR must aim to be the custodian of the 'deal' – the moral bargain or psychological contract between an employer anxious to enlist employee engagement around the business purpose and an employee who will be readier to engage more if she is given an animating reason to do so.

If employee engagement in the wider purpose of the organization is a desirable outcome that can be reinforced, rather than undermined, by reward then there may a strong case for deepening and extending employee share-ownership schemes. Employee share-ownership schemes seem to work best when they connect the employees to the purpose and values of the business and avoid annual 'windfall' payments that employees are grateful to receive but do not connect to the effort they have made. For example, the Treasury in the largest study of share ownership ever to have been undertaken in Britain (Oxera Consulting, 2007), found that 'on average, across the whole sample, the effect of tax-advantaged share schemes is significant and increases productivity by 2.5 per cent in the long run'. Different schemes reinforced the effect and it found that schemes chosen by firms without tax advantages tended to pay out more than those with tax breaks. This suggests that if cash is just the motivation, it works less well than a determined effort to signal that what matters to management is inclusion, engagement and fairness. When workers are given their due desert within a system of due process, leading them to believe that they are being treated fairly, they work harder.

DUNCAN BROWN

THE TOTAL REWARDS/BEST PLACE to work rhetoric that many large employers still use has become unsuited to an era of austerity and market-copying at best, and at worst has been a cover for significant curbing of the value of employee benefits and reductions in real earnings.

Rewards in future need to be demonstrably based on a few core values including a shared but genuine commitment to employee well-being and welfare; they need to be evidence-based, so we can assess the delivery of these values and principles in practice; the reward package requires investment by firms, particularly in a decent base pay level; and there needs to be brilliant two-way communications, given that despite the explosion in cheap communication forms employers have generally become more secretive about their rewards in recent years.

Some link between rewards and performance/contribution has become unavoidable and does correlate with high organizational performance, with research generally more positive on variable pay/bonuses than performance-related base pay, particularly collective bonuses such as gainsharing. However in future we believe we need to be much more creative in how variable pay is used, particularly as a recognition and 'sharing in success' vehicle, and schemes need to be much more specifically focused on key outcomes with a business case and clear life cycle. We summarize the direction of travel as:

- greater, in some cases exclusive, focus on the customer;

- clearer incentive principles and architecture within large employers, acting as a framework for greater variety and numbers of plans;

- improved measurement internally and fuller external comparisons (e.g. KPI library);

- more and more genuinely variable pay;

- wider variety of total rewards used to engage employees to perform highly, individually and collectively;

- improved business cases and evaluation of plan returns and effectiveness;

- more switching 'on' and 'off' of plans and more market variety (including 'no bonus' approaches?);

- something new: lottery or unexpected gift element? (*New Evidence on Gift Exchange from a Field Experiment*, Duncan Gilchrist, Michael Luca, and Deepak Malhotra)

Of course you can't reward performance unless you can manage and measure it. Performance management is one of the most interesting areas in the workplace at present in the UK, with firms finally seeming to accept that the all-singing, all-dancing multi-purpose process fails to be implemented effectively in most organizations. And while Yahoo! and Shell have shifted to more aggressive differentiation, Microsoft and others have abandoned rank and yank and are focusing more on the development/improvement aspects of the process. Middle-of-the-road HR is finding it tough to ignore the debate and rightly having to think more about what really creates high performance in their organization.

We characterize the process as moving in future towards:

- a less ambitious, more *disaggregated* and looser process:
  - shorter, more frequent meetings;
  - more separation of the development and reward, past and future dimensions;
  - more variation by business unit and staff groupings;
  - simpler processes and paperwork;
- a better *managed* process:
  - better management development and support;
  - but also holding managers more to account and compulsion;
  - improved leadership and example setting;
  - improved data support and performance metrics;
- a more *engaging* process:
  - technology supporting not controlling;
  - employee more in control/responsible;
  - improved employee education and support.

Reward futures: towards a new collectivism?

The decline in trade-union membership, a major force in the collectivization of pay determination and co-ordinated wage bargaining, has coincided with a shift towards greater individualization of pay. Of course, there are arguments on both sides about whether setting pay through these traditional mechanisms are efficient, fair or transparent. Ideology plays a strong part in these debates to the extent that objective analysis can be difficult. Much of the terrain, despite the evidence, remains contested – does contingent reward motivate improved performance, does collective bargaining drive wage inflation and 'freeloading', do non-pay rewards motivate as much as cash and does profit-sharing or employee share ownership give employees a 'stake' in the future of the organization and its longer-term performance?

In the current era of relatively weak unions, low labour productivity, stagnant real wage growth and historically low inflation that, nonetheless, still outstrips wage increases, organizations need to re-think their approaches to reward or temper their expectations of the leverage reward can give them over performance.

Part of the answer may lie in a more contemporary approach to collectivization. One of the primary objections to the growth in individualized pay is that is implicitly underplays the fact that many work teams achieve results through collective effort that is driven by collective rewards. Do 300 people in a call centre all doing broadly the same work really need to have individualized performance-related pay to get them to achieve their targets? The managerial bandwidth required to set and monitor progress towards these targets may well, it could be argued, wipe out any benefits such arrangements deliver. In this example, it may make more sense to set collective or team targets and to reflect these in the variable or contingent reward which is available. With this kind of arrangement, measures which factor in customer satisfaction and quality can also play a part in determining the 'pot' of rewards that is then distributed among the workforce, ensuring that the collective performance reflects the values and purpose of the organization.

It is this connectedness to the wider purpose of the organization and the need to reflect the expectations of its stakeholders where new opportunities for calibrating more collective approaches to reward in the future may exist. Loyalty, alignment and engagement are increasingly difficult to achieve with more highly educated workforces who demand consent and expect to influence important decisions that affect their future. In terms of rewards, this has never been more true and to avoid employers' reward strategies appearing parsimonious, secretive, mean-spirited and transactional, it may be that more imagination and flexibility in the use of open, democratic and transparent approaches such as employee ownership, profit- or gain-sharing schemes and share schemes where employees feel they can influence the outcome can play a more prominent part in the future reward landscape.

8

The future of the ageing workforce

One of the bigger underlying demographic changes that will shape the future of work is that the workforce is getting older and people over 50 are now much more likely to be in a job than in the mid-1990s. As we showed in Chapter 2, increases in the employment rate of older people has been a consistent trend in the UK and across most OECD economies. This rise has been driven by three underlying structural factors and more recent changes on pension policy. The most obvious is that life expectancy has increased and this in turn has increased the share of older people in the population. It has also allowed people to work longer. Both these developments make the concept of normal working ages of 16 to 64 obsolete. In addition, improvements in educational levels and the rise in the share of better educated workers has worked its way through the workforce, and on average the better educated are much more likely to be in employment for longer than the poorly educated.

Successive governments have introduced changes in pension provision and employment law that have removed the ability of employers to enforce fixed retirement ages, pushed state pension retirement ages up and made it easier for people to continue to work, reducing the cliff-edge still faced by many older workers. There is also some evidence that many older workers want to stay on in jobs they enjoy, albeit not necessarily on a full-time basis.

Without rising employment among those over 50, the UK labour market would have been in serious trouble. Between 1994 and 2014 the employment rate was essentially flat, after taking account of the dip caused by the Great Recession. The employment rate for women has also been flat over the past decade. Employment rates for men between the ages of 50 and 64 are now, for the first time, overtaking those of men between the ages of 20 and 24, while those for older women are fast catching up the employment rates for younger women. This is shown in Figure 8.1. Had older workers' participation not increased the UK would have been faced with a falling employment rate – with adverse consequences for economic growth prospects.

This positive story also has a darker side, however. Some older workers struggle on in poorly paid jobs out of necessity rather than choice. And the labour market has been a harsh place for those older workers who become

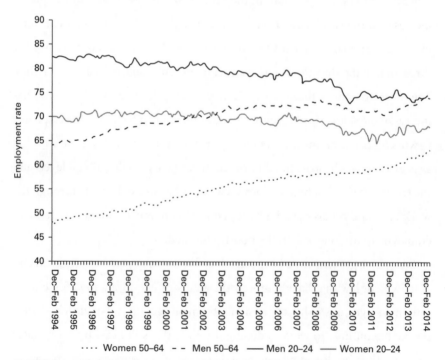

FIGURE 8.1 *Employment rates for older workers in the UK, 1994–2014.*
Source: Office for National Statistics, Labour Market Release, Reference Table A.05.

unemployed and do not have the skills or relevant experience or live in areas of high unemployment and find it hard to get back into a job. Others who might have continued in work with more support despite the development of chronic physical and mental conditions have instead dropped out of the labour market. For example, in the UK between April and June 2014 there were 750,000 people between the ages of 50 and 64 who were classified as 'economically inactive' who said they would like a job. Of course, part of this aspiration gap might be explained by the fact that there may be some residual prejudice among some employers against the employment of older workers, despite a recent strengthening of UK age discrimination legislation. In the same period, about 46 per cent of all unemployed over 50 had been out of work for more than a year and nearly 30 per cent for more than two years. This is an improvement on the position in the 1990s at roughly the same point in the labour-market recovery, but also tells us that long-term unemployment is a serious and persistent problem for some of the over-50s as well as for the young.

There are two persistent beliefs about the increase in older workers, neither of which is true. One is that older workers are displacing younger workers. The OECD (2013a) has demonstrated that there is no link between increasing employment rates for older workers and youth unemployment: 'on average across the OECD increases in the employment rate of older workers are either associated with increases in the youth employment rate or have no impact at all.' This is the so-called 'lump of labour' fallacy which, among other things, is based on the erroneous belief that there is a fixed number of jobs in the economy and that an increase in employment among one group automatically reduces employment prospects for others. The second widely held belief is that older workers become less productive as they age – perhaps due to greater health problems at work and as a result of a deterioration in relevant skills. Research by Professor Gary Burtless on the US labour market shows that relative wages of older workers have been increasing – hardly compatible with declining productivity as we age (Burtless, 2013). He concludes that if labour markets are selectively excluding those with less education, the impact of rising numbers of the old in work could increase productivity:

> If less productive workers selectively exit the workforce at younger ages, the average productivity of the older workers who remain may compare favourably to the average productivity of the young. A surge in the percentage of the potential workforce that is old may simply increase the proportion of the workforce that consists of comparatively skilled older workers.

An additional dimension of the ageing agenda is the growth in the number of people working beyond state-pension age (SPA). In the UK, this cohort is the fastest growing group in the labour force. Figure 8.2 below indicates that between 2008 and 2014 the number of over-65s in the UK labour market grew to over 1 million.

To a greater or lesser extent, the same trend can be seen across many developed economies. Data from the Study of Health, Ageing and Retirement

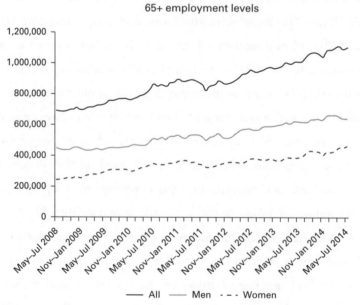

FIGURE 8.2 *Over-65-year-olds in the UK labour market, 2008–2014.*
Source: ONS (2015).

in Europe (SHARE) show that 1 in 10 men and 1 in 20 women are now working beyond the age of 65. Among women, the proportion who are working as employees at older ages (between 65 and 70) is a little higher – at 75 per cent – than during the years of working life (70 per cent), whereas among men the proportionate change is greatest among the self-employed, where the proportion doubles from 10 per cent among the under-60s to 20 per cent among the over-65s. So, most over-65-year-old workers are employees or self-employed men (Blane, 2015). Looking at the hours and job security of those working beyond 65, the SHARE data show that most are working full time and have permanent contracts. Part-time workers are only about one-third of the total and less than one-fifth have short-term contracts. When we compare the people who continue working after age 65 years with those at younger ages, the SHARE data suggest that older workers tend to avoid jobs with high effort–reward imbalance and those that have low autonomy and job control.

Workforce ageing and, in particular, extending the working lives of older workers has become a policy priority for many OECD and EU countries. It has been estimated that approximately one-third of the UK labour force will be aged 50 or over by 2020 (Taylor, 2007). Ignoring the skills, knowledge and contribution that older workers are capable of making to organizational performance has been described as a high-risk strategy (Barry and Friedli, 2008). The number of working-age adults across Europe has begun to decline, and despite the recessionary impact of the financial crisis (and the slow recovery), some sectors of the European economy are already suffering from skills shortages. In response, many European governments have increased SPAs or reduced the generosity of state pensions to address this issue (Sinclair et al., 2013).

In response to these demographic pressures the UK government, along with many others in developed Western economies, have increased the SPA. In the UK this is projected to rise in line with life expectancy, with many of us likely to be working up until the age of 70 and beyond. The wider economy also depends heavily on the skills and experience of older workers and, in parallel with the economic and social arguments for extending working lives, there is also a productivity and competitiveness argument. In the recent report *Missing Million – Recommendations for Action* (Business in the Community, 2015) it was estimated that, between 2012 and 2022, in the region of 12.5 million jobs will be opened up through people leaving the workforce and an additional two million new jobs will be created, yet only seven million new young people will enter the workforce to fill these jobs. This represents a significant skills gap across the UK labour market.

The numbers leaving work before SPA are also significant – on average, men leave the labour market earlier now than they did in the 1950s and 1960s. We also know that older people who fall out of the labour market are much less likely to find work again than younger people, although they are equally likely to be made redundant as younger people. Analysis by the Department for Work and Pensions (DWP) shows that 47 per cent of unemployed older people had been out of work for a year or more compared with 40 per cent of 25–49-year-olds, and only 33 per cent of unemployed 18–24-year-olds (Department for Work and Pensions, 2015). With the risk of a large-scale pensions crisis growing, and widespread pensioner poverty, the UK has made considerable efforts to discourage older workers from retiring early and to extend their working lives at least up to, and preferably, beyond SPA. However, DWP analysis shows that:

- There are 2.9 million people out of work aged between 50 and SPA. Of these, only 0.7 million see themselves as retired, yet 1.7 million think it is unlikely that they will ever work again. Many of this group have long-term illnesses or are disabled.

- Early (i.e. pre-SPA) withdrawal from the labour force can have serious financial consequences for individuals. For example, there are

12 million people of working age who are likely to have inadequate retirement incomes and foreshortening working lives through early retirement is contributing to the problem. Early withdrawal can also have financial consequences for the public purse – people between 50 years old and the SPA are paid in the region of £7 billion each year in out-of-work benefits.

The UK has been making progress, however. For example, since 2000, employment rates among people aged between 50 and SPA have increased by five percentage points to around 72 per cent, whilst employment rates among those above SPA have increased by four percentage points, to around 12 per cent. International data suggest that the UK has performed better than some of its OECD competitors, but still lags behind several countries who either started at a higher baseline level or who have adopted more radical policies.

Table 8.1 shows data calculated by Guillemard (2013) using Eurostat and OECD data to illustrate the progress made by EU countries towards improving employment rates among 55–64-year-olds since 1996.

These data show that, while employment rates for older workers in the UK remain consistently higher than the average in the EU-15, the rate of improvement (20 per cent between 1996 and 2011) has been slower that in the EU as a whole and much lower than other countries such as the Netherlands (86 per cent) and Finland (63 per cent). Both these countries introduced a range of policy changes in the late 1990s that are widely regarded as accounting for much of the improvement in employment rates of over-55s. In Finland the government was keen to promote 'experience as a national asset' and introduced over 40 measures to support improvements in career management, older worker health and well-being, access to training, the organization of work, working conditions, working time/flexible working and education/information.

Guillemard (2013) seeks to explain some of the differences in progress with an analysis of the policy 'thrust' of different countries. This analysis is presented

TABLE 8.1 *Change in employment activity rates of 55–64-year-olds in the EU, 1996–2011*

	1996	2011	% Variation
B	21.9	38.7	60
DK	49.1	59.5	17
FL	35.4	57	63
F	29.4	41.5	35
D	37.9	59.9	53
I	28.6	37.9	28
NL	30.5	56.1	86
P	47.3	47.9	4
ES	33.2	44.5	31
SE	63.4	72.3	14
UK	47.7	56.7	20
EU–15	**36.3**	**47.4**	**35**

Source: Guillemard (2013).

in Figure 8.3. It identifies the conditionality of out-of-work benefits as one of the important differentiating factors, contrasting those countries (such as France) which have historically sought to incentivize early exit from work among older workers – in the mistaken belief that this would allow the redistribution of work to younger people – with countries like Japan which have paid employers subsidies to retain older workers for longer.

While the location of the UK as a 'Type 4 – Reject or Retain' country (relying on changing patterns of demand for older worker as the buoyancy of the labour market fluctuates) may understate the range of policies that the UK has adopted in recent years, it is true that the UK has been less 'interventionist'

Level of welfare coverage for economic inactivity

Active Labour-Market Policies	Low	High
Few policy instruments for keeping older workers in the labour market	Type 4 'Reject or Retain' Older workers are ejected from, or retained in, work depending on the buoyancy of the labour market United States/UK	Type 1 'Depreciate & Eject' Older workers are depreciated and then pushed (or incentivized) to leave the labour force France and Belgium (Netherlands and Finland until 1998; Germany until 2005)
Many policy instruments for keeping older workers in the labour market	Type 3 'Retain' Older workers are kept in the labour force through employer incentives and subsidies, and no compensation for early exit Japan/Singapore	Type 2 'Integrate or Reintegrate' Older workers are retained or brought back into work through tighter benefit conditionality and ALMPs Sweden and Denmark

FIGURE 8.3 *International policy approaches to extending working lives.*
Adapted from Guillemard (2013).

with employers than some other countries. This is despite new age discrimination legislation and changes to the SPA.

Ageing, work and health

The health of the working population is vital to the economy and to society, but due to changing demographics of the workforce, Western societies are facing great challenges to maintain economic growth and competitiveness. The workforce is ageing; in the UK it has been estimated that approximately one-third of the labour force will be aged 50 or over by 2020 (Taylor, 2007). Ignoring the skills, knowledge and contribution that older workers are capable of making to organizational performance has been described as a high-risk strategy (Barry and Friedli, 2008). The number of working-age adults across Europe has begun to decline, and despite the recession some sectors of the European economy already suffer from skills shortages. Thus, many European governments have increased SPAs or reduced the generosity of state pensions to address this issue (Sinclair et al., 2013). As a result, the workforce is older and sicker with more people living with a longstanding health problem or disability: according to The Labour Force Survey (2011), of 7.2 million aged 50–64 who are employed, 42 per cent are living with a health condition or disability in the UK (Sinclair et al., 2013). It is likely that chronic disease rates will continue to rise; much of this is due to an increase in poor lifestyle factors, such as poor diet, smoking and lack of exercise.

Ill health represents a major economic burden for society due to increased health-care costs, loss in productivity and sickness absence. Although absence rates have been falling in recent years, it has been estimated that annual costs of sickness absence for UK businesses is nearly £14 billion a year (Vaughan-Jones and Barham, 2010). Although the largest cause of absenteeism at work is short-term, non-certified absence, both males and females over the age of 55 take more days off work due to self-reported ill-health caused or made worse by work. The most common sources of new cases of work-related illness reported were musculoskeletal complaints and stress, depression or anxiety, with those over 45 having the highest estimated prevalence rate (Crawford et al., 2010). Mental ill-health is associated with both physical and mental decline which is more common among older groups (Barry and Friedli, 2008). Besides poor health, the reasons for ceasing economic activity at age 50-plus include limited skills and increased caring responsibilities (Marmot, 2010).

Another age-related health factor is so-called 'co-morbidity' – the increasing likelihood that older workers will have more than one chronic condition at the same time. Figure 8.4 shows how steeply such a risk can grow.

Despite these barriers, the number of employed people of SPA and above has nearly doubled over the past decades, from 753,000 in 1993 to 1.4 million in 2011 (ONS, 2012). An evidence-based review on the health, safety and

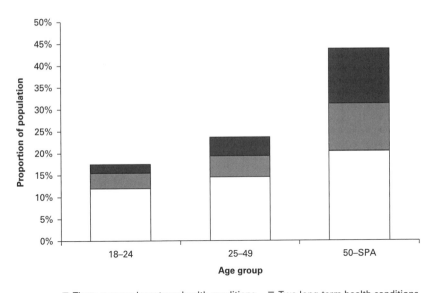

FIGURE 8.4 *Risk of having comorbid health conditions increases with age.*
Source: Labour Force Survey (2013).

health promotion needs of older workers (Crawford et al., 2010) identified that although there is an increased risk with age of developing a disease, this is not necessarily a reason to exclude an individual from work. Certain diseases, such as heart disease or diabetes, can be controlled and reasonable adjustments can be made to keep the individual at work.

Many people who develop physical or mental health issues during their working lives are able to maintain employment without additional assistance, although this differs significantly by condition. The most prevalent health conditions affecting those people aged 50–64 (see Figure 8.5) are related to musculoskeletal (21 per cent) and cardiovascular (17 per cent) conditions, and depression and anxiety (8 per cent). Whereas 83 per cent of people with no long-term condition aged 50–NSPA are employed, 54 per cent of those with musculoskeletal problems are in employment, 67 per cent with circulatory problems and only 43 per cent of those with mental health issues such as

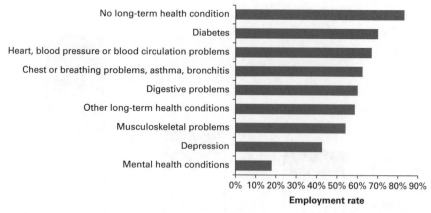

FIGURE 8.5 *Employment rate of older workers (50–64) with health conditions.*
Source: Labour Force Survey 3 quarter average 2013 Q2–Q4.

depression and anxiety (half the rate of 'healthy' people of comparable age). This last statistic suggests that the barriers to maintaining employment for those who have or develop a mental health condition are more significant than for those with other long-term conditions (Heron et al., 2016).

This has important implications since the proportion of people over 50 reporting long-term health problems or disability is projected to increase substantially from 43 per cent in 2004 to 58 per cent by 2020 (Pillai et al., 2007).

The fact that fewer than one in three UK employees with a long-term condition have discussed it with their employer suggests that there may also be stigma associated with chronic conditions in workers (Steadman et al., 2015). According to Age UK (Harrop and Jopling, 2009) 65 per cent of older workers (people over the age of 65 years, unless otherwise specified) believe age discrimination still exists in the workplace. A UK telephone study of 50–75-year-olds (Maitland, 2010) identified attitudes and structure rather than health as barriers to continued employment. Age discrimination and unconscious bias result in both positive and negative stereotypes; older workers may be described by some as more loyal, reliable and diligent, and by others as less flexible, less productive and slower to adapt to new technology than younger workers.

Of course, some work can itself be damaging to health. Workers aged over 55 years report the highest rates of illness caused or made worse by their work (4,620/4,580 per 100,000 employed) (HSE, 2015). Rates of self-reported stress, depression or anxiety caused or made worse by work are highest for men and women in the age band 45–54. A significant number of cancers diagnosed in people aged 50–70 are attributable to work; over half the melanomas occurring between 50 and 70 years of age could be prevented by tackling occupational exposures in outdoor workers (Rushton and Hutchings, 2015); for lung and breast cancer alone, approximately 2,500 cancers could be prevented (each year) by controlling exposure to workplace hazards (ONS, 2013).

Furthermore, the health impacts from an early exit from the labour market are not evenly borne; for those in lower socio-economic groups, compulsory retirement or economic insecurity in retirement may adversely affect health, well-being and survival, whereas planned early retirement may bring health benefits to those in higher socio-economic groups, particularly those who are economically secure (Mein et al., 2003; Waddell and Burton, 2006).

The health of employees is a major factor in an organization's competitiveness. Employees in good health can be up to three times as productive as those in poor health; they can experience fewer motivational problems; they are more resilient to change; and they are more likely to be engaged with the business's priorities (Vaughan-Jones and Barham, 2010). In Dame Carol Black's review of the health of Britain's working-age population it was calculated that improved workplace health could generate cost savings to the government of over £60 billion – the equivalent of nearly two-thirds of the NHS budget for England (Black, 2008).

It has been recognized that improved workplace health has the potential to make a significant contribution to the economy, to public finances and to reducing levels of disease and illness in society (Waddell and Burton, 2006).

Employers play a key role in helping to protect health and prevent future ill health of the working population and NICE Public Health Guidelines (2009) recommend a strategic and co-ordinated approach to promoting employees' mental health well-being. One of the biggest challenges facing the working-longer agenda is poor health of older workers. However, relatively few initiatives by governments or employers have been established to explicitly improve the health of older workers (Sinclair et al., 2013). In fact, according to research from the Chartered Institute of Personnel and Development (CIPD) and the Chartered Management Institute (CMI) into age management, UK employers are still 'woefully unprepared for the impact workforce demographics will have on their businesses' (Macleod et al., 2010).

Survey research of 1,500 older workers by the Equality and Human Rights Commission (Smeaton et al., 2009) found that 60 per cent of older workers wanted to carry on working after retirement age either in the same or different jobs. This is often because they cannot afford to retire. Whilst economic considerations are a key factor, personal fulfilment is also important to older workers, with re-entering the workforce for enjoyment or company at work (Parry and Harris, 2011). The decision of whether or not to continue working is complex and influenced not only by a combination of individual factors but also by organizational culture and policies.

Workplace health programmes are more likely to be effective in organizations that promote good-quality work (Vaughan-Jones and Barham, 2010). Evidence has shown that being in good-quality work is good for your physical and mental health resulting in better self-esteem and quality of life (Waddell and Burton, 2006). Promoting good-quality work involves giving consideration to issues of working practices and job design (Bevan, 2010). Even though the evidence is limited, interventions for occupational health and health promotion can be effective in protecting the needs of older workers (Crawford et al., 2010). There is particular scope for the extension and development of 'pre-retirement' training (Barry and Friedli, 2008). However, even though research results have suggested that job performance does not decline with age, many negative stereotypes about 'trainability' of older workers among employers exist that may reduce access to training and its effectiveness among older workers (Hsu, 2013).

A case study involving several large organizations in the UK that had policies in place for ageing workers found that the main positive impacts of policies at the company level were healthier and happier staff and staff retention. In fact, many companies that were reviewed put the greatest emphasis on retention. The retention policies included flexible working schemes that allowed employees to combine salary reward with pension. The programmes that were the most successful were those that had senior management's whole-hearted commitment. However, whatever management commitment was involved, if the financial impact of policies did not benefit employees, then they were unlikely to succeed. The lack of interest by employees in flexible working was often the result of employees' fear of losing some of their pension entitlement. At the organizational level, the positive approaches that some organizations had taken to their cohort of older employees tended to fade away when faced with external factors that demanded labour-force reductions (Eurofound, 2007).

In addition to interventions intended to improve the quality of working life, it is important to understand the impact of effective and less effective transitions from working life to retirement. Concerns about poverty and social isolation of older people with consequent negative effects for mental and physical health and attendant costs for health and social care are a significant social policy issue (see, e.g., Cacioppo and Patrick, 2008). This is heightened by ongoing reform to retirement ages and pension regulation and must be set in a context where large proportions of the population have made inadequate investment in pensions. The workplace is an ideal site for delivering pre-retirement planning interventions to help workers make suitable retirement provision. A number of studies have examined the impact of pre-retirement training and advice sessions. A meta-analysis of 99 studies drawn internationally found that participation in retirement planning was positively and significantly associated with improved mental/physical health, a more effective bridging process from employment and higher life satisfaction, and a positive but non-significant association with retirement satisfaction (Topa et al., 2009). An experimental study in the US involving groups of around 25 people exposed to delivery of financial information about retirement combined or separate from goal-setting support showed that provision of financial information alone had a positive impact on financial planning activities (e.g. savings and investment behaviours), retirement goal clarity (e.g. setting goals, having clear plan/vision) and average percentage of monthly income saved, compared with a control group receiving no intervention (Hershey et al., 2003). A longitudinal survey between 1992 and 2004 of US citizens showed that financial planning predicted retirement satisfaction and physical health and those who attended training/seminars had higher levels of psychological health, although this was moderated by discussion of retirement plans with a spouse (Noone et al., 2009). A very quick follow-up study of the impact of retirement planning training on knowledge and understanding of the issues conducted two weeks after training among 395 employees in five organizations found that 69 per cent showed improvement in financial awareness and knowledge of retirement options, with the largest gains for those who initially had poor levels of awareness/knowledge (Clark et al., 2009). This brief exploration of the literature demonstrates the potentially beneficial effect of retirement planning but highlights that the characteristics of effective programmes and their precise costs and benefits would benefit from a more detailed review.

A better understanding and more effective handling of diversity, such as ethnicity and gender, in the workplace have become key success factors for organizations around the world. Despite several reviews and meta-analyses of effects of diversity in the workplace, systematic knowledge of age diversity is still limited (Kunze and Boehm, 2013). Organizations currently have only a vague idea of how diversity will affect their internal processes and states, including their older employees' well-being, commitment and performance. Due to the relative recentness of the labour market trend of an ageing workforce, the management of age diversity is not yet an established component of corporate training or development initiatives. A systematic evaluation of the best approach to the best management practices for age diversity at the workplace is lacking. Therefore a NICE-sponsored systematic evaluation of the evidence on the effective policies and approaches for promoting and protecting the health of older workers is timely. As more employers recognize the need to promote the health and well-being of ageing employees, it is important that they have access to guidelines that help them to provide healthy and good-quality working environments in a cost-effective way and using evidence-based interventions.

Ageing, cognitive decline and work

Contrary to popular mythology, older workers do not have significantly more sick days than their younger colleagues, but they sometimes have chronic and fluctuating health conditions that affect their functional capacity at work, or increase their risk of having to leave work prematurely. Despite that fact that the over-65s are the fastest growing segment of the workforce, the numbers leaving work before SPA – often for health reasons – are still significant. Of course, conditions such as cancer, cardiovascular disease, stroke and arthritis feature prominently among the causes of premature job loss or early retirement. However, it is the spectre of early cognitive decline associated with dementia among working-age adults that is giving increasing cause for concern.

The World Health Organization (WHO, 2012) estimates that 10 per cent of the 35.6 million people worldwide with dementia are aged under 65 years old. The number of people with dementia in the UK is forecast to increase to over 1 million by 2025 and over 2 million by 2051. According to the Alzheimer's

Society, which has produced an excellent guide for employers, there are currently over 40,000 people with dementia under the age of 65 in the UK and 18 per cent of them continue to work after a diagnosis of dementia is confirmed (Alzheimer's Society, 2015). This 'time bomb' is likely to have serious social and economic consequences, with impacts on productivity and social inclusion (Frahm-Falkenburg et al., 2016). But the idea that nothing can be done to support people living and working with this condition is being challenged (Ritchie et al., 2015). There are excellent examples of jobs being redesigned around the capabilities of people working with dementia and the adoption of simple adjustments such allocating mentors or 'buddies', increasing signage and labelling in workplaces to help people find places and resources, creating quiet spaces and soundproofing, and adapting working hours to accommodate fluctuations in symptoms or to help manage the impact of medication.

In knowledge-based organizations the tacit knowledge, skills, experience and know-how of older workers should be a major asset both to employers and the wider economy. While it remains largely an intangible asset to which it is hard to ascribe a financial value, it is clear that extending the productive working lives of older workers makes sense from both an economic and social perspective. Even dementia should not be a barrier to having a full, fulfilling and extended working life. Every organization has the challenge of capturing and building on the wisdom of its older workers before they edge towards retirement and 'dementia-friendly' workplaces need to become routine and unremarkable arenas within which we make this possible on a larger scale (Scottish TUC, 2016).

Many people with dementia are, especially in the early years, able to continue working and choose to do so. Additionally, many people, and especially those with early onset dementia under the age of 65, have financial commitments such as mortgages or dependent children and so are anxious to stay in paid employment for as long as they are able (Robertson, 2013; Evans, 2016). Early assessment and diagnosis is important in preventing problems arising at work and enabling people to continue to work even after a diagnosis. However, currently fewer than half of people with dementia (48 per cent) receive a formal diagnosis. This can be because people are either reluctant to talk to their doctor and seek help, or because health professionals are not confident in making a diagnosis.

Employees with early onset dementia can often experience delays receiving a diagnosis because, as the condition is relatively rare in people under 65, the symptoms are often attributed to stress or depression. As a result, it is likely that there are a significant number of people working with dementia who are unaware of their developing condition.

Coupled with this, in 2013 the dementia Direct Enhanced Service (DES) was introduced to the GP contract to help tackle the low rates of dementia diagnosis. The DES promotes a case-finding approach where clinicians ask those who are at a higher risk of developing dementia if they are worried about their memory so they can be referred for appropriate tests. As a consequence, people can be diagnosed at an earlier stage, when they may still be functioning well and are able to cope at work with relatively few changes.

Various studies chronicling the experiences of workers living and working with dementia suggest that prior to getting a diagnosis, they were left questioning why they were struggling to complete routine tasks at work or having difficulty remembering the details of instructions they had been given (Chaplin and Davidson, 2016). In some cases, the employee may notice differences in cognition but ascribe these changes to work pressure, changes in work roles, or changes attributed to the ageing process (e.g. declining physical strength or stamina, poor eyesight, forgetfulness and hearing loss). As a woman who had been a nursing assistant told Chaplin and Davidson (2016: 151): 'All through my life I had been a good speller and I even got to the point one day when I spelled my own name wrong and at that point I did become concerned.'

However, once people have a diagnosis of dementia they can start to put the problems they may have experienced at work into context. They can begin to make plans, such as considering how long they want to carry on working, and they can have conversations with their employer about how they are able to support them to stay at work. Early diagnosis can also assist employers to provide support and seek specialist advice from services such as occupational health (OH) about how best to support that individual and plan for the future. It should also be recognized that work can, in some circumstances, have therapeutic benefits for workers in the early stages of cognitive decline. A systematic review by McCulloch et al. (2016) found evidence for a number of health benefits of continuing to engage in meaningful work. Indeed, previous research among 430,000 self-employed French workers by Dufouil et al. (2014) found a potentially preventative impact, with evidence of 'a significant decrease in the risk of developing dementia associated with older age at retirement'. The authors concluded that their evidence lent support to the so-called 'use it or lose it hypothesis' of cognitive decline.

People who develop dementia while working, irrespective of their age, often fear going to their GP to get a diagnosis because they feel that they have everything to lose. Employers can help by having clear and open policies about how the organization will support people who develop dementia and encourage staff to be aware of the condition. The Alzheimer's Society runs Dementia Friends information sessions for businesses to help staff learn about dementia and the steps they can take to make a difference to the lives of people with the condition.

The kind of workplace support that employers might consider will depend on the nature, severity and job-relatedness of the cognitive impairment. Sachs and Redd (1993) offer a simple framework that can be adapted to a range of organizational contexts (see Table 8.2).

Eventually, it may no longer be possible for employers to make workplace adjustments to keep a person at work – or the individual may be ready to leave by choice. The guide produced by the Alzheimer's Society (2015) recommends employers avoid using capability and disciplinary procedures, but follow

TABLE 8.2 *Examples of cognitive difficulties and potential workplace accommodations*

Cognitive impairment	Potential workplace solution
Short-term memory	• Present information through multiple modes, e.g. visually and verbally. For example, instead of simply telling your employee what to do, also give them a note that states the instructions. • Allow use of memory aids. For example, encourage the use of checklists, notes and voice recorders. • Repeat instructions and demonstrate tasks multiple times if required.
Reduced speed/fatigue	• Give the employee extra time to meet deadlines. • Allow them to take more breaks as needed. • Allow flexible hours.
Attention/distractibility	• Highlight important information with the use of colours and illustrations. • Allow the employee to work in a less distracting office or area. • Clear the desk surface of only the things that are essential to performing the task. • Reduce extraneous noises in the workplace, modify lighting as needed.
Sequencing/planning	• Colour code or number job duties to assist with organization and structure. • Provide models or samples of completed work so that the employee can reference it as he/she works.

Source: Sachs and Redd (1993).

instead a 'dignified exit package and strategy'. As a former heavy goods vehicle driver told Chaplin and Davidson (2016: 155), this can be a difficult time and can leave the employee feeling embittered and even betrayed: 'They said there were no jobs I could do, safety wise, in the depot. The will wasn't there really was it?'

Dementia frightens people, in part because it is progressive and is currently resisting attempts to prevent or treat it. But as most of us will now be compelled to work much longer before we retire it is inevitable that more workplaces will need to have policies, adaptations and levels of awareness and compassion to deal with the consequences of a doubling of dementia cases in the UK, either because employees have caring responsibilities for elderly relatives or because they receive a diagnosis themselves while they are still of working age. Sadly, this not a domain where we have much choice because the demographic and epidemiological trends don't lie. The sooner employers get to grips with developing policies and practices that make them dementia friendly, the better equipped they will be to play their part in making the lives of those affected directly or indirectly by dementia more dignified and less isolated.

Ageing and the employment deal

FRANCES O'GRADY

ENSURING THAT OLDER WORKERS ARE able to fully participate in the labour market will be essential to securing strong economic performance in the years ahead. With demographic change leading to growing pressures on the public finances, securing higher employment rates across the board will be an essential means to provide a progressive solution to future fiscal challenges. But of course higher rates of employment are not simply a requirement for future economic success – they will also be essential to securing the livelihoods of older workers and their families.

The 'risks' of an ageing workforce has been a major policy issue over the last decade, but it could be argued that extending the working lives of an ageing workforce can lead to increased opportunities, both for the individual and the employer. What has to be considered is the 'employment deal' and ensuring that the ageing workforce has the same access to 'good work' as the rest of the working age population. Ignoring the skills, knowledge and contribution of the older workforce can be a high-risk strategy and, thus, it is important that employers begin to focus on what can be done in organizations to enhance older workers' experience of work, so that work remains fulfilling for them. If this does not happen, then the UK (and other countries) are at risk of approaching a skills gap across the labour market.

A recent evidence review, conducted by Marvell and Cox (2017), argued that there is an economic and societal need to support fulfilling work for the older workforce. They highlighted that there are clear benefits for employers in retaining and engaging an ageing workforce. Just because an individual is ageing, their ability to work does not automatically diminish, and the experience and skills that older workers have make a substantial contribution to the workforce and organizational outputs. The authors argue that older workers have highly developed communication skills, are adept at problem solving, have unique insights and good judgement as a result of their experience, and can, if given the opportunity, work well in teams. How employers behave towards the ageing workforce should not differ from their actions towards the rest of the workforce – if older workers have fulfilling work and are engaged in their roles, older workers will be loyal to their organization and increase their tenure. If, therefore, employers would like to maintain organizational productivity, employers must ensure that the employment deal is fulfilled, as this will result in older workers being more willing to be motivated towards organizational goals, provide their unique insights and remain productive.

Workplace attachment and work content

Bevan et al. (unpublished) undertook a rapid evidence review in terms of how to retain the ageing workforce and found that there were a number of factors that contributed to an older worker's attachment to the workplace. The main factors identified included:

- friendships and personal relationships with colleagues (McNair, 2006; Macleod et al., 2010; Mountford, 2013; Jenkins et al., 2014);

- contribution to self-esteem and identity (Bernard and Phillips, 2007; Carmichae et al., 2013);

- opportunity to use creativity and intellectual capacity (Shacklock, 2006);

- good match between job content and personal skill profile (McNair, 2006);

- opportunity that work provides to help others (Shacklock, 2006);

- personal fulfilment (Macleod et al., 2010).

In terms of job content, Marvell and Cox (2017) highlighted that older workers valued the same factors as other ages in the workplace, in terms of work that is fulfilling, challenges their intellectual capacity, is stimulating and provides the opportunity for skill use and development. Skill utilization and ensuring a positive match between the skills demanded and used by the job was seen as important for job satisfaction. Crawford et al. (2010) reported that there was increased work attachment and job satisfaction displayed when older workers were able to use their professional skills at work, aided by good matches between the employees' skill profile and the job content. For older workers, remaining at work also provided the opportunity to strengthen old or develop new skills, particularly those related to technology, an ever increasing demand in the current workplace (and one that will inevitably increase in the future workplace). Reynolds et al. (2012) argued that not only would this mean that these new skills will enhance their opportunities to remain active players in the workforce, but it could also help them in wider society. Having a certain skills set also provided an older worker a sense of contribution or personal identity in the workplace as they could have been viewed as an expert, or have the ability to mentor younger workers. As with other age cohorts in the workplace, if work was repetitive, mundane or did not utilize their skills effectively, they would disengage themselves from the workplace, which could have negative effects for both the individual and the organization. Marvell and Cox (2017) also found that having greater autonomy and control over their role led to greater fulfilment and job satisfaction. Having control over the work they did, and how they did it and whether they could be more entrepreneurial in their role.

Job content also included the friendship and personal relationships that older workers develop with their colleagues. Jenkins et al. (2014) reported that the social contact that work provided made older workers feel valued, and reduced the disengagement from society that those in unemployment may experience. The CIPD (2014) also reported that the social side of work was something that the ageing workforce really appreciated – the social interaction that work provides can help older workers extend their social networks, and it is often the social aspect of work that those in retirement report missing the most.

However, do older workers experience 'good work'? In a survey study conducted by The Work Foundation (unpublished), there is evidence to suggest that this may not always be the case, and more needs to be done to encourage older workers to remain in work and enhance their experience of work. For example, 30 per cent of those surveyed did not feel that their achievements were recognized in the workplace, with a similar proportion of older workers reporting they did not feel valued, recognized and appreciated at work. Additionally, 24 per cent responded they did not have suitable levels of autonomy, and 48 per cent felt they were not involved in organizational decision-making.

Workplace culture

As in work content, the current literature pertaining to the ageing workforce highlights that the procedures for effectively managing and enhancing employee retention and motivation of older workers are the same as for any other generation in the workforce, although there are some factors that may require more focused employer attention.

As in other areas of workforce management, the employment relationship and how older workers are effectively managed is a key factor in influencing employees' attachment to the workplace and their motivation to work. However, Davies et al. (2013) reported that line managers frequently had not received the training required to have age-sensitive conversations, especially in relation to retirement. Pillay et al. (2010) also discussed the importance of the employment relationship, as they argued that relationship is critical to allow for open discussions about their well-being, opinions on current work practices, and their confidence to discuss any other factors that could be having an impact on their ability to work. The line-managerial relationship, and the effect on employees' resultant job satisfaction, has been reported as a factor in retirement decisions.

However, the employment relationship forms only one part of a supportive organizational culture. The CIPD (2014) also reported that managers have an important role in developing good relationships between older and younger workers – especially needed in the current workplace where there is the possibility to have up to four or five generations working alongside each other. Kunze and Menges (2016) noted that in organizations where intergenerational conflict was experienced, there was a reduction in work productivity and older workers were also more likely to report emotional disengagement from the employer.

Unfortunately, a number of common stereotypes still exist regarding the ageing workforce; for example, that they can't or won't learn new skills, they take more days of sickness absence than younger workers, they are not flexible or adaptable in the work they are willing to undertake and will burnout, or get tired in their roles more quickly. However, there is evidence to suggest that older workers are now actively looking for employers and organizations who do not hold these inaccurate prejudices or stereotypes towards the ageing workforce (e.g. ILC-UK, 2015). Marvell and Cox (2017) commented that older workers valued having both a supportive and open organizational culture, where there was transparency in communication, where all employees had the opportunity to express their views openly and clearly, and where the needs of all employees were accommodated. Boot et al. (2016) believed that older workers (similarly, it could be argued that all employees) would be more likely to perform at their best when there was a positive work environment.

There is now an increasing amount of evidence showing that older workers want equal access to workplace training and development as their younger counterparts (Marvell and Cox, 2017). However, the likelihood of their receiving such training could in some part be related to the attitude of their employers or line managers. For example, there is evidence to suggest that employers perceive older workers as lacking confidence in their ability to be trained, have less interest in being trained, are more reluctant to request training and are less likely to identify their own training needs (Loretto and White, 2006). Martin et al. (2014) found that most managers believed that younger workers are more willing to learn, and that at the age of 45 most workers should be able to recognize the training needs and further support they require. This may be true, but if older workers perceive themselves to be in an unsupportive workplace, they may be unwilling to ask for training, for fear of refusal, or being seen as inadequate in undertaking their role.

A common perception exists that older workers are less likely or less able to adapt to learning how to use new technology – the 'you can't teach an old dog new tricks' stereotype. However, Carmichael et al. (2013) indicated that training older workers in new technology and the ICT competencies needed to complete their roles could maximize their potential (and consequently improve organizational productivity) and improves opportunities for further skills and career development. Providing training for ICT to older workers also then reduces any gaps in knowledge between the younger and older generation – the younger generation often classed as being 'digitally native', having grown up with this technology. However, training should be adapted to fit the preferences of older workers; for example using practical hands-on tasks, and recognizing the competencies and experiences that individuals already have and building upon these (Marvell and Cox, 2017).

Providing older workers with access to training and development opportunities, as with their younger counterparts, helps to improve their job satisfaction and job performance which could both have implications for organizational outcomes. NIACE (2015) reported that when employers do invest both time and money in training for the ageing workforce, it suggests that they recognize that older workers are still worth investing in. Older workers appreciate the investment and the chance to develop skills to improve their opportunities for personal development, rather than extending their working lives by being downshifted to less demanding roles (which could lead to reduced motivation and disengagement). However, in the survey undertaken by The Work Foundation (unpublished) there is evidence to suggest that older people are increasingly likely to be overlooked for training, as 31 per cent of those surveyed responded that they were not encouraged to engage in professional development, and 27 per cent noting that they did not have the opportunity to learn.

Workplace flexibility and workplace adjustments

As the workforce ages, so is the likelihood of people living and working with long-term health conditions. In 2013, of the 7.2 million people aged between 50 and 64 who were in employment, 42 per cent were living with a health condition or disability (Taskila et al., 2015). Early interventions need to be considered to reduce the opportunity of some long-term health conditions developing, but for older employees already in the workplace, employers can implement workplace adjustments that could help employees remain in the workforce and also improve their job satisfaction. It is important that the health and well-being of the ageing workforce is considered, as health has one of the largest effects on an older employee's decision regarding remaining in the workforce, and Marvell and Cox (2017) commented that this could be more influential than job satisfaction or job quality. This is especially the case if both the physical and emotional job demands (it is important to consider both mental and physical health) become too great for an employee to cope with; this can exacerbate stress (one of the most common reasons for sickness absence) or their physical pain, which could lead employees to consider changing their roles, or leaving the workforce altogether (Eurofound, 2012).

Although health conditions can occur in the workplace at any age, there are some conditions that have been reported to be more prevalent in the older workforce, including: cardiovascular conditions, occupational cancers (e.g. cancers related to asbestos), deterioration in eyesight (which can occur on its own, or be a side-effect of a co-morbid condition), a reduction in muscle strength and now increasingly dementia. Other conditions that are increasingly prevalent among the ageing population include stress, anxiety and musculoskeletal conditions (which could be further aggravated by repetitive movements, heavy lifting, or roles that include changing shift patterns and night shifts). An employee's line manager is often the first port of call in relation to how such conditions are dealt with in an organization. But the CIPD (2014) reported that older workers perceived that health conditions are not effectively or sufficiently considered by managers, even though some simple workplace adjustments could make the difference between making work sustainable and aid retention for older workers. In fact, implementing a workplace adjustment could be a signal to older workers that their skills and experience are valuable, increasing their engagement and motivation, and encouraging them to remain (e.g. CIPD, 2014; NIACE, 2015). It is important to recognize that individual needs must be taken into account, as chronic conditions can affect employees differently (especially if it is a fluctuating condition), and consequently older employees (or any employees with chronic conditions) may require different types or levels of adjustments.

One workplace adjustment that has attracted a lot of attention in the literature is the provision of flexible working arrangements. Eurofound (2012) reported that older workers who have been offered flexible work have demonstrated an increasingly positive view of their work, increased organizational and role commitment, enhanced organizational goodwill and importantly an improved work–life balance. In the UK in June 2014, the government made changes to the 'Right to Request' legislation, so that any employee with 26 weeks of employment in an organization is entitled to make a request for flexible work. Although an organization does not have to grant them this request, they must respond to employees within four weeks and provide a strong business case as to why the request has been rejected. Even with this change in legislation (although there has been little evaluation as to its effects), employees have reported that they perceive access to flexible work is still limited (NIACE, 2015).

Bevan et al. (unpublished), in their evidence review, recognized a number of factors that have been reported to facilitate the implementation of flexible work for older workers. These included:

- adequate planning and resourcing (Alden, 2012);

- integration of flexible working for older staff as part of a broader diversity policy (Employers Forum on Age and IFF, 2006);

- trust between managers and employees (Employers Forum on Age and IFF, 2006; Bernard and Phillips, 2007; Alden, 2012);

- support from colleagues (Bernard and Phillips, 2007);

- effective communication of policies to workers, including avoidance of jargon (Employers Forum on Age and IFF, 2006);

- use of workplace champions (Employers Forum on Age and IFF, 2006);

- provision of expert advice to workers (Employers Forum on Age and IFF, 2006);

- effective liaison between HR staff and pension fund staff (Employers Forum on Age and IFF, 2006);

- awareness of costs and benefits of the policy (Employers Forum on Age and IFF 2006).

The provision of flexible employment has been seen to lead to positive implications, both for the individual and the organization. Evidence suggests when those over 50 work more flexible or part-time hours they report increased positive attitudes and job satisfaction in comparison with those who work full-time hours (McNair, 2006). Working fewer hours can also improve the health of those over 50 in the workplace (Carmichael et al., 2013 reported that employees who worked in inflexible organizations in terms of working hours suffered increased health problems, with their only option being to leave employment), and can lead to other benefits such as positive work and home–life perceptions, enhanced commitment and self-reported goodwill towards the organization.

However, just as the evidence from Bevan et al. (unpublished) indicated factors that contributed to the positive implementation of flexible work, there is also a large body of evidence highlighting a number of barriers to the implementation of flexible working for older staff. These included:

- negative attitudes of managers (Employers Forum on Age and IFF, 2006);

- communicating working time options in a way that was clearly understood by staff (Employers Forum on Age and IFF, 2006);

- overcoming jargon associated with financial aspects of retirement such as pensions planning for staff (Employers Forum on Age and IFF, 2006);

- later rather than earlier discussions between HR and pensions fund staff (Employers Forum on Age and IFF, 2006);

- managing employee expectations that flexible working would be available to all staff seeking phased retirement (Employers Forum on Age and IFF, 2006);

- employee reluctance to downshift and reduce responsibility (Employers Forum on Age and IFF, 2006);

- operational pressures on business provision (Alden, 2012), economic conditions (Smeaton et al., 2009), the nature of the job (Smeaton et al., 2009), requiring attendance at the place of work (Talbot et al., 2011) which impede provision of flexible hours and/or home working;

- succession planning and the need to adapt to the business cycle (Smeaton et al., 2009);

- workers' lack of understanding of provisions and their individual eligibility (Bernard and Phillips, 2007);

- organizational cultures deterring staff from disclosing information about personal circumstances and motivations for seeking flexible working (Bernard and Phillips, 2007);

- having problems recruiting machinery operators, drivers and labourers (Taylor et al., 2013);

- organizations reporting experiencing increases in job stress (Taylor et al., 2013);

- workers lacking requisite IT equipment which prevented home-working (Talbot et al., 2011).

One other issue that is affecting the ageing workforce is caring responsibilities (both for ageing parents and for grandchildren), and although this is going to become an increasingly prevalent issue, the CIPD (2014) reported that a lot of organizations do not have provisions or policies in place to fully support carers – which could be a reason why helping to remove the barriers of flexible working could become of greater importance. Policies can be simple considerations such as allowing employees to carry mobiles on them at all times (especially if they are not allowed to do so usually) in case of emergencies (Marvell and Cox, 2017).

Marvell and Cox (2017) identified a number of factors that employers could implement that might help to create a fulfilling and age-friendly workplace, where older workers feel valued. As was identified, older workers still want to use their skills, and consequently both HR and line managers can ensure personal aspirations and job roles are matched to organizational objectives, and that employees have autonomy in their role to complete the work where and how they wish. Additionally, employers could provide opportunities for older workers to mentor younger employees so that their skills, experience and organizational knowledge/memory can be transferred to others in the organization. However, as older employees still wish to learn, and are very capable of learning new skills (including ICT), to help older workers feel valued employers should provide training and opportunities to learn new skills. Finally, employers need to provide older workers with workplace adjustments (e.g. flexible work, OH and well-being support) so that they can extend their working life if they wish. Most importantly, as with employees of any age, older employees would like to feel valued, and thus ensuring a positive 'employment deal' is just as important for this age group as any other in the workplace.

Decisions regarding retirement

FRANCES O'GRADY

FAR MORE ATTENTION WILL ALSO need to be paid to the importance of supporting older workers to update their skills, given the increasing length of working lives, speed of technological change and the growing number of jobs most people are likely to undertake throughout their careers.

The TUC's learning organization, Union Learn, has been involved in piloting a government funded project on mid-life development reviews run by union learning representatives. This involves providing employees with the opportunity to review and take stock of their career with a focus on developing a strategy to develop their future employment opportunities.

Older employees in France already have an entitlement to a review along these lines and a similar right would be welcome in the UK.

But such initiatives will be undermined if current approaches to skills funding continue, as there has been a marked decline in participation of mature higher-education students since the introduction of higher tuition fees. The introduction of further-education loans for those aged over 24 has had a similar impact on the numbers of adults undertaking occupational/vocational courses. Putting the financial onus to fund upskilling wholly on individuals will constrain the choice of many to even consider a new career, as they see it (correctly) as simply a device to connect to their (and other people's) data in the cloud .... Recognizing and using this gives an organization such as Fujitsu an opportunity and an advantage – that of reverse mentoring – or to put it more emotively 'learning from the young'.

For many people the ageing workforce may be synonymous with discussions surrounding retirement. However, Beehr (2014) points out that for many older employees now the choice to retire is not a dichotomous choice – there are now other opportunities to either to remain fully in employment or fully retire. In fact, the decision to retire can be viewed as a complex issue, and could be related to a number of factors: economic decisions (retirement is usually associated with a reduction in income/wages); social decisions (retirement could either mean a reduction in social contacts from the workplace, the everyday social interactions of the workplace and potential post-work socials, or could be associated with an increased opportunity to socialize with other colleagues who are also retired and have time to do the activities that work had hindered); and psychological decisions (retirement could lead to a loss of their identity if this was in relation to their organizational membership or role).

Oakman and Howie (2013) commented that retirement had previously been defined as either working or not working, with no transitional period in between. However, this notion is now changing, with evidence suggesting that people no longer work in life-long roles, and there are new patterns of retirement emerging (e.g. part-time working, reduction in hours, short-term contracts or consultancy work with periods of non-work in between). Beehr (2014) argued that retirement has become more of a process rather than a one-time event in a person's life, and that retirement can have three phases (p. 1100):

1   Imagining the possibility of their future life during retirement. Employees can imagine their retired life at any time in their careers, and those in this stage may not yet be making any realistic plans for retirement, but they may be imagining some activities that they may not currently have time to do. Those who are considered to be 'nearing retirement', but before any plans are actually made, they may begin to assess their work history, consider if they have accomplished everything they had wanted to, and may be starting to understand that they will be retiring one day.

2   Assessing the past to help decide when to retire. After considering their past, employees may then begin to plan how and when they retire in the future, and decide when they want to/will leave their job. How this is done may differ between individuals; some may view it as letting go of their past, while others could view this as having the opportunity to do something new with their lives.

3   The transition to retire, or enacting retirement plans. When an individual reaches this stage, they have usually made some firm decision regarding what they are going to do, and they announce their retirement in some way (i.e. by telling their employer). The act of retirement here is thought to be a clear and rational decision.

Retirement decision-making

A number of factors have been discussed as to why individuals make a decision to retire. One theory often proposed is an economic theory, with the assumption that individuals may not want to work, but have to as they need the income that employment provides. Bevan et al. (unpublished) reviewed evidence suggesting that retirement decisions are related to an employee's financial status. For example, there was evidence suggesting that those with a higher current income or potential pension pot were more likely to both make their retirement plans and retire earlier than those with a more limited income (e.g. Smeaton et al., 2009; Noone et al., 2013). Davey (2008) undertook a mixed-method study in New Zealand of workers aged between 50 and 70, finding that an employee's financial position did have an important influence for retirement decision-making. Another survey (Noone et al., 2013) found that those who had higher levels of financial preparedness for retirement also had more positive perceptions regarding the retirement process, had improved levels of financial preparedness and had more positive perceptions regarding retirement. Further evidence to support this view has come from Australian studies which have found that retirement planning is more likely among those in higher socio-economic groups, or who had better overall labour-market positions (Quine et al., 2006; Cobb-Clark and Stillman, 2009). There is some evidence from the UK that economic decisions play an important role in retirement, as Smeaton et al. (2009) reported evidence from a telephone survey of older workers, finding that those who were employed in skills trades, sales and other personal service jobs were increasingly likely to be planning to delay their retirement in comparison with employees in other occupational groups (which reflected lower income levels than those in higher-skilled managerial and professional occupations).

Beehr (2014) commented that one of the most prominent non-economic theories for predicting retirement is the health and well-being of the individual. Although some have remarked that the process of retirement in itself is a stressor (and that readjustment for retirement can in itself be stressful), an employee's health status before retirement is likely to be a major factor in the retirement decision. Evidence suggests that poorer health conditions, including mental health, were one of the main reasons that led to retirement decisions among older workers (e.g. Brown et al., 2006; Rice et al., 2011; Carmichael et al., 2013). However, Pond et al. (2010) in their study found that decisions to retire related to ill health formed a more complex relationship, as they reported that some employees chose to retire while they were still healthy (so that they could enjoy their retirement), while others did retire early because of their ill health, or to reduce the possibility for their health to worsen further (including mental health conditions). In a four-year cohort study undertaken in the UK, Rice et al. (2011) found that fair or poor self-rated health was associated with work exit. In addition, the research also found that symptomatic depression was also a predictor for early work exit. This finding was supported by research undertaken by Hill et al. (2010), who reported in a qualitative study that depression was the main reason for early retirement, followed by musculoskeletal conditions and then specific skin conditions (the sample was UK dentists, thus skin conditions could have had a greater impact on their role than in other professions). Brown et al. (2006), in their study of teachers, also reported that mental health was the most common reason for ill-health-related retirement, followed by musculoskeletal conditions. Pond et al. (2010) found in their study employees in New Zealand used a number of different pathways to retirement associated with their health and well-being. These included an 'impaired health pathway' (where health or disability affected an employee's ability to work), a 'maximization of life pathway' (where individuals retire when they are healthy so that they can fulfil life goals that they would still like to achieve) and finally a 'protective pathway' (this is when employees are motivated in their retirement decisions by the need to both protect and promote their health).

There is some evidence to suggest that how satisfied older workers are with their job could have an impact on retirement decisions. For example, a UK household survey found that 39 per cent of workers aged 51 to 70 who were still in employment were working even though they could afford to retire

(McNair, 2006). All of these people said they enjoyed working with colleagues and that their job was well suited to their skills. Additionally, research from Australia found that enjoyment at work was an incentive to remain in the workforce (Quine et al., 2006), with another study among older public service employees in Australia finding that as employees aged they placed greater importance on job satisfaction as a reason to stay in work, particularly when their financial situation enabled them to make choices about when to retire (Oakman and Howie, 2013). However, a study using data from an Australian household survey found that individuals who were uncertain about retirement plans or never expected to retire were not significantly happier in their jobs than those forming retirement plans (Cobb-Clark and Stillman, 2009). Oakman and Howie (2013) reported in their qualitative study that job satisfaction was thought to be extremely important in the decision as to when to retire. They found that employees who experienced high levels of job satisfaction were more likely to stay in work, especially if their work was still generating successful results. Their study also confirmed that support from work colleagues and the level of control they had over their work also had an impact on the level of job satisfaction reported, which highlighted the important influence of work factors on retirement decisions and how influential organizational policies can be in relation to retirement decisions.

Work factors, especially the role of the line manager and their impact on the decision that older workers made about retirement were discussed by Davies et al. (2013). The line manager was viewed as important in negotiating with the employee factors that will help the individual–organizational fit. Davies et al. (2013) found that line managers do acknowledge that they have some level of responsibility in an older worker's retirement decision, especially in relation to workforce planning and resource allocation, but only 38 per cent of line managers thought it was their role to ensure that older workers were aware of training and development opportunities that were relevant to them. Although

70 per cent of line managers acknowledged that they had discretion over the way that retirement is managed in their organization, only 45 per cent had received training regarding how to deal with these issues. The authors argued that this suggested that retirement management was not yet perceived to be a mainstream managerial concern and not required for inclusion in management training programmes. The study also reported that there were certain characteristics of line managers that helped play a role in helping older workers with their retirement decisions, which included those who had a positive employment relationship with their employees, line managers more familiar working with the older generation and those who understood the value of older workers continuing to work in the workplace. Morrell and Tennant (2010) found that the provision of information regarding retirement policies and procedures, different retirement options and pathways could enable employees make more informed retirement choices, encourage them to think about what would be best for them and reduce the effects of potential undesirable retirement outcomes. If they were more informed about the options open to them, then this helped individuals feel part of the decision-making process and make any readjustments to retirement expectations if this was needed. One aspect of information provision that needs improvement is the understanding of financial products – especially in relation to pensions and other financial issues that will help to improve informed decision-making (Barnes and Taylor, 2006).

One aspect of retirement that has been discussed in the literature is gradual retirement, thought to aid the transition into retirement. However, as Bevan et al. (unpublished) found in their review of the ageing literature, there is in fact mixed evidence regarding the benefits of gradual retirement. De Vaus et al. (2007) found that gradual retirement was positively associated with improved health after 12 months into retirement, but those who had retired gradually were significantly less satisfied with their retirement in comparison to those who has abruptly retired. It is therefore clear that more research needs to be conducted to see what factors aid gradual retirement, and whether this is an option that needs further organizational study.

Finally, it is worth considering the concept of 'unretirement'. Data from a number of cohort studies in the UK suggest that up to 25 per cent of people who retire return to paid employment within 15 years – though mostly within eight years (Glaser et al., 2017). The 'Wellbeing, Health, Retirement and the Lifecourse' (WHERL) project is an international collaboration looking, among other things, at retirement decisions among older workers. Among this 'unretired' group, the majority were healthy, relatively prosperous and exercising a positive choice to return to work. These data suggest that it would be wrong to regard retirement as a single, permanent and irreversible event any longer. Indeed, it appears to be more of a process that can vary substantially by individual and that can mean that the later career can be characterized by interruptions, reversal and significant changes in direction – most often discretionary. Of course, some (though still the minority) 'un-retirement' has financial need at its core. It might be possible that, over the longer term, a larger proportion of the cohorts of workers in the future with poor or no adequate pension provision might be more likely to adjust their retirement plans and trajectories owing to financial issues. This suggests that, while 'un-retirement' may become more common, its days as a mainly discretionary choice may be numbered.

Ageing at work: future directions

While so much about the future of work remains uncertain, demographics is one of the most reliable disciplines on which we can draw if we wish, with some certainty, to know what the future holds. In general, we know that the pressure to support job retention among older people will continue. We also know that, if we want to make the extension of working lives as fulfilling and as healthy as possible for older workers, we need to attend to the quality of jobs as well as their quantity.

With this in mind, therefore, what gaps exist in either our knowledge or in the interventions we have at our disposal to ensure that working longer works well for people? Here are a few suggestions:

1   *Job retention among unskilled and low-paid non-learners.* There is good evidence that the use of flexible working, access to learning and training opportunities and work adaptations can have a positive impact on job retention. However, very little of this evidence looks specifically at older workers in low-paid and unskilled work, at older workers with little motivation or disposition towards learning or those in jobs with challenging physical or psycho-social demands. Efforts to maximize access to fuller working lives need to be successful and inclusive for groups of older workers (including women and minority ethnic older workers) in industries, occupations or labour-market settings that may perpetuate disadvantage and more evidence of 'what works' for these groups would be beneficial.

2   *Work-based preventative screening tools for work ability.* The 'technology' of work ability measurement has been established for some time, and there is good evidence about work ability among older workers. However, research about the workplace prediction and prevention of health or functional capacity-related job loss is weaker and less accessible to HR professional and line managers – especially if workplace adaptations to job demands or working time are required. Research focusing on the simplest screening tools that give maximum predictive and preventative power would be beneficial to practitioners and OH professionals alike, especially if this research also focused on economic return on investment.

3   *Aligning flexible working and rostering with business needs.* Much of the research on flexible working for older workers focuses on access and acceptability to the worker. However, there is less evidence on how to

embed greater flexibility into the 'rhythm' of the way businesses operate, the demands of customers and the need to maximize staff availability for operational reasons. More evidence of how a growing proportion of older workers having access to flexible working, self-rostering and so on can be accommodated by businesses would help the demand for flexibility to be met more readily.

4   *Job retention among the older self-employed.* The DWP's Sickness Absence Review identified that in the region of 90,000 (mainly older) self-employed people in the UK move from self-employment onto Employment & Support Allowance (ESA) each year. These people are not eligible for support from the new Fit for Work Service and we know too little about them, their needs and what measures might help them stay active in the labour market.

5   *Mitigating the impact of seniority pay.* The issue of seniority pay is mentioned in several studies as a potential barrier to job retention, yet there is very little evidence of the nature and scale of its impact. Even in organizations that have broken the link between service, age and pay progression many employers are still concerned that older workers cost more. Research to map the nature and extent of this problem and to identify innovative ways of mitigating it (e.g. through total reward schemes, salary sacrifice and other forms of pay and pension flexibility) would help enhance both understanding and organizational practice.

There are fundamental and, at least in the foreseeable future, irreversible shifts in the age profile of many major economies. Along with technological advances, demography promises to be one of the major and most consistent drivers of change in the world of work. Within the space of 40 or 50 years we have moved from retirement being a short period between the end of our working lives and death to retirement representing something approaching a third of our lives. This means, among other things, that we will need to re-frame the societal, citizen, employer and policy-maker expectations of the course that our working and non-working lives will take. In addition, the concept of 'retirement' as we currently think of it, and the way that job content, careers, pensions and financial planning among older workers will need to be managed in the future will need a major re-think.

PETER CHEESE

WHAT IS THE FUTURE OF work, the kinds of jobs we will be doing, and the sorts of organizations or workplaces we will work in? All key questions, but it's not just about the nature of jobs or the work we might do from an economic sense. It's also about the social and societal importance of work, and understanding how we create a better future of work that is the best it can be for people, for our well-being and happiness, and for cohesive and thriving societies. Whatever the future of work will be, the future of work is human.

Besides the continuing macro-economic and geopolitical uncertainties, there are many systemic shifts happening in the nature of work (jobs, roles, skills needed), the workplace (where and how we work), and the workforce itself (demographics, diversity, attitudes) that are impacting on all of us. For many of these shifts, the trends for the future are already observable or, to coin a phrase, the future is already here, it's just unevenly distributed.

So what are the observable trends and where are they pointing?

Too many trends pointing in the wrong direction

From both an economic as well as a social and societal (or human) context, we are at an inflection point in the world of work. Technology is continuing to disrupt, enabling many new businesses, challenging old, but also changing the nature of jobs and work. Survey after survey points to how many jobs could be done by AI or robots in the future.

But if these predictions are true, what will be the nature of work or jobs that people do, and how many people would be working? Will the predictions by John Maynard Keynes of almost 100 years ago of 15-hour weeks become the norm?

Or will new jobs be created much as they have in the past, and all the various trends of recent years just continue?

Whatever the outcome, we should aim to be creating better work and working lives for more people. We have to figure out how to work smarter and not just harder. For many, work seems to be getting less satisfying[1] and more intense.[2] The majority of people are seemingly not engaged at work, stress is becoming almost endemic, and many feeling that they have less autonomy or control.[3] Technology has enriched our lives in so many ways outside work, but inside work has too often deskilled, disempowered or even dehumanized, and created an 'always on' working culture blurring the boundaries between our work and home lives, and extending our working hours.

Reward is our primary individual outcome of work, yet too many are in low-skill, low-wage jobs, and evidence is growing of rising in-work poverty,[4] with limited progression opportunities at work. And there is a growing mismatch of jobs with the higher levels of education and qualification of the workforce.

We have to make better use of the diversity and differences in our workforces, both for economic and societal reasons. We have to ensure a greater sense of fairness and support for people at work and address the vital issue of the declining trust in institutions and leaders. The most recent Edelman Trust Barometer[5] described a 'yawning trust gap that is emerging between elite and mass populations'. This gap has been exacerbated by corporate behaviours misaligned to stated values or their wider social responsibilities, fuelled by the continued short-term focus on financial returns and reward as the key metric of business and of economies more widely.

So we need a much more fundamental debate than just what jobs might be done by robots, and we have to consciously design for a future of work that makes the best of and for people.

Emergence of new models and ideas

The good news, however, is that we are also seeing now a lot more innovation and variety in ways of working, in organizational forms, in jobs and roles and careers, in people management and development practices, and a greater focus on and understanding of engagement and well-being. This is happening not just in some of the more celebrated examples of start-ups or high-tech firms, but more and more across a wide range of organizations. These are also some of the trends that can shape the future, to address the challenges we face and to make work better.

So the future of work will see much more diversity – in how and where we work, in the organizations, jobs and roles we do, and the careers we build. We have to move away from the notion of best practice and the more homogeneous views of business of the past, to develop best-fit practice that suits the context of the organization or the nature of work being done, or the workforce or skills that needs to be attracted and retained.

To rebuild trust and to better align the interests of business with the wider interests of society, we need also to develop a better set of defining principles and measures to hold ourselves more accountable to all our stakeholders – employees, customers, suppliers, regulators, the environment and the societies we serve and operate as part of. There needs to be more transparency and perhaps less accounting and more accountability – a move from market capitalism to inclusive capitalism.

The fundamental economics of work

A key part of the future of work must be to keep improving productivity and output growth. As the economist Paul Krugman said in 1994, 'productivity isn't everything, but in the long run it's almost everything. A country's ability to improve its standard of living over time depends almost entirely on its ability to raise its output per worker.' As we stand, real earnings and household incomes in the US, UK and Europe have either not grown or declined since 2008, and some economists are now pointing to signs of shrinking of the middle classes and a view that the younger generations may be the first not to exceed their parents' standard of living.[6]

Productivity growth in general has stagnated, and in the UK has flatlined since 2008. This makes the UK now amongst the least productive in the G20, as much as 30 per cent less productive than the US and 20 per cent less than its European neighbours, encouraging the headline that if the French stopped working on Fridays they would still be more productive than us.

The productivity issue has become a key focus for governments, particularly for the UK in a post-Brexit world, and various views are being put forward, the main one of which is that we need to improve 'management' in the UK workplace. Good people management is clearly a key driver and an enabler of team performance, engagement, and even lower stress and improved well-being. The 2009 MacLeod report on engagement 'Engage for Success' highlighted many of these connections and is being taken forward through the Engage for Success movement.[7]

But management is also about how work is organized, and how skills are developed and utilized, which will also greatly impact overall performance and productivity. A key reason is that the UK has too much taken the route of utilizing and retaining cheap labour rather than capital investment in the workplace, developing jobs and progression routes that utilize the skills of a high skill workforce, or even properly investing in people's skills and capabilities.

A consequence of this over the years has been the steady hollowing out of mid-skill jobs and the emergence of the so-called 'egg-timer'-shaped jobs economy. The OECD estimates that more than 20 per cent of jobs in the UK require little more than a primary school education, we have too few mid-skill jobs to support progression (usually defined as Level 3 or 4 or GCSE to A level equivalent), and an increasing challenge in high-skill jobs that we can't fill. The sheer volume of low-skill and low-wage jobs is starkly reinforced by the Office of Budget Responsibility estimating that raising of the minimum wage to £9 per hour by 2020 will impact on 6 million workers or one in five in the workforce.

With productivity growth as a key driver, investment in technology in the workplace is likely only to increase, particularly as the price points for more and more sophisticated robotics and artificial intelligence (AI) continue to drop much in line with Moore's Law – which translates to the power of microchips roughly doubling every 18 months. Many sectors see greater use of automation and reducing the need for labour as the way in which they will improve labour productivity as labour costs continue to rise. The first impact may therefore be fewer lower-skill jobs and a reshaping of the jobs and skills market.

Skills mismatches and inefficiency of the labour markets

So it seems that whilst we have been pushing the skills and qualifications of the workforce for several decades, improving standards and participation rates in secondary and tertiary education, we haven't been creating the kinds of jobs that will make best use of these skills and provide the breadth and depth of opportunities for progression. With the number of young people in full-time education doubling in the last 20 years and now over 50 per cent going into higher education, the UK now has amongst the highest rates of education in the OECD.[8]

CIPD research[9] recently reported almost 60 per cent of graduates were working in jobs not requiring this level of qualification, and this was up from around 40 per cent back in 2004. The UK in this regard has amongst the worst skills mismatches, but we're not alone. According to CEDEFOP research[10] across the EU, 25 per cent of young adults are working in jobs they are over-qualified for, and 27 per cent see themselves in 'dead end' jobs with little opportunity to develop or grow.

Simultaneously we also have a growing proportion of organizations finding they can't fill the jobs or vacancies they do have. Now 40 per cent of enterprises say they cannot meet their needs for labour and skills, particularly for skilled trade occupations and in technical and high-skill jobs. UKCES recently reported that job vacancies have risen by 130 per cent in the last four years, and that there will be an additional 5 million high-skill jobs in the next decade equivalent to a 60 per cent increase.[11]

Looking ahead, a recent research report from City & Guilds and EMSI[12] suggested that by 2022 less than one-third of jobs will require a university degree yet more than two-thirds of young people plan to go to university. The same report highlighted what many other surveys have shown the growing mismatch of young people's aspirations with the jobs market.

Addressing skills mismatches will become more and more critical as technology impacts on jobs and skills needs more and more in the future. We will have to adapt, upskill and reskill people during their working lives much more frequently to keep up. Learning and development in the workplace must become much more agile and efficient in how we develop new skills, but most of all we have to figure out how to reverse the trends of low or slowing investment in skills development in the adult workforce. Recent CIPD research showed that the UK may be investing as much as a third less in workforce development than our European neighbours.[13] The Eurostat Adult Education Survey of 2012[14] shows that the UK ranks 20th out of the EU28 countries for participation in adult learning, and 23rd out of 26 countries on the job-related employer training measure. Participation has fallen significantly, from 49 per cent to 36 per cent on the general measure and from 35 per cent to 25 per cent in the last ten years since the global financial crisis. In contrast, the EU28 average participation rate has increased from 35 per cent to 40 per cent on the general measure and from 34 per cent to 41 per cent on the job-related measure.

Shifts needed in learning and education

These trends are unsustainable. Youth unemployment (16 to 24) continues to average around two to three times higher than adult unemployment. And the future doesn't look encouraging with the need for older workers to stay in work given demographic trends and the trends in the job markets.

In work learning, apprenticeships, internships and traineeships are all getting more attention, and provide not only very tangible and economically efficient routes into work, but also benefits for employers from recruitment, to productivity gains, and even customers encouraging this practice. Government targets in the UK have been raised, but we are starting from a very low base with only 4 per cent of apprenticeships starts being higher level (level 4 or above), and that being less than 5 per cent of those applying to University (ONS data for England).

A more profound shift in mindset and policy from both education and the world of work will be needed. Employers have to be pushed a lot further on apprenticeships and in work learning programmes, designing and recruiting for jobs that give more opportunity, and better connection to schools and universities. Education has to adapt, there should be more accountability for outcomes (i.e. where students end up), better development of employability and core life skills, together with much better careers advice and guidance.

We will also need to create much more of a culture of lifelong learning, particularly in the context of a world of work where people are likely to have many different jobs and careers during a longer working life in the future, and where jobs and skills needs will change much more rapidly. Education will need to better equip people for a world where not all the jobs can be predicted, but we can say for sure that most of us will need core skills such as critical thinking, curiosity and learning, empathy and ability to work with others, alongside essential literacy, numeracy and digital skills.

So what about how work is changing and the jobs we may do in the future? The big game changer is going to continue to be technology.

New jobs and fear of becoming obsolete (#FOBO)

There have been a rash of recent surveys pointing to how many jobs might be done by artificial intelligence or robots, some suggesting as much as 50 per cent of jobs we do today in the next 20 years (e.g. Frey and Osborne, 2013).

The World Economic Forum recently forecast a net loss of over 5 million jobs in 15 major developed and emerging economies by 2020. The British Retail Consortium recently predicted that one in three jobs in the sector (which employs one in six people in the workforce today) would go with a stronger focus on automation and productivity, in part to cover the increased costs of labour with a rising minimum wage and other labour costs. And if not directly replacing existing jobs, then most jobs and the skills needed will be impacted on. According to some views, this is already happening with the top ten in demand jobs in 2014 not having existed in 2004, or that two out of three of the jobs that school children today will end up doing have not yet been invented. Hard to ascertain, but certainly thought provoking.

Added together across almost every sector, the implications in the future of automation taking many jobs is a possible scenario that we have to consider. However, many commentators have criticized the analysis or implied projections from these sorts of predictions. They point to the past where technology has almost always resulted in old jobs going but new ones taking their place, and that today we have high levels of employment that in most countries have recovered from the pre-recession levels, so where is the current evidence of jobs disappearing?

But as we know the past is not always a good predictor of the future. Artificial intelligence, machine learning, robotics, the internet of things and 3D printing are all advancing at a huge pace, and the technologists and the innovators see little that can't ultimately be accomplished by technology in the future. These new technology 's' curves are more far-reaching in impacting on not just lower-skill jobs or administrative tasks, but high-skill jobs and into the professions, and are truly ubiquitous in their nature and application. And they are accelerating.

If we do end up in the future with a lot fewer jobs, then this creates huge challenges for policymakers, welfare systems and economies that have for decades been built on models of high employment and growth opportunity. Whilst no one can say with certainty what the future of jobs will be, we have to at least consider these possibilities and work more together on the possible implications as part of strategic thinking within organizations, but also across economies.

Most importantly though, we must work together with technology to ensure we are creating jobs, roles and opportunities that get the best out of people. Klaus Schwab, the founder of the World Economic Forum, has coined the term 'the fourth industrial revolution', and talks about the real emergence of cyber physical systems – people working more and more with technology, where we must aim to get the best out of both.

The death of the 'average' job, the 'average' worker, the 'average' career

Technology, amongst other drivers, is also enabling and impacting on different ways of working and different organizational forms. The majority of new jobs being created are in small or micro enterprises with less than ten employees, with 58 per cent of all jobs growth across the EU between 2002 and 2010.[15]

In response, larger enterprises are focusing more on creating more agile business models – more cross-functional teams, more matrixed working and movement away from traditional corporate hierarchies, and rapid access to specialist skills on an as needed basis, creating more job movement and even jobs becoming more like time-based roles.

There has been significant growth in flexi-working and irregular hours working, partly driven by individual choice but also by the growing demands of our 24/7 consumer driven economies. There has also been significant growth in freelance employment and the self-employed. Data and measurement are inconsistent, but most estimates put the proportion at between 15 and 30 per cent of the workforce today, and predict these forms of working are on the rise and could account for 40 per cent or more of the workforce in the future.

This has led to the emergence of the so-called gig economy, supported through the growing number of on-demand job sites and creating the growth of new business models exemplified by the likes of Uber. There has been much excitement about this as a future trend, but on the downside there is the real risk of the commoditization of people and work in such a system, and much less security of work. Mixed-mode employment models also make it harder for organizations to sustain consistent cultures, for managers to connect and engage with their teams, and can be seen as higher risk.

However, flexi-working has many positives, particularly in helping people work around other life commitments, such as caring responsibilities. Almost half the growth in women in the workforce since 2008 are as contractors or self-employed (ONS data), and according to the Bank of England, half the increase in self-employed between 2004 and 2014 was linked to the ageing workforce.

Ultimately, this should be about creating greater choice in where and how we work – the individualization of work, balanced with the needs of organizations and productive output. But there is much need for adaptation of our processes, practices, laws, organizational systems, welfare and support systems, and what we measure and account for to meet these trends.

The changing nature of the workforce

The changing attitudes and shifting workforce demographics are also a factor in driving the changes that have been occurring in where and how we work.

Generational differences have received much attention in recent years, and Gen Y have been challenging many of the old norms of work. According to many surveys more than half of young people say they expect eventually to work independently or in small enterprises, and as many as two out of three say they intend to leave their organization by 2020,[16] reinforcing their more mobile career expectations and the shift from a job for life to a life of jobs.

At the same time, the overall workforce in most Western economies is ageing. The over–50s in the UK will grow from about 29 per cent of the workforce to 35 per cent within the next ten years. At least this is not as dramatic as China where due to the one child per family policy only recently repealed, by 2050 more than one-third of the population will be over 60 compared with 12 per cent today. As people age but also live longer, we will have to adapt work, culturally and practically, to engage and retain older workers. Not only will they have valuable skills, but they themselves will increasingly want to remain active in forms of work for economic as well as social reasons.

With an ever-increasing diversity of the wider working population, not only is it important societally that we create opportunities and support more diverse workforces, but it is important economically to fill the skills gaps, make best use of our people and reflect the societies we work in.

However, almost universally we still struggle with one of the most basic dimensions of diversity, and that is gender. More women than men complete higher education (although not in science, technology, engineering and maths (STEM) subjects), and whilst the gap between female and male employment is now down to around 10 per cent in the UK, men still significantly dominate in senior executive roles and in many of the higher-skill and higher-paid roles – for example in the IT sector (a point related to fewer female STEM graduates). A recent McKinsey report suggested that as much as $12 trillion could be added to the global economy by 2025 by advancing women's equality in the workplace.[17]

So in the next ten years managing retirement rates, attracting and retaining young people, and doing a better job of diversity and inclusion will grow significantly as workforce planning priorities.

Voice, employee relationship and representation

With the combination of diverse ways of working, the demographics and expectations of the new workforce, and the need for greater inclusion and building trust, employee voice and development of the employee relationship has never been more important.

Employee relations have changed substantially in the last 30 years. The biggest shift has been from collective forms of employment relations to individualized forms. Trade-union membership in the UK has halved since the 1970s when it peaked, to around 7 million today. Changing union legislation has impacted on this as well, but only 6 per cent of private-sector workplaces engage now in collective bargaining and only 14 per cent have employees who are part of a trade union.[18]

Unions need to continue to modernize and play their part, but there are now many other channels, including through social media now for employee voice. Glassdoor and similar sites are getting over a million hits a month and are providing very different forums for employees to express their feelings about work. But we still need to work harder in training and developing managers to listen more to their employees, and recognize that they are one of the key influencers of individual employee engagement.

Employee voice and engagement is also about how much autonomy or power individuals have over the work they do, and their working environment, but also how they contribute more broadly. 'Democratization' of the workplace has been an emergent theme for a while, seeking to break the mould of command and control, and driving more collaborative learning and growth cultures. At the extreme have been the much-cited examples[19] of 'holacracies' or 'bossless' environments where employees decide how and what to work on within transparent rules.

Decades of behavioural research and experience remind us that you can't drive better behaviour by writing more rules. Yet the paradigm of work for so long has been to write rules and policies, and engineer processes as the means to control people and outcomes. It's about us shifting from a rule-based world that seeks to drive an ethics of obedience, to an ethics of care and ultimately an ethics of reason[20] – help people understand the wider implications of their decisions and actions, make them more accountable and they are more likely to behave accordingly. And they will be more engaged.

Fairness, opportunity and reward

Finally, we will also need to address the growing disparities in income and opportunity, and the sense of fairness that has been a key ingredient in undermining trust in the establishment and large corporations in particular. Fairness is an important if somewhat complex notion. It can be looked at within an organization, or it can be considered across societies and economies. People do react to perceived fairness very strongly, either by leaving their job or by disengaging and becoming less motivated. It is also a key element of trust.

A multi-year study on fairness at work by Lancaster University, the Work Foundation and the CIPD[21] found that 41 per cent of people surveyed said they had encountered things they thought were unfair in their workplace in the last year, and 59 per cent believed that the rules and procedures are not applied consistently and 49 per cent believe rewards are not distributed fairly.

Pay itself is the greatest cause of perceived unfairness, and reward systems and outcomes must continue to come under greater scrutiny. The growth of in-work poverty, and of lack of opportunity has to be countered. Not only has there been very little real growth in average earnings over the last decade, but according to a 2016 report by Timewise and the Joseph Rowntree Foundation, almost 2 million people in the UK were unable to get part-time jobs enough to achieve the minimum standard of living.

This doesn't sit well with the fact that those at the top have seen their rewards grow. The economist Emmanuel Saez in the US caused much consternation with his estimates that the top 1 per cent of earners had benefited from 65 per cent of income gains from economic growth since 2001. In the UK, according to the High Pay Centre, last year in the UK FTSE100 CEO pay had increased to 183 times average employee pay, up from 47 times in 1998.

Again, these trends are not sustainable, and without more specific actions are only likely to get worse. People with valuable skills in short supply, or the owners of capital and leaders of businesses will likely continue to do well, but as technology works its inevitable way across many workplaces perhaps proportionately displacing more in the lower-skill jobs, we have to find ways to more fairly distribute wealth. Whether Bill Gates's idea of taxing robots is part of the solution, or the increasingly touted views of universal basic income, we need to actively consider these future scenarios sooner rather than later.

Conclusions

The trends driving the future of work over the next ten or so years are already here now. They are characterized by increasing diversity in where and how we work, in the nature of our workforces and organizations, and the jobs we will do. And as has been observed before, the best way to predict the future is to create it.

So we will have to actively design work and organizations for this future, and to challenge and innovate more in our ways of working and our management practices, to improve work and working lives. HR as a function in particular has a big role to play and has to step up.

We must also work more to common principles: to the principle of valuing and supporting diversity of all kinds; to valuing the individual; to engaging and supporting our people more; to increasing well-being; to making work meaningful; to ensuring technology enables the best in humans; to greater fairness and transparency; to building trust and acting ethically; to thinking and working more holistically; and to taking more responsibility for all our stakeholders. These are what should guide our future of work and be enshrined in our corporate governance.

There are also scenarios that could unfold and create a more radically different future. If long-term economic growth really slows and automation takes out many low- and mid-skill level jobs of today, how do we then balance our economies and ensure fairness and financial well-being or prosperity for all? This would require profound debate and change across our education and welfare systems, legislation and taxation, business policy and industrial strategy. We would have to actively design for this possible future, reduce norms of working hours, shift our reward mechanisms, and work out how to share wealth more widely.

Perhaps this is our longer-term future. That we are finally able to really reduce the burden of work for all and to provide for more balanced and fulfilled lives. As the Dalai Lama observed, we sacrifice our health to make money and sacrifice money to recuperate our health. And it was Aristotle who first posited the idea that happiness should be a central purpose and goal of humanity, and that idea has echoed down the centuries. The future of work really should drive to these outcomes as well.

9

Working futures

What will work be 'for' in the rest of the twenty-first century?

Our conception of 'work' has undergone a transformation, at least in developed economies, over the last century. In part, this has been because of technological progress and seismic changes to the structure of our economies. The growth in the service sector and the so-called knowledge-based industries has shifted the balance of economic activity and the demand for skills. One hundred years ago there was much more manual work in sectors such as agriculture, heavy manufacturing and extractive industries. The work was often physically demanding and dangerous, and was conducted during long hours and primarily to earn income. The workplace was too frequently a battleground for tussles over power, control, dignity and fairness. In addition, retirement, if workers lived long enough, was usually short.

Now work is, for a much larger proportion of us, as much a social act as an economic one – work helps define us as individuals, provides social networks, support and community, and, if we are lucky, a connection to a wider purpose. There are more women in work than ever before and, although progress has been slow, more women in senior positions. Workplaces are now more likely than ever before to take seriously their obligations to widen opportunities for employees from diverse ethnic and cultural backgrounds and those with disabilities. Again, much more remains to be done, but there is at least visible progress on which to build. Compared with a century ago the size, sophistication and dominance of the so-called professional class is also noteworthy, as is the substantial increase in the qualifications and know-how of the workforce. This means that the skill base from which modern employers can draw is unrecognizably rich. The quid pro quo, however, is that the modern workforce has a much higher expectation of being informed about major decisions, having a voice and having its consent sought than was ever dreamed of a century ago.

In this book, we have looked at a number of the macro and micro challenges that will shape the workforce and the workplace for the remainder of the twenty-first century. In this final chapter, we set out our assessment of the primary forces that will shape the future of work in modern societies. We will argue that it is only by harnessing these forces, and taking action to make sure that the way labour markets operate and employers manage their people, that the world of work can evolve into an economically efficient, productive and socially inclusive arena.

The productivity puzzle and the workplace

We have identified productivity as a major factor in this vision of the future of work. This may seem an oddly prosaic theme on which to focus in such a book, especially with its associations with traditional manufacturing industry and the imperative to quantify and measure work outputs. However, despite its elusive nature, so much of what we collectively want from work is dependent on steady, evenly distributed and sustainable productivity growth. Improving living standards, rising real wages, economic competitiveness, investment in public services and job security are among the highly valued work-related commodities on which workers and their families rely.

Traditionally, productivity has been a high-level measure of the aggregate performance of an important part of the economy – the part that measures, in a standardized way, how much economic output can be generated by an hour of labour. At an individual level, labour productivity can, of course, be an aggregation of the skills of a worker, how well she is led and managed, how sophisticated the tools and technology which she has to work with, and motivation she has to direct all of her efforts into doing a great job for an employer whose values and purpose she believes in. Despite the focus of both policymakers and employers on these challenges, the era of relatively low productivity growth has been stubbornly long and we have no obvious levers to pull to get it moving again.

In Chapter 2 we briefly examined the origins and consequences of this productivity puzzle – the massive slowdown in productivity growth during the 2008 crash and the subsequent recovery. We still have at best only a partial explanation and as a result few forecasters, analysts and commentators know with any confidence when or even if productivity growth will move back to the long-run pre-crash average. There is not space here to go into all the details, but at least part of the missing pieces to the puzzle lie in what is going on inside firms and we have only limited insights into how this might have changed and why.

Over the past decade employers have kept many more people on their payroll during the recession than they did in any previous downturn. And despite having surplus labour available at the start of the recovery, they then started to hire in large numbers despite the fact that the efficiency of labour was falling with productivity growth close to zero.

Policymakers and academics are deeply interested in productivity but hardly any organization sets out to explicitly improve productivity directly. Firms' annual reports talk mostly about competitiveness, growing market share and profitability, and how this will lead to better returns for shareholders. It can be argued that if firms collectively are good at doing all these things then higher productivity will follow – except that it clearly has not. Firms are profit maximizers, not productivity maximizers. If reasonable profits can be made with low productivity growth, then until conditions change there is no great incentive to maximize productivity growth.

One possibility is that labour-market dynamism is slowing down with less movement than in the past. The result is that in many OECD economies average job tenures have been going up. This could be for good reasons – for example, firms investing more in training, better hiring decisions and good workforce practices – in which case we would expect productivity to improve. Or it could be for bad reasons – employers getting more cautious about hiring employees and more cautious about moving, which will tend to depress labour-market efficiency. Recent research from the US (Molloy et al., 2016) suggests that the decline in dynamism is not driven by good reasons or by the ageing of the workforce (older workers tend to be more cautious about moving). The researchers make the intriguing suggestion that declines in social trust and social networks may be part of the explanation. This is still inconclusive – there are few consistent measures of trust that show changes over time and the researchers used just one question about whether people trusted strangers or not. They nonetheless found an association at the US state level between falls in the extent of social trust and labour-market dynamism, allowing for other factors.

But if there is some truth in the linkages, it may be that a decline in social trust and the scarcity of high-trust workplaces – including the disintegration of the social contract between senior managers and the workforce – are also part of the explanation for the long-term decline in productivity across many OECD economies. What is clear is that we have spent vast sums over the past decade providing the best educated workforce working with the most advanced technologies operating in the most global markets in the post-war period and have got less productive.[1] More of the same seems unlikely to deliver a different result.

Time, surely, to think more seriously about the wider social context and what is actually going on in workplaces, knowing how and why managers make the decisions they do, how employees respond, and whether things are really done more efficiently as a result. Governments in the past placed productivity at the centre of their economic and industrial strategies, but focused on the conventional supply-side levers of research and development (R&D), producing more graduates and on support for the high-tech sectors. Making workplace productivity – including low-pay workplaces – a major priority for policymakers over the next five years would be a good start. The relative neglect of the workplace and workplace organization in the productivity debate needs to be remedied. Government and public organization research budgets need to be brought together in a single initiative that engages the social partners and other organizations able to influence workplace outcomes from the start.

Just managing to manage

Perhaps part of the answer to the productivity problem, therefore, lies as much as with the quality of management in modern workplaces as the way we use technology. As we have seen, several empirical studies have suggested that the quality of management and more specifically people-management practices relating to work organization, job design, performance management and monitoring can differentiate between high-performing businesses and those lagging behind. Of course, management as a discipline is very varied and covers a range of areas from strategy, marketing and operations where technical or professional expertise is the primary entry route and can, in addition, define a specific career path. For example, engineers, accountants, doctors and teachers all have access to well-defined career structures that allow vertical progression up a hierarchy which matches increasing responsibility with advancement in pay. The common features of increasing managerial responsibility – in any discipline – and the climb up the 'greasy pole' of organizational hierarchy are that accountability for financial and people matters also grow in weight and criticality. Despite the proliferation of business schools and management qualifications, which are often dominated by modules on financial accounting and analysis, it seems that the people aspects of management most closely related to high-productivity work practices still have relatively low priority.

This is not a new problem and some might argue, with some justification, that the increase in the skills and education of the workforce have reduced (though not eliminated) the number of managers who adopt the techniques of the stereotypical Victorian mill owner. But we should set our sights higher than this. Although there have been attempts to professionalize management, to award managers 'chartered' status or to elevate the status of management above that of a role one performs in addition to one's professional discipline, too much of management practice is stuck in a low-expectations and low-status equilibrium that all but guarantees that it hardly ever receives the investment or priority it both merits and desperately needs.

As we have seen in previous chapters, a great manager has the potential, the power and the reach to provide employees with an 'animating purpose' to perform at their best, to motivate, involve, engage and develop individuals and teams to collaborate, innovate and excel, to nurture skills, talent and potential, to promote physical and mental health in the workplace and to ensure that employees have all the technology and tools they need to perform at their best. It is hard to imagine that any organization able to call upon managers who are consistently delivering working environments with these characteristics would not also be delivering sustained high-energy, high-output, high-quality and high-productivity results. This is not to paint an idealistic picture of management as a kind of unattainable alchemy. The characteristics of managers who do this daily have been scrutinized and deconstructed many times and the 'genome' of high-class management is prominently in the public domain. It is no longer a mystery but too few organizations have enough faith in its transformative potential to invest in it without reservation.

The rewards that are likely to accrue to organizations brave enough to encourage and incentivize managers with these skills to emerge and flourish are considerable. Profits, market share and investor confidence are but some of them. Indeed, the evidence is that over time the effects will radiate out into the performance of sectors, local economies and ultimately into the productivity and GDP figures. Yet there are many cultural and other barriers to overcome if organizations of the future are to benefit. The first is the low status of management. In the UK, the number of managers working in the NHS is seen as a simple proxy for the density of the time-wasting, clay layer of bureaucracy that is holding back the performance of the whole system. It has become axiomatic that too much management is a bad thing and that managers must be doing more harm than good because they crowd out investment in front-line staff such as nurses. Of course, incompetent or poorly deployed managers can be a liability to any organization. But managers who are energized, skilled, trusted, empowered and clear-sighted can infect employees with the capacity to deploy their professional and technical skills with great effectiveness.

For the workforce and for workplaces over the next 50 years and beyond, our individual and collective experiences of 'good' work, the success of our organizations and the productivity, inclusiveness and living standards of the wider economy depend on whether we have faith in the ability of managers to step up to the challenge in the future.

What about the workers? The future of collectivism and voice at work

The decline in trade-union membership has been accompanied by workplace practices that, deliberately or not, have individualized the employment relationship. The now mainstream use of the annual performance appraisal and the sometimes ideological enthusiasm for individual performance-related pay have placed the 'deal' between the individual and the employer is now more important than the collective relationship. In Chapter 3 we looked at changes in collective organization across the OECD, including the significant falls in union membership, organization and influence in the UK. In some ways, UK unions have been more resilient than a focus just on historical trends might suggest. Unionization in the UK is higher than in Germany, France, the US and Japan, and the much higher coverage of collective bargaining in countries like Germany, France, and Italy owes more to legal support than any obvious superiority in organizational ability. Union influence is also largely within the gift of the government of the day, although also influenced by the willingness of employing organizations to engage.

As neither a revival in the share of membership or bargaining coverage appears very likely in the UK, the future for unions lies in influence, exercised through social partner institutions and in changing the nature of the collective bargaining agenda. The role of trade unions in workplace health and safety has been relatively uncontroversial and seems set to continue. Trade unions have also influenced the delivery of vocational training and education, but could be expanded much more to increase the effectiveness of measures intended to reach the adult workforce. This is a role that successive governments have under-valued. In the UK, unions have had a significant role in overseeing and setting the national minimum wage through the Low Pay Commission.

But other opportunities exist, as the nature of work in some parts of the labour market changes. Some specialized trade unions have always provided services for the self-employed. The rise of 'gig economy' digital platforms and the creation of more people who might be called 'near employees' offers new opportunities to provide a collective voice for people who at the moment have none.

Changing the collective-bargaining agenda away from a narrow focus on pay and conditions has been attempted, with only mixed success as there are significant barriers identified in the 2011 WERS survey. One is that on some issues there may be a preference among individuals to represent themselves or seek support from supervisors. However, where union structures are available most employees and most union members use them. Another is while relatively few workplace managers are actively hostile to unions, the vast majority (80 per cent) would rather consult employees directly, suggesting a lack of enthusiasm for giving unions a stronger role in the consultation process.

Overall, there has been some contraction in collective representative structures since 2004, but not in routes for individual representation and it is the latter that is now the norm in UK workplaces. Other forms of representation have not taken off to any great extent – neither managers nor organized labour have shown any great enthusiasm for Works Councils, and employer-sponsored staff associations once promoted as a 'modern' alternative to trade unions remain a rarity that too often focus only on minor workplace issues.

How far has the retreat from collective voice weakened employee influence and voice? The evidence from the 2004 and the 2011 WERS tells us that employers have got better at providing employees with the means to engage, especially around information sharing, with just over half rating mangers good or very good at seeking their views in 2011. But a much smaller share – 35 per cent – said they were satisfied with their ability to influence decisions and this share has barely changed since 2004.

Most measures of employee commitment have increased between 2004 and 2011, with at least two-thirds saying they identified with their organization's values, felt loyalty to the organization, or would feel proud to tell people where they worked. However, there is a very strong association between people expressing these positive views and their satisfaction with being able to influence decisions. Among the satisfied, the shares increase to 90 per cent and among the dissatisfied they fall to between 40 and 50 per cent.

The impression is that some workplace relationships got stuck between 2004 and 2011, with increased effort by managers to engage not translating into employees being able to exercise significant influence on actual decisions despite the clear evidence that doing so secures very high levels of employee commitment. We also have little hard evidence on how things might have changed during the past five years, but it is not obvious that there has been a significant overall increase in employee voice. It all looks like another decade of much the same to come.

The relationship between government and trade unions over the past 30 years has settled down to a mix of low-level hostility, indifference, and mild encouragement and support depending on the issue, the governing political party and ministerial incumbent. This seems unlikely to change. Developing a more constructive and systematic long-term relationship at the national level with the trade unions and employer organizations, focusing on adult training and education, employee voice, productivity and effective social partner institutions has been dabbled with in the past with limited lasting results. It nonetheless remains a viable option for future governments of all political persuasions as one of the relatively few levers remaining to influence the development of workplace practice.

The risk pendulum

As we showed in previous chapters, the shift towards contingent work in the UK economy and beyond has been somewhat overstated. Nonetheless, there have been significant transfers of risk away from organizations to individuals. The most obvious has been in pension provision, where the shift from defined benefit schemes where the organization took the risk and paid the pension regardless of economic circumstances at the time of retirement to defined contribution schemes where the value of the pension goes up and down with the stock market and how much you get on retirement can vary depending on the state of the market at the point of retirement. We can also see it in the provision of highly skilled labour, where over time firms have cut back the volume of training as huge numbers of graduates became available paid for largely by the taxpayer and more recently by individuals themselves.

Even if the overall shares of contingent work have not changed much we can see a number of trends where risk is further being transferred to individuals. Zero-hours contracts in theory mean a sharing of risk – workers risk that work will not be available on any given day, but employers risk that workers will not turn up when needed. In practice, these relationships are likely to be much more in the favour of the employer, as relatively few zero-hours workers are likely to be in a position to turn down work other than under exceptional circumstances. The rise of the gig and sharing economies discussed in Chapter 3 has seen the increase in professional freelancing and the increase in what we have described as 'near employees' typified by the Uber cab driver or Deliveroo cyclist.

We also have the recent rise of self-employment in some low-pay areas such as cleaning and office services, where it is likely that people are moving or being forced to move to self-employment status to secure sub-contracted work at lower prices. This is sometimes called 'bogus self-employed'. The latter is historically associated with the construction industry, where self-employment for some became a mechanism both for employers to avoid employment responsibilities but also for employees to illegally reduce their tax liabilities. In the UK, the Taylor Review in 2017 started to shine a light on these practices and suggested that the worst excesses of exploitation may need a regulatory response.

These changes are not always bad for workers, with risk being offset by other perceived benefits. Many professional freelancers and self-employed prefer their employment status compared with being conventional employees. People on zero-hours contracts and people working for lower value-added services in the gig and sharing economy have more ambivalent attitudes, with some saying they like the flexibility and significant minorities expressing deep dissatisfaction. In particular, large numbers of people working in the sharing economy want what they would see as a more equitable relationship with the digital platform providers on issues such as benefits and training and risk sharing.

There have been proposals to limit or even ban zero-hours contracts, although it seems unlikely these will be introduced into the UK labour market in the near future. The UK has historically focused on applying employee rights equally across all forms of employee contracts, so an outright ban on one particular form of contract would be a significant departure. Moreover, those employers who want to use such contracts in an exploitative way have many other options, including designating people as self-employed sub-contractors. And those who like the flexibility of zero-hours contracts and have an employer who treats them fairly would lose out.

That said, zero hours are associated in the public mind with some of the worst excesses in the labour market. Few would want to see zero-hours contracts become the norm as it is likely that the numbers on them out of necessity rather than choice would sky-rocket. The recent announcement by McDonald's that it is shifting away from zero hours may be a sign that fears of damage to corporate reputation are starting to self-limit the growth of zero hours. If we had to answer the question, what share of zero hours in the labour market would be most desirable in, say, ten years' time, we would say greater than zero but less than it is today. In an ideal labour market, the only people doing zero hours would be those who for whatever reason want to or are indifferent to whether they are on a zero-hours or regular contract.

Efforts to limit or even ban the development of 'gig economy' digital platforms services also seem misplaced, not least because restricting new service innovations is usually costly in both economic and employment terms.

First, most of the growth and certainly the vast majority of participants are professional freelancers, and most of these are doing it out of choice. Second, rather like zero hours, digital platform workers providing lower-value services such as taxi-driving or concierge services seem split between those who like the flexibility and those who are dissatisfied.

The big issues here are whether such people should count as employees or self-employed and whether they get a fair deal from the platform providers. The first can only really be settled by the courts. The second is partly in the hands of the platform providers whose collective response so far has been less than impressive. But giving gig economy workers a stronger voice through professional associations and trade unions could also help – as we noted above, trade unions have an opportunity to build representation in other areas of the labour market than employees.

So far we have talked about changes in the composition of employment, but the biggest risks faced by most people are the threat of job loss and the risk that they will not find a new one. As we noted in earlier chapters, the UK is a contradiction – the OECD measures of labour-market insecurity based on 'hard' labour-market data shows insecurity in the UK much higher than in France and Germany, whereas questions about worker perceptions on the ease of getting another job at the same wage give the reverse impression. As we discussed in Chapter 2, this may reflect the complex relationship between job protection and perceptions of job insecurity, where in some labour markets high levels of protection for some increases anxieties about the consequences of job loss among protected workers.

Further deregulation in this area is unlikely to generate further benefits, but could increase the scope for unfair and harsh treatment of workers with little bargaining power. A modest increase in protections to restore the pre–2010 status quo, for example, is very unlikely to have an adverse impact on jobs. Either way, legislation that is easy to understand and enforce remains the key to effective intervention.

Moving outside the historic parameters would be risky – we might well end up with higher protections for some but no improvement in perceptions of job security and fewer and poorer quality jobs for others. Overall, it is very unlikely that the UK is going to significantly deviate from its historic position as a labour market with relatively low levels of employment protection and providing the same employment rights for most forms of employee contract rather than banning particular working arrangements.

Pay and rations: just deserts?

As we have seen, the story about pay in modern workplaces has at least two dimensions. At the top end of the wage distribution we have seen CEOs and other senior executives enjoying continued earnings growth. This has been through basic pay increases and long-term incentive plans, other bonuses and share options. Perhaps too often, the relationship between these reward packages and the company performance they are intended to reflect is too opaque or tenuous to command public confidence. Even among free-market-friendly governments, there is concern that widening pay dispersion between top pay in companies and the pay of the average worker has gone too far and requires intervention. For example, among FTSE 100 companies in the UK the ratio of CEO pay to average pay in 1998 was 47:1. By 2015 this gap had increased to 128:1. For comparison, the 2015 figure among CEOs in the US was 335:1. Whether such disparities are justified in terms of the labour market for CEOs, or whether concern about them is rooted more in envy rather than anxiety about inequality, the challenge of restraining top pay is put into sharp relief by the near stagnation of wage growth among the lowest paid. The widening of the gap has not been slowed down significantly by the financial crisis and shows no sign of diminishing over the next decade. So is this an issue that governments should worry themselves about in the future?

The wider social consequences of income, wealth and health inequality are more closely linked than is generally appreciated and, insofar as governments have an interest in what employers pay their employees, any negative or corrosive social consequences of widening pay dispersion at the bottom of the labour market will need to be considered in the future. The rhetoric embedded in the welfare policies of many Western governments is that work is the best route out of poverty and that limiting income from welfare payments among the unemployed will provide a powerful incentive to find work. One of the problems with this rhetoric is that most people who do not have enough money to live on are in work already. In the UK, for example, about 75 per cent of working-age adults in low-income households are in work. There is a similar picture in the US where for men in full-time employment the lower 50 per cent of earners have experienced a fall in real income. Further, in the US, it has been estimated that 95 per cent of all the income growth between 2010 and 2012 went to the top 1 per cent of the income distribution.

Of course the gap between the top and the average pay is only one pay gap that has been resistant to attempts at narrowing. The gender pay gap, despite legislation dating back decades, remains in the region of 18–20 per cent in both the UK and the US and at the current rate will only close to zero in 85 years' time. New regulations requiring UK employers to publish details of their gender pay gaps may help slowly to raise awareness and change practices, although resistance, institutional bias and inertia remain powerful barriers to rapid change.

History tells us that pay gaps get wider if left unchecked and, once widened, are very hard to close. If this tendency extends into the future, then the social and public health consequences may be serious. One problem with pay gaps is that, even if we ignore serious and relevant debates about fairness, proportionality and incentivization, they reinforce the wider societal challenge of the so-called social gradient. Up to a point, income inequality can be the consequence of political choices. The calibration of minimum wages, the setting of progressive or regressive income tax rates and the targeting of welfare benefits often reflect the political choices and philosophy not just of governments but of society as a whole. What is clear from the evidence is that income inequality is strongly related to wider social outcomes such as health inequalities, mortality rates, educational outcomes, productivity, social mobility and social inclusion. Of course, employers have a part to play in this story too, but will most often only change course if the regulatory environment forces them to.

In this context – in which the forces that widen pay disparities systematically 'outgun' the pressures to narrow them – one of the policy areas of current interest that may emerge as a serious option in the future is the Universal Basic Income (UBI). The UBI concept is that all citizens receive a regular, unconditional sum of money, either from a government or some other public institution, independent of any other income. This is not a new idea, nor is it uncontested. In 1969, President Richard Nixon's proposal for a 'Family Assistance Plan' – involving a basic income for all families with children – passed a vote in the House of Representatives but was defeated in the Senate. Contemporary trials and pilots of various models of UBI are currently being undertaken in Finland, India, California and elsewhere. Each involves paying everyone a basic monthly income set at or just below subsistence level. The income is not means-tested and is retained regardless of what is earned through employment. In some models it replaces some (but not all) basic welfare benefit entitlements. The UBI is an unusual policy option in that it has some (but not unequivocal) support from both the left and the right of the political divide. Those on the left are attracted by the prospect of an underpinning income that might significantly reduce poverty and support people as they manage the transition between employment and unemployment. Those on the right are attracted by the idea that UBI can help get control over complex welfare systems that may disincentivize work. The Finnish pilot involves 2000 citizens and pays each of them a monthly income of $580. It is being closely monitored both within and outside Finland to see if it might be the basis for a wider and larger scale roll-out.

Another reason for interest in this approach is that it is hoped by some that a UBI could provide some protection against any future precariousness or job insecurity in the labour market and any potentially disruptive effects of automation. Others have argued that UBI might begin a wider debate about whether, for some people, the dominant financial imperative to work might be softened to allow more people to choose work that satisfies a wider social purpose or that uses their skills and talents in different ways.

If widening income inequality, wage stagnation, more fragile pension provision and ballooning household debt are to remain powerful and dominant features of the world of work for decades to come, pressure for regulatory reform or bold social experiments such as the Universal Basic Income are likely to intensify.

The end of retirement?

Before Otto von Bismarck first introduced a scheme of financial support for older people in 1881 the concept of retirement was unknown. In general, if you were alive, you worked. The scheme which was eventually introduced was only available for people over 70 years old which, given the low life expectancy of the time, meant that few people lived long enough to benefit. Many other countries adopted similar schemes, though most linked retirement ages broadly to life expectancy, keeping their costs down but their social value high. The notion that retirement pensions might be paid by the state for 20 or even 30 years after retirement from work was never considered, yet is part of the current landscape that policymakers, employers and individuals have to navigate. There is a neat symmetry to the notion that a pension age of 70 years set by von Bismarck in the 1880s should be mirrored by the prospect of contemporary governments edging retirement ages up to the same level on the grounds of affordability some 150 years or so later.

The challenge today, and over the next 50 years, is to prevent the whole system of state pensions from collapsing completely under the weight of longer life expectancy, lower mortality rates and a pervasive desire among most individuals to either retire completely in their early to mid-sixties, or to scale down both the intensity or hours of what remains of their working lives. The way we manage retirement in the future is, at least in part, framed by some basic economics. The numbers are sobering. For example, in the UK, only 35 per cent of adults – the lowest for 60 years – are members of an occupational pension scheme (with an average 'pot' to buy an annuity of £25,800) and half of all people with a defined contribution pension pot aged over the age of 55 will not be able to secure an adequate income unless they use non-pension assets or get other benefits in addition to the state pension. In 2015 the average weekly pre-tax income received by single pensioners was £156 (just over £8,112 per annum) and this income, supplemented by the state pension, will need to sustain people for far longer than von Bismarck or anyone else ever anticipated. For example, by 2050 the average remaining life expectancy for 65-year-olds in the UK will be 27 years for women and 25 years for men.

The financial pressure on both the state and on retired individuals and their families is likely to intensify, even with policy innovations such as auto-enrolment. Fewer young people are saving enough to make adequate provision for their retirement and, to do so, a 30-year-old employee today would need to save £12,000 a year, or £1,000 per month, each year until retirement. The future, on almost any scenario, can feel unremittingly gloomy. One conclusion, especially if retirement saving is not going to increase appreciably, is that more needs to be done to make it easier, more congenial and financially beneficial to work longer. This means consigning retirement, as we have grown to know and love it since the 1880s, to the history books. Taking a more positive, appreciative, approach there is a compelling logic to the notion that countries will want to secure a longer-term return on their investment in human capital and its productive capacity by helping older citizens to remain active and fulfilled at work for much longer. Already in the UK the over-65s are the fastest growing cohort in the labour market and up to 25 per cent of people who retire from paid employment 'un-retire' within 15 years of doing so – mainly out of choice rather than poverty.

Perhaps the idea of the 'end of retirement' may not catch on entirely, especially as the proportion of older workers with chronic illnesses is also set to increase. More realistically it is likely that retirement will cease to be a clear-cut, age-defined, binary, never-go-back 'cliff-edge' between work and leisure. The last decade or so of our working lives will, however, need more active management. Already some countries provide mid-career reviews for workers in their 50s, helping individuals and their partners think ahead, plan their finances and working patterns well in advance so that they can exercise more choice about the roles they take on, the training and skill development they will need and the extent to which they want to 'ramp down' into retirement in a dignified manner. As we highlighted earlier, pensions is one of the main areas of employment practice that illustrates the choice by employers to transfer risk from the business to the individual. Perhaps now it is down to these same employers – as a quid pro quo – to allow the extension of fulfilling working lives to be more widely available to the next few generations of workers.

Workforce health and well-being

Given the dramatic changes that have taken place in the workplace over the last decade as a result of the financial crisis, the impact on employee, organizational and societal health has been dramatic. This is likely to continue over the next few decades as the workforce ages and increases its susceptibility to chronic illnesses resulting from lifestyle change and increased life expectancy.

In the recent UK government Foresight project on Mental Capital and Wellbeing (Cooper et al., 2009), the cost to the UK economy of stress-related and mental ill health deriving from absenteeism, presenteeism and turnover alone is £25.9 billion (Sainsbury Centre for Mental Health (SCMH), 2007). This does not take into account incapacity benefit which is around £12 billion, with 40 per cent of that attributed to stress and mental ill health. This does not even take into account the substantial, but difficult-to-calculate, costs of lost productive value to our services and products because of excessive pressure and stress, and the substantial cost to the NHS of treating those who are unable to cope. While the direct costs are high, the human costs are profound for the individuals concerned, their families and the community (Cooper, 2009). For a more comprehensive assessment of the total costs of depleted mental capital and well-being at work, see Cooper and Dewe (2008).

So how has work changed? Cooper (2009) highlighted the changing nature of work and the impact of the recent severe recession. The 1980s were the start of the 'enterprise culture' where we in the UK and some other European countries began to Americanize their workplaces, with privatizations of the public sector, many more cross-national mergers and acquisitions, and the beginnings of the process of changing the nature of the psychological contract between employee and employer. In the 1990s and during most of the first decade of the 2000s, we saw the 'short-term contract' culture, with its intrinsic job insecurity, outsourcing of labour, major restructurings, long-hours working environments and more 'bottom-line' management styles. This trend towards what is euphemistically labelled the 'flexible workforce' started in Britain and Ireland, and spread more slowly across Western Europe, but was more strongly embraced in the UK than elsewhere. The UK was in effect a metaphorical 'causeway' to the US in our changing workplace attitudes and behaviours. The psychological contract of the past, where employees showed commitment and loyalty in return for reasonable job security was gone and the concepts of 'outsourcing', 'market testing', 'downsizing', 'restructurings' and the like became common parlance.

So this scenario of a 'leaner and meaner' culture, a flexible worker ('no jobs for life'), a long-hours culture and a more assertive management style began to have an adverse impact on employee health and well-being, and on employees' levels of motivation, morale, loyalty and the like.

What has been the impact of the immediate recession? Not only has work changed over the last few decades but the recent and severe recession has had even more profound effects on the health and well-being of individuals and organizations. Worrall and Cooper (2013) in their CMI Quality of Working Life survey of a representative cohort of 10,000 managers from shop floor to top floor found the following impact on the health of employees from 2007 to 2012:

- Job satisfaction declined from 62 per cent to 55 per cent.

- The percentage of managers who felt fairly treated by their organization declined from 60 to 54 per cent.

- The percentage that thought that their organization was a good employer declined from 69 to 64 per cent.

- The percentage that thought senior managers were managing change well declined from 45 to 30 per cent.

- The percentage that thought senior managers were committed to promoting employee well-being declined from 55 to 39 per cent.

- The percentage working two hours or more per day over contract increased from 38 to 46 per cent.

- The percentage suffering from symptoms of stress increased from 35 to 42 per cent.

- The percentage suffering from depression increased from 15 to 18 per cent.

- While managers were more likely to have reported symptoms for ill health, they were less likely to have taken time off work than in 2007.

- Managers were less likely to think that employees were treated sympathetically by their organizations if they took time off work sick.

- There was a marked increase in presenteeism with fewer managers being prepared to take time off work even if they were ill.

The authors conclude:

A comparison of 2007 and 2012 reveals that many organizations have taken a step backward on measures that are generally seen as desirable and indicative of good management practice; respondents felt less fairly treated; levels of mutual trust declined; managers' sense of empowerment declined; and top managers were seen as less committed to promoting well-being and less favourably as effective managers of change. It is not surprising that job satisfaction declined. The impact of the post–2007 recession on the UK economy has been profound and it has sent shock waves through many organisations.

So what needs to be done to enhance well-being in the workplace over the next decade to minimize employee ill health, to increase productivity and to create more liveable working environments? Cooper (2009) has suggested a three-pronged approach. First, the evidence suggested that how people manage other people at work, whether in the private or the public sector, is critical not only to their effective performance, but also to their health and well-being. This requires better social and interpersonal skills among managers, which means enhanced training to emphasize the 'people-management' skills and competences, and not just the technical parts of their job (i.e. marketing, operational management, human resources policies/law, etc.). This can be done by a partnership between employers and government, where each shares part of the training costs (where government and organizations themselves contribute equally to the training costs) as in the Industrial Training Boards of the 1980s. This is particularly important for the small and medium-sized enterprises (SMEs), where training budgets are very small or non-existent.

Second, most organizations are so fast moving and focused on immediate returns that they lose touch with their employees' concerns and issues. One way to track the health and well-being aspects of work is to engage in regular well-being or stress audits screening through psychometric measures already available (see *Management Standards on Workplace Stress*, Health and Safety Executive, 2003; or Faragher et al., 2004). The evidence is that performing regular audits by collecting the views (anonymously) of employees on how they perceive their job, their organization, their management and so on, and then systematically intervening to deal with the problems highlighted, can have a major impact of reducing stress, sickness absence, turnover and enhancing mental well-being. This is currently good practice in a small number of global companies and larger public-sector bodies, but not very prevalent in most SMEs or public-sector bodies (Robertson and Cooper, 2010).

Third, the evidence shows that working long hours can damage people's mental well-being, particularly at a time when the average family is a two-earner family. Long hours can adversely affect health, performance and family relationships (Burke and Cooper, 2008). One answer to this is 'flexible working arrangements', or at least 'the right to request' these arrangements. In the UK, all employees have the right to request flexible working but we need organizations to encourage it and not inhibit free choice.

Managing the health and well-being of our working population is vital not only for the individual but also for the bottom line of our organizations, whether in the public (e.g. health service, education) or private sector. The costs of doing nothing runs to billions of pounds in terms of sickness absence, presenteeism and lost productive value. As Studs Terkel suggested about the quality of working life more generally in his acclaimed book *Working* in the 1970s, 'work should be about a search for daily meaning as well as daily bread, for recognition as well as cash, for astonishment rather than torpor, in short, for a sort of life rather than a Monday through Friday sort of dying'. This is our challenge in the field of stress.

Work is here to stay

There are, as ever, some powerful and irresistible forces that will continue to shape the landscape of work for the remainder of the twenty-first century. Some, such as demographics and technological change, will have a direct and pervasive effect on the nature of work and who is available to do it. Others, such as globalization and climate change, will frame the context within which governments and businesses function. Throughout this book we have sought to embrace and interpret these challenges more through sober analysis than through alarmism. In general, our view is that commentary on the world of work has a tendency to overstate and even over-dramatize the short-term impact of these forces and to underestimate their long-term effects. In part, this explains our reluctance to push the 'panic' button about the disruptive impact of the so-called 'gig economy' or digitization and automation at work.

This sobriety should unequivocally not be taken as complacency. The long-term impact of demographic and technological change will, of course, transform much of what we have come to accept as the normal operation of labour markets, business models, social welfare systems and financial markets. But the precise focus and pace of these changes is far harder to anticipate. We must remain open, therefore, to new models of working and, indeed, to the possibility that the nature and meaning of work itself will change as our need for it evolves and our demands of it transform. Despite the many historical and Utopian forecasts that leisure will largely replace work in our lives, our conclusion is that our need for work as both a social and an economic activity will remain. The task for those of us who work is to have the confidence, imagination and vision boldly to shape its future for ourselves and the generations that follow.

NOTES

2 The changing labour market: myths and reality

1   Some also include part-time work. We think this is anachronistic given part-time work has been an established part of the labour market for many years and most part-time jobs are permanent.

2   Jobs defined by the researchers as having at least four positive attributes.

3 The global workforce

1   Peter Drucker, often described as a 'guru' on the future of management, hated the term: 'I have been saying for many years that we are using the word "guru" only because "charlatan" is too long to fit into a headline.' We agree. www.gurteen.com/gurteen/gurteen.nsf/id/gurus-charlatans

5 Better managers in the future workplace

1   The former chairperson and CEO of Xerox.

2   https://hbr.org/2004/01/managers-and-leaders-are-they-different

3   For more information and a good introduction to the methodology see: http://cep.lse.ac.uk/pubs/download/occasional/op041.pdf

4   See Tamkin and Ni Luanaigh (2016: 28) for more examples of the Cox et al. (2012) model.

5   www.blogs.hbr.org/2012/12/why-do-we-wait-so-long-to-trai/

6   www2.cipd.co.uk/pm/peoplemanagement/b/weblog/archive/2015/08/25/almost-half-of-workers-have-left-a-job-because-of-a-bad-boss-survey-finds.aspx#

7   www.bbc.co.uk/news/business–28220312

8 www.bbc.co.uk/news/technology–16314901

9 www.hrmagazine.co.uk/article-details/should-uk-employers-offer-the-right-to-disconnect

10 http://gender.bitc.org.uk/all-resources/factsheets/women-and-work-facts

6 The future health of the workforce

1 https://inews.co.uk/essentials/news/health/simon-stevens-nhs-life-expectancy-pressure/

2 www.ons.gov.uk/employmentandlabourmarket/peopleinwork/labourproductivity/articles/sicknessabsenceinthelabourmarket/2016

3 www.weforum.org/agenda/2016/02/how-can-we-achieve-universal-health-coverage/

4 World Economic Forum 2010 Global Risks Report, www3.weforum.org/docs/WEF_GlobalRisks_Report_2010.pdf

5 www.who.int/occupational_health/publications/global_plan/en/

7 The future of pay and reward: the triumph of faith over evidence?

1 Even the Swiss population, where income inequality is perhaps less extreme than elsewhere, was animated enough on the issue of pay dispersion to force a national referendum, in November 2013, on a 12:1 ratio between pay at the top and pay at the bottom. The proposal was narrowly defeated.

8 The future of the ageing workforce

1 EVS Foundation (2008). *Longitudinal data file 1981–2008.*

2 Chartered Institute of Personnel and Development (CIPD) (2014). *Absence management survey.* London: CIPD.

3 Ref. Kenexa, Aon Hewitt, Hay Group engagement surveys.

4 Joseph Rowntree Foundation.

5   Edelman Trust Barometer (2016).

6   For example, Gordon, R. (2016). *The Rise and Fall of American Growth*. Princeton, NJ: Princeton University Press.

7   MacLeod, D. and Clarke, N. (2009). *Engaging for Success: Enhancing performance through employee engagement*. London: Department for Business Innovation and Skills.

8   OECD (2013). *Long-term growth scenarios*. Paris: OECD.

9   Chartered Institute of Personnel and Development (CIPD) (2015). *Over-qualification and skills mismatch in the graduate labour market*, August. London: CIPD.

10 European Centre for the Development of Vocational Training (CEDEFOP) (2015). *European skills and jobs survey*. Thessaloniki: CEDEFOP.

11 UKCES Working Futures Dataset.

12 City & Guilds (2015). *Future jobs market*, EMSI Report 2015.

13 Chartered Institute of Personnel and Development (CIPD) (2017). *From inadequate to outstanding: Making the UK skills system world class*. London: CIPD.

14 Eurostat AES 2002.

15 EU Commission (2002). *Growth – Internal market, industry, entrepreneurship and SMEs*, January.

16 Deloitte (2016). *The Deloitte Millennial Survey 2016*. London: Deloitte.

17 McKinsey Global Institute (2015). *How advancing women's equality can add $12 trillion to global growth*. Available at: https://www.mckinsey.com/global-themes/employment-and-growth/how-advancing-womens-equality-can-add-12-trillion-to-global-growth

18 WERS (2013). *The 2011 Workplace Employment Relations Study*. London: BIS.

19 For example, Zappos, WL Gore, Morning Star.

20 Steare, R. (2012). *Ethicability*. London: Roger Steare Consulting Ltd.

21 Chartered Institute of Personnel and Development (CIPD) (2013). *The changing contours of fairness*. London: CIPD.

9 Working futures

1   A recent report commissioned by the UK Department of Business Enterprise Innovation and Skills (BEIS) suggests that skills – mainly the increasing share of graduates in the workforce – have continued to boost productivity, but these positive impacts have been offset by other factors.

REFERENCES

Agarwal, S. and Wang, F. (2009). *Perverse incentives at the banks? Evidence from a natural experiment.* Working Paper #WP–09–08. Chicago, IL: Federal Reserve Bank of Chicago.

Aguinis, H., Joo, H. and Gottfredson, R. (2011). Why we hate performance management – and why we should love it. *Business Horizons*, 54, 503–507.

Alden, E. (2012). *Flexible employment: How employment and the use of flexibility policies through the life course can affect later life occupation and financial outcomes.* London: Age UK.

Altmann, R. (2014). *A new vision for older workers: Retain, retrain, recruit.* London: Department for Work and Pensions. Available at: https://www.gov.uk/government/uploads/system/uploads/attachment_data/file/411420/a-new-vision-for-older-workers.pdf

Alzheimer's Society (2015). *Creating a dementia-friendly workplace: A practical guide for employers.* London: Alzheimer's Society. Available at: https://www.alzheimers.org.uk/download/downloads/id/2619/creating_a_dementia-friendly_workplace.pdf

Anand, G. (2011). India graduates millions, but too few are fit to hire. *The Wall Street Journal* [online]. Available at: https://www.wsj.com/articles/SB1000142405274870351550457614209286321982

Andrews, D., Criscuolo, C. and Gal, P.N. (2016). *The best versus the rest: The global productivity slowdown, divergence across firms and the role of public policy.* OECD Productivity Working Paper #5. Paris: OECD. Available at: www.oecd-ilibrary.org/economics/the-best-versus-the-rest_63629cc9-en

Appleyard, B. (2014). Why futurologists are always wrong – and why we should be sceptical of techno-utopians. *New Statesman* [online]. Available at: http://www.newstatesman.com/culture/2014/04/why-futurologists-are-always-wrong-and-why-we-should-be-sceptical-techno-utopians

Arntz, M., Gregory, T. and Zierahn, V. (2016). *The risk of automation for jobs in OECD countries: A comparative analysis.* OECD Social, Employment and Migration Working Paper #189. Paris: OECD. Available at: http://www.ifuturo.org/sites/default/files/docs/automation.pdf

Association of Chambers of Commerce and Industry of India (ASSOCHAM) (2016). *B and C category B-schools producing un-employable pass-outs* [online]. New Delhi: ASSOCHAM. Available at: http://www.assocham.org/newsdetail.php?id=5651

Autor, D. (2015). Why are there still so many jobs? The history and future of workplace automation. *Journal of Economic Perspectives*, 29 (3), pp. 3–30 [online]. Available at: https://economics.mit.edu/files/11563

Awano, G., Heffernan, A. and Robinson, H. (2017). *Management practices and productivity among manufacturing businesses in Great Britain: Experimental estimates for 2015.*

London: ONS. Available at: www.ons.gov.uk/employmentandlabourmarket/peopleinwork/labourproductivity/articles/experimentaldataonthemanagement practicesofmanufacturingbusinessesingreatbritain/experimentalestimatesfor2015

Bajorek, Z. and Bevan, S.M. (2015). Performance-related-pay in the UK public sector: A review of the recent evidence on effectiveness and value for money. *Journal of Organizational Effectiveness: People and Performance*, 2 (2), 94–109.

Bajorek, Z., Donnaloja, V. and McEnhill, L. (2016). *Don't stop me now: Supporting young people with chronic conditions from education to employment*. London: The Work Foundation. Available at: http://www.theworkfoundation.com/wp-content/uploads/2016/11/399_Dont_stop_me_now_main_report.pdf

Bajorek, Z., Shreeve, V., Bevan, S. and Taskilla, T. (2014). *The way forward: Policy options for improving workforce health in the UK*. London: The Work Foundation. Available at: http://www.theworkfoundation.com/wp-content/uploads/2016/11/372_The-Way-Forward-FINAL.pdf

Baldwin, R. (2006). *Globalisation: The great unbundling(s)*. Economic Council of Finland. Available at: http://graduateinstitute.ch/files/live/sites/iheid/files/sites/ctei/shared/CTEI/Baldwin/Publications/Chapters/Globalization/Baldwin_06–09–20.pdf

Baptiste, R.N. (2008). Tightening the link between employee wellbeing at work and performance: A new dimension for HRM. *Management Decision*, 46, 284–309.

Barber, L., Hayday, S. and Bevan, S. (1999). *From people to profit*. IES Report #355. Brighton: IES. Available at: http://www.employment-studies.co.uk/system/files/resources/files/355.pdf

Barnes, H. and Taylor, R.F. (2006). *Work, saving and retirement among ethnic minorities: A qualitative study*. Department for Work and Pensions Research Report #396. London: DWP. Available at: http://webarchive.nationalarchives.gov.uk/20090605235538/http://www.dwp.gov.uk/asd/asd5/rports2005–2006/rrep396.pdf

Barry, M. and Friedli, L. (2008) *Mental capital and wellbeing: Making the most of ourselves in the 21st century. State-of-Science Review #SR-B3: The influence of social, demographic and physical factors on positive mental health in children, adults and older people*. London: Government Office for Science. Available at: http://webarchive.nationalarchives.gov.uk/20121204182719/http://bis.gov.uk/assets/foresight/docs/mental-capital/sr-b3_mcw.pdf

Bebchuk, L. and Fried, J.M. (2004). *Pay Without Performance: The unfulfilled promise of executive compensation*. Cambridge, MA: Harvard University Press.

Beehr, T.A. (2014). To retire or not to retire: That is not the question. *Journal of Organizational Behavior*, 35, 1093–1108.

Belt, V. and Giles, L. (2009). *High performance working: A synthesis of the key literature*. Evidence Report #4. London: UCKES. Available at: http://webarchive.nationalarchives.gov.uk/20140108131537/http://www.ukces.org.uk/assets/ukces/docs/publications/evidence-report–4-high-performance-working-key-literature.pdf

Beltratti, A. and Stulz, R.M. (2010). *The credit crisis around the globe: Why did some banks perform better?* Charles A. Dice Center Working Paper #2010–05. Columbus, OH: Fisher College of Business.

Bernard, M. and Phillips, J.E. (2007). Working carers of older adults: What helps and what hinders in juggling work and care? *Community, Work and Family*, 10 (2), 139–160.

Bernhardt, A. (2014). *Labor standards and the reorganization of work: Gaps in data and research* [online]. Berkeley, CA: Institute for Research on Labor and Employment. Available at: http://irle.berkeley.edu/files/2014/Labor-Standards-and-the-Reorganization-of-Work.pdf

Bernhardt, A. and Thomason, S. (2017). *What do we know about gig work in California? An analysis of independent contracting* [online]. Berkeley, CA: Labor Center. Available at: http://laborcenter.berkeley.edu/what-do-we-know-about-gig-work-in-california/

Bevan, S. (2010). *The business case for employee health and wellbeing.* London: The Work Foundation. Available at: http://investorsinpeople.ph/wp-content/uploads/2013/08/The-Business-Case-for-Employee-Health-and-Wellbeing-Feb–2010.pdf

Bevan S. (2013). *Compensation culture: Is executive pay excessive? Does it matter?* London: The Work Foundation.

Bevan, S. (2014a). Unemployed? You shouldn't just take any job. *The Washington Post*, 16 December. Available at: https://www.washingtonpost.com/posteverything/wp/2014/12/16/unemployed-you-shouldnt-just-take-any-job/

Bevan, S. (2014b). *Performance management:* HR *thoroughbred or beast of burden?* London: The Work Foundation. Available at: http://www.theworkfoundation.com/wp-content/uploads/2016/11/376_Performance-Management.pdf

Bevan, S. (2015). *Back to work: Exploring the benefits of early interventions which help people with chronic illness remain in work.* London: The Work Foundation. Available at: http://www.theworkfoundation.com/wp-content/uploads/2016/11/F152_Economics-of-Early-Intervention-FINAL.pdf

Bevan, S., Bajorek, Z. and Laghini, M. (unpublished). *Rapid review of evidence on retaining older people in the workplace.* Unpublished paper. London: The Work Foundation.

Bevan S et al. (2009). *Musculoskeletal Disorders and Labour Market Participation in Europe.* London: The Work Foundation.

Bevan, S., Zheltoukhova, K., Summers, K., Bajorek, Z., O'Dea, L. and Gulliford, J. (2013). *Life and employment opportunities of young people with chronic conditions.* London: The Work Foundation.

Black, C. (2008). *Working for a healthier tomorrow.* London: The Stationery Office. Available at: https://www.gov.uk/government/uploads/system/uploads/attachment_data/file/209782/hwwb-working-for-a-healthier-tomorrow.pdf

Blane, D. (2015). *Working longer: Paid employment beyond age 65 years.* ICLS Occasional Paper #16.1. London: The International Centre for Lifecourse Studies in Society and Health. Available at: https://www.ucl.ac.uk/icls/publications/op/op16_1.pdf

Bloom, M. and Michel, J. (2002). The relationships among organizational context, pay dispersion, and among managerial turnover. *Academy of Management Journal*, 45 (1), 33–42.

Bloom, N., Dorgan, S., Dowdy, J. and Van Reenen, J. (2007). *Management practice & productivity: Why they matter.* London: Centre for Economic Performance, LSE/McKinsey and Co. Available at: http://cep.lse.ac.uk/management/Management_Practice_and_Productivity.pdf

Bloom, N., Genakos, C., Sadun, R. and Van Reenen, J. (2012). Management practices across firms and countries. *Academy of Management Perspectives*, 26 (1), 12–33.

Bloom, N., Propper, C., Seiler, S. and Van Reenen, J. (2010). *The impact of competition on management quality: Evidence from public hospitals*. CEP Discussion Paper #983, revised November 2014. Available at: http://cep.lse.ac.uk/pubs/download/dp0983.pdf

Boot, C., de Kruif, A., Shaw, W., van der Beek, A., Deeg, D. and Abma, T. (2016). Factors important for work participation among older workers with depression, cardiovascular disease, and osteoarthritis: A mixed-method study. *Journal of Occupational Rehabilitation*, 26, 160–172.

Borman, W.C. and Motowidlo, S.J. (1993). Expanding the criterion domain to include elements of contextual performance. In N. Schmitt and W.C. Borman (eds.), *Personnel Selection in Organizations* (pp. 71–98). San Francisco, CA: Jossey-Bass.

Bosworth, D.L., Davies, R. and Wilson, R.A. (2002). *Skills, high level work practices and enterprise performance*. IER Research Report. Warwick: University of Warwick.

Bowen, D. and Ostroff, C. (2004). Understanding HRM–firm performance linkages: The role of the strength of the HRM system. *Academy of Management Review*, 29, 203–221.

Bowles, J. (2014). *The computerisation of European jobs* [blog]. Bruegel. Available at: http://bruegel.org/2014/07/the-computerisation-of-european-jobs/

Boxall, P. and Purcell, J. (2003). *Strategy and Human Resource Management*. Basingstoke: Palgrave Macmillan.

Boyatzis, R.E. (1982). *The Competent Manager: A model for effective performance*. New York: Wiley.

Bramley-Harker, E., Hughes, G. and Farahnik, J. (2006). *Sharing the costs – Reaping the benefits. Incentivising return to work initiatives*. A report for Norwich Union Healthcare. London: NERA Economic Consulting.

Brinkley, I. (2008). *The knowledge economy: How knowledge is reshaping the economic life of nations*. London: The Work Foundation. Available at: http://www.theworkfoundation.com/Reports/213/Knowledge-Workers-and-Knowledge-Work

Brinkley, I. (2016). *In search of the gig economy*. London: The Work Foundation. Available at: http://www.theworkfoundation.com/wp-content/uploads/2016/11/407_In-search-of-the-gig-economy_June2016.pdf

Brown, J., Gilmour, W.H. and Macdonald, E.B. (2006). Ill health retirement in Scottish teachers: process, outcomes and re-employment. *International Archives of Occupational and Environmental Health*, 79 (5), 433–440.

Bryman, A. (1992). *Charisma and Leadership in Organisations*. London: Sage.

Burgess, S.M. and Rees, H.J.B. (1996). Job tenure in Britain 1975–1992. *Economic Journal*, 106, 334–344. Available at: http://research-information.bristol.ac.uk/en/publications/job-tenure-in-britain–19751992(39552f6e–3aa6–44d1-a77b–043cb0e9db6b).html

Burke, R. and Cooper, C.L. (2008). *The Long Working Hours Culture*. Bingley: Emerald.

Burtless, G. (2013). *The impact of population ageing and retirement on productivity*. Washington, DC: Brookings Center for Retirement Research. Available at: www.brookings.edu/research/papers/2013/05/impacting-aging-population-workforce-productivity

Bush, V. (1945). As we may think. *The Atlantic*, July.

Butterworth, P., Leach, L., McManus, S. and Stansfeld, S. (2013). Common mental disorders, unemployment and psychosocial job quality: Is a poor job better than no job at all? *Psychological Medicine*, 43 (8), 1763–1772.

Cacioppo, J. and Patrick, W. (2008). *Loneliness: Human nature and the need for social connection*. New York: W.W. Norton.

Cain, S. (2012). *Quiet: The power of introverts in a world that can't stop talking*. London: Penguin Books.

Campbell, J.P., McClay, R.A., Oppler, S.H. and Seger, C.E. (1993). A theory of performance. In N. Schmitt, W.C. Boorman and Associates (eds.), *Personnel Selections in Organizations*. San Francisco, CA: Jossey-Bass.

Carers UK (2014). *Supporting employees who are caring for someone with dementia*. Available at: https://www.carersuk.org/for-professionals/policy/policy-library/ supporting-employees-who-are-caring-for-someone-with-dementia (accessed 14 November 2016).

Carmichael, F., Hulme, C. and Porcellato, L. (2013). Older age and ill-health: Links to work and worklessness. *International Journal of Workplace Health Management*, 6 (1), 54–65.

Chaplin, R. and Davidson, I. (2016). What are the experiences of people with dementia in employment? *Dementia*, 15 (2), 147–161.

Chartered Institute of Personnel and Development (CIPD) (2013). *Employee outlook: Focus on trust in leaders*. London: CIPD. Available at: https://www.cipd.co.uk/Images/ employee-outlook_2013-autumn-trust-leaders_tcm18–9571.pdf

Chartered Institute of Personnel and Development (CIPD) (2014a). *Managing an age-diverse workforce: Employer and employee views*. London: CIPD. Available at: https://www.cipd.co.uk/Images/managing-an-age-diverse-workforce_2014_tcm18– 10838.PDF

Chartered Institute of Personnel and Development (CIPD) (2014b). *Learning and development survey*. London: CIPD. Available at: https://www.cipd.co.uk/Images/ learning-and-development_2014_tcm18–11296.pdf

Chartered Institute of Personnel and Development (CIPD) (2015a). *Productivity: Getting the best out of people*. London: CIPD. Available at: https://www.cipd.co.uk/Images/ learning-and-development_2014_tcm18–11296.pdf

Chartered Institute of Personnel and Development (CIPD) (2015b). *Absence management 2015*. London: CIPD. Available at: www.cipd.co.uk/binaries/ absencemanagement_2015.pdf

Chartered Institute of Personnel and Development (CIPD) (2015c). *Employment regulation and the labour market*. London: CIPD. Available at: https://www.cipd.co.uk/ knowledge/work/trends/labour-market-regulations

Chartered Institute of Personnel and Development (CIPD) (2016). *Employee outlook: Employer views on working life*. London: CIPD. Available at: https://www.cipd.co.uk/ knowledge/fundamentals/relations/engagement/employee-outlook-reports

Chartered Institute of Personnel and Development (CIPD) (2017a). *From 'inadequate' to 'outstanding': Making the UK's skills system world class*. London: CIPD. Available at: https://www.cipd.co.uk/knowledge/work/skills/uk-skills-system-report

Chartered Institute of Personnel and Development (CIPD) (2017b). *To gig or not to gig? Stories from the modern economy*. London: CIPD. Available at: https://www.cipd.co.uk/knowledge/work/trends/gig-economy-report

Chartered Institute of Personnel and Development (CIPD)D (2017c). *HR outlook: Views of our profession*. London: CIPD. Available at: https://www.cipd.co.uk/knowledge/strategy/hr/outlook-reports

Chartered Management Institute (CMI) (2008). *Management futures – The world in 2018*. London: CMI. Available at: http://www.managers.org.uk/insights/research/current-research/2008/march/management-futures-the-world-in-2018

Chartered Management Institute (CMI) (2014). *Management 2020: Leadership to unlock long-term growth*. London: CMI. Available at: https://www.managers.org.uk/~/media/Files/PDF/M2020/Management%202020%20-%20Leadership%20to%20unlock%20long-term%20growth

Cherns, A. (1975). Perspectives on the quality of life. *Journal of Occupational Psychology*, 48, 155–167.

Chua, J., Chrisman, J. and Chang, E. (2004). Are family firms born or made? An exploratory investigation. *Family Business Review*, 17 (1), 37–55.

Clark, G.L., Knox-Hayes, J. and Strauss, K. (2009). Financial sophistication, salience, and the scale of deliberation in UK retirement planning. *Environment and Planning A*, 41 (10), 2496–2515.

Cobb-Clark, D.A. and Stillman, S. (2009). The retirement expectations of middle-aged Australians. *Economic Record*, 85 (269), 146–163.

Colley, J. (2017). Silicon Valley firms are over-valued – here's why a correction is coming. *The Conversation* [online]. *Business and Economy*. Available at: https://theconversation.com/silicon-valley-firms-are-over-valued-heres-why-a-correction-is-coming-81572

Collinson, D. (2002). Managing humour. *Journal of Management Studies*, 39 (3), 269–288.

Combs, J., Liu, Y., Hall, A. and Ketchen, D. (2006). How much do high work practices matter? A meta-analysis of their effects on organisational performance. *Personnel Psychology*, 59, 501–528.

Connor, S. (2011). US Science Chief warns: 'China will eat our lunch'. *Independent* [online]. Available at: http://www.independent.co.uk/news/science/us-science-chief-warns-china-will-eat-our-lunch-2219974.html

Conway, N. and Briner, B. (2005). *Understanding Psychological Contracts at Work: A critical evaluation of theory and research*. Oxford: Oxford University Press.

Conway, N., Guest, D. and Trenberth, L. (2011). Testing the differential effects of changes in psychological contract breach and fulfilment. *Journal of Vocational Behavior*, 79, 267–276.

Conyon, M., Fernandes, N., Ferreira, M.A., Matos, P. and Murphy, K.J. (2011). *The executive compensation controversy: A transatlantic analysis*. ICS–2011002. Ithaca, NY: Institute for Compensation Studies, Cornell University. Available at: http://digitalcommons.ilr.cornell.edu/ics/5/

Conyon, M., Peck, S.I. and Sadler, G.V. (2009). Compensation consultants and executive pay: Evidence from the United States and the United Kingdom. *Academy of Management Perspectives*, 23, 43–55.

Cooper, C.L. (2009). The changing nature of work: Enhancing mental capital and well-being of the workplace. *21st Century Society*, 4 (3), 269–275.

Cooper, C. and Bevan, S. (2014). Business benefits of a healthy workforce. In A. Day, K. Kelloway and J. Hurrell (eds.), *Workplace Well-being: How to build psychologically healthy workplaces*. Chichester: Wiley.

Cooper, C.L. and Dewe, P. (2008). Wellbeing – absenteeism and presenteeism, costs and challenges. *Occupational Medicine*, 58, 522–524.

Cooper, C.L., Field, J., Goswami, U., Jenkins, R. and Sahakian, B. (2009). *Mental Capital and Wellbeing*. Oxford: Wiley Blackwell.

Corporate Leadership Council (2002). *Building the High-Performance Workforce: A quantitative analysis of the effectiveness of performance management strategies*. Washington, DC: Corporate Leadership Council.

Cox, A., Rickard, C. and Tamkin, P. (2012). *Work organisation and innovation*. European Foundation for the Improvement of Living and Working Conditions. Available at: https://www.eurofound.europa.eu/sites/default/files/ef_publication/field_ef_document/ef1272en.pdf

Cox, P. (2010). *Spedan's Partnership: The story of John Lewis and Waitrose*. Cambridge: Labatie Books.

Cranfield University School of Management (2013). *The new vocational currency: Investing for success*. Bedford: Cranfield University School of Management. Available at: https://dspace.lib.cranfield.ac.uk/bitstream/1826/9032/1/New_Vocational_Currency.pdf

Crawford, J.O., Graveling, R.A., Cowie, H.A. and Dixon, K. (2010). The health safety and health promotion needs of older workers. *Occupational Medicine*, 60 (3), 184–192.

Cropanzano, R. and Mitchell, M.S. (2005). Social exchange theory: An interdisciplinary review. *Journal of Management*, 31, 874–900.

Davey, J. (2008). What influences retirement decisions? *Social Policy Journal of New Zealand/Te Puna Whakaaro*, 3, 110–125.

Davies, E.M.M., Dhingra, K. and Stephenson, J. (2013) *The role of line managers in retirement management and their perceptions of their role of the timing of employee retirement*. Netspar Discussion Paper #05/2013–019. Available at: http://arno.uvt.nl/show.cgi?fid=130485

De Backer, K., Desnoyers-James, I. and Moussiegt, L. (2015). 'Manufacturing services – That is (not) the question': *The role of manufacturing and services in OECD economies*. OECD Science, Technology and Industry Policy Papers #19. Paris: OECD. Available at: http://www.oecd-ilibrary.org/science-and-technology/manufacturing-or-services-that-is-not-the-question_5js64ks09dmn-en

Deci, E.L. (1971). Effects *of* externally mediated rewards on intrinsic motivation. *Journal of Personality and Social Psychology*, 18, 105–115.

Deci, E.L., Koestner, R. and Ryan, R.M (1999). A meta-analytic review of experiments examining the effects of extrinsic rewards on intrinsic motivation. *Psychological Bulletin*, 125, 627–668.

Dellot, B. (2014). *Salvation in a start-up? The origins and nature of the self-employment bloom* [online]. London: RSA Action and Research Centre. Available at: https://www.thersa.org/globalassets/pdfs/blogs/salvation-in-a-start-up-report-180714.pdf

Deloitte (2014). *Big demands and high expectations: The Deloitte Millennial Survey.* London: Deloitte. Available at: https://www2.deloitte.com/content/dam/Deloitte/global/Documents/About-Deloitte/gx-dttl-2014-millennial-survey-report.pdf

Department for Business, Innovation and Skills (BIS) (2012). *Leadership and management in the UK – The key to sustainable growth.* London: BIS. Available at: https://www.gov.uk/government/uploads/system/uploads/attachment_data/file/32327/12–923-leadership-management-key-to-sustainable-growth-evidence.pdf

Department for Business, Innovation and Skills (BIS) (2013). *Hollowing out and the future of the labour market.* London: BIS. Research Paper #134. London: Department of Business, Innovation and Skills. Available at: https://www.gov.uk/government/uploads/system/uploads/attachment_data/file/250206/bis–13–1213-hollowing-out-and-future-of-the-labour-market.pdf

Department for Business, Innovation and Skills (BIS) (2015). *UK skills and productivity in the international context.* London: Business Innovation and Skills. Research Paper #262. London: BIS. Available at: https://www.gov.uk/government/uploads/system/uploads/attachment_data/file/486500/BIS–15–704-UK-skills-and-productivity-in-an-international_context.pdf

Department of Work and Pensions (DWP) (2015). *Attitudes of the over 50s to fuller working lives.* DWP ad hoc Research Report #15. London: DWP. Available at: https://www.gov.uk/government/publications/attitudes-of-the-over–50s-to-fuller-working-lives

De Vaus, D., Wells, Y., Kendig, H. and Quine, S. (2007). Does gradual retirement have better outcomes than abrupt retirement? Results from an Australian panel study. *Ageing and Society,* 27 (5), 667–682.

Dobbs, R., Madgavkar, A., Barton, D., Labaye, E., Manyika, J., Roxburgh, C., Lund, S. and Madhav, S. (2012). *The world at work: Jobs, pay, and skills for 3.5 billion people.* McKinsey Global Institute. Available at: http://www.madrimasd.org/empleo/documentos/doc/MGI-Global_labor_Full_Report_June_2012.pdf

Donald, B. (2013). Stanford scholars find varying quality of science and tech education in Brazil, Russia, India and China. *Stanford News* [online]. Available at: http://news.stanford.edu/news/2013/august/bric-higher-ed–081913.html

Donaldson-Fielder, E., Munir, F. and Lewis, R. (2013). Leadership and employee well-being. In H. Skipton Leonard, R. Lewis, A.M. Freedman and J. Passmore (eds.), *The Wiley-Blackwell Handbook of the Psychology of Leadership, Change and Organizational Development.* London: Wiley.

Drucker, P.F. (2002). They're not employees, they're people. *Harvard Business Review,* 80, 70–77.

Dufouil, C., Pereira, E., Chêne, G., Glymour, M.M., Alpérovitch, A., Saubusse, E., Risse-Fleury, M., Heuls, B., Salord, J.-C., Brieu, M.-A. and Forette, F. (2014). Older age at retirement is associated with decreased risk of dementia. *European Journal of Epidemiology,* 29 (5), 353–361.

EEF/Jelf (2015). *Sickness Absence Survey 2015.* Available at: https://www.eef.org.uk/about-eef/media-news-and-insights/media-releases/2015/jul/government-fit-note-fails-to-deliver–5-years-on

Eisenberger, R. and Cameron, J. (1996). Detrimental effects of reward: Reality or myth? *Journal of the American Psychological Association*, 51, 1153–1166.

Employers Forum on Age and IFF Research Ltd. (2006). *Flexible retirement: A snapshot of employer practices 2006*. London: Age Partnership Group.

Equalities and Human Rights Commission (EHRC) (2007). *Enter the Time Lords: Transforming work to meet the future*. London: EHRC.

Eurofound (2007). *Annual review of working conditions in the EU 2006–2007*. Dublin: Eurofound. Available at: https://www.eurofound.europa.eu/observatories/eurwork/comparative-information/annual-review-of-working-conditions-in-the-eu–2006–2007

Eurofound (2012). *Sustainable work and the ageing workforce*. A report based on the 5th European Working Conditions Survey. Luxembourg: Publications Office of the European Union. Available at: https://www.eurofound.europa.eu/sites/default/files/ef_publication/field_ef_document/ef1266en.pdf

Eurofound (2015). *Sixth European Working Conditions Survey: 2015*. Available at: https://www.eurofound.europa.eu/surveys/european-working-conditions-surveys/sixth-european-working-conditions-survey–2015

Evans, D. (2016). An exploration of the impact of younger-onset dementia on employment. *Dementia*, 15 (2), 147–161.

Fahlenbrach, R. and Stulz, R. (2011). Bank CEO incentives and the credit crisis. *Journal of Financial Economics*, 99 (1), 11–26.

Faragher, E.B., Cooper, C.L. and Cartwright, S. (2004). ASSET: A shortened stress evaluation tool. *Stress and Health*, 20, 189–201.

Farmer, M., Brown, D., Reilly, P. and Bevan, S.M. (2013). Executive remuneration in the United Kingdom: Will the Coalition Government's latest reforms secure improvement and what else is required? *Compensation and Benefits Review*, 45 (1), 26–33.

Farmer, M.A., Alexandrou, G. and Archbold, S. (2010). New evidence of relative performance evaluation (RPE) in UK chief executive realised incentive compensation. *Corporate Law: Corporate Governance eJournal*, 2.

Felstead, A., Gallie, D., Green, F. and Inanc, H. (2013). *Work intensification in Britain: First findings from the Skills and Employment Survey, 2012*. London: Centre for Learning and Life Chances in Knowledge Economies and Societies, Institute of Education. Available at: http://www.llakes.ac.uk/sites/default/files/5.%20Work%20Intensification%20in%20Britain%20-%20mini-report.pdf

Figlio, D.N. and Kenny, L. (2007). Individual teacher incentives and student performance. *Journal of Public Economics*, 91, 901–914.

Forth, J., Bryson, A., Humphris, A., Koumenta, M. and Kleiner, M. (2011). *A review of occupational regulation and its impact*. Evidence Report #40. London: UKCES. Available at: http://dera.ioe.ac.uk/12298/1/evidence-report–40-occupational-regulation-impact.pdf

Frahm-Falkenburg, S., Ibsen, R., Kjellberg, J. and Jennum, P. (2016). Health, social and economic consequences of dementias: A comparative national cohort study. *European Journal of Neurology*, 23, 1400–1407.

Fredrickson, J.W., Davis-Blake, A. and Sanders, W.M.G. (2010). Sharing the wealth: Social comparisons and pay dispersion in the CEO's top team. *Strategic Management Journal*, 31 (10), 1031–1053.

Freeman, R. (1998). *On the divergence in unionism among developing countries.* NBER Working Paper #2817. Cambridge, MA: NBER. Available at: http://core.ac.uk/download/pdf/6708175.pdf

Freeman, R. (2006). *The Great Doubling: The challenge of the new global labor market* [online]. Berkeley, CA. Available at: http://eml.berkeley.edu/~webfac/eichengreen/e183_sp07/great_doub.pdf

Frey, C. and Osborne, M. (2013). *The future of employment: How susceptible are jobs to computerisation?* Oxford [online]. Available at: http://www.oxfordmartin.ox.ac.uk/downloads/academic/The_Future_of_Employment.pdf

Furnham, A. (1996). *The Myths of Management: Forty fables from the world of management.* London: Whurr.

Furnham, A. (2005) *The Psychology of Behaviour at Work: The individual in the organization.* Hove: Psychology Press.

Gallie, D., Felstead, A. and Green, F. (2004). Changing patterns of task discretion in Britain. *Work, Employment and Society*, 18 (2), 243–266.

Gallie, D., Felstead, A., Green, F. and Inanc, H. (2013). *Fear at work in Britain: First findings from the Skills and Employment Survey, 2012.* London: Centre for Learning and Life Chances in Knowledge Economies and Societies, Institute of Education. Available at: http://www.llakes.ac.uk/sites/default/files/4.%20Fear%20at%20Work%20in%20Britain%20-%20mini-report.pdf

Gallie, D., Felstead, A., Green, F. and Inanc, H. (2016). The hidden face of job insecurity. *Work, Employment and Society*, 31 (1), 36–53.

Garner, C., Forbes, P. and Sheldon, H. (2016). *Working anywhere: A winning formula for good work?* London: The Work Foundation. Available at: http://www.theworkfoundation.com/Reports/398/Working-Anywhere

George, J.M. and Brief, A.P. (1992). Feeling good–doing well: A conceptual analysis of the mood at work–organizational spontaneity relationship. *Psychology Bulletin*, 112, 310–329.

Gerhart, B. and Rynes, S.L. (2003). *Compensation: Theory, evidence, and strategic implications.* Thousand Oaks, CA: Sage.

Giang, V. (2013). Ranking America's biggest companies by turnover rate. *Business Insider: Slate* [online]. Available at: http://www.slate.com/blogs/business_insider/2013/07/28/turnover_rates_by_company_how_amazon_google_and_others_stack_up.html

Gilbert, C., De Winne, S. and Sels, L. (2011). The influence of line managers and HR department on employees' affective commitment. *International Journal of Human Resources Management*, 22, 1618–1637.

Gittleman, M. and Kleiner, M. (2013). *Wage effects of unionization and occupational licensing coverage in the United States.* BLS Working Paper #464. Washington, DC: US Bureau of Labor Statistics. Available at: https://www.bls.gov/ore/pdf/ec130040.pdf

Gladwell, M. (2002), The social life of paper: Looking for method in the mess. *New Yorker Magazine*, 25 March.

Glaser, K., Price, D. and McDonough, P. (2017). *The Wellbeing, Health, Retirement and Lifecourse project*. London: The Pensions Policy Institute. Available at: http://www.pensionspolicyinstitute.org.uk/publications/reports/the-wellbeing,-health,-retirement-and-the-lifecourse-project

Global Corporate Challenge (2013). *2013 Global workplace health and wellness report: A global analysis of how organisations are implementing global initiatives to create long-term employee health behaviour change*. London: Global Corporate Challenge. Available at: https://gccmarketing.blob.core.windows.net/sitecontent/2013_Global_Workplace_Health_and_Wellness_Report.pdf

GMI Ratings (2013). *2013 CEO pay survey*. Available at: https://www.scribd.com/document/178268688/GMI-Ratings–2013-CEO-Pay-Survey

Goodman, S. and Turner, L. (2009). *Teacher incentive pay and educational outcomes: Evidence from the NYC Bonus Program*. Program on Education Policy and Governance Working Papers Series, Columbia University. Available at: http://educationnext.org/files/ednext_20112_GoodmanTurner_Unabridged.pdf

Goos, M. and Manning, A. (2003). *Lousy and lovely jobs: The rising polarization of work in Britain*. London: Centre for Economic Performance, LSE. Available at: http://eprints.lse.ac.uk/20002/1/Lousy_and_Lovely_Jobs_the_Rising_Polarization_of_Work_in_Britain.pdf

Gosling, T. (2017). *The Purposeful Company Executive Remuneration Report*. London: The Big Innovation Centre.

Green, F. (2013). *Is Britain such a bad place to work? The level and dispersion of job quality in comparative European perspective*. LLAKES Research Paper #40. London: Centre for Learning and Life Chances in Knowledge Economies and Societies, Institute of Education. Available at: http://www.llakes.ac.uk/sites/default/files/Francis%20Green%20paper.pdf

Green, F. and Mostafa, T. (2012). *Trends in job quality in Europe*. Available at: https://www.eurofound.europa.eu/publications/report/2012/working-conditions/trends-in-job-quality-in-europe

Green, F., Mostafa, T., Parent-Thirion, A., Vermeylen, G., Van Houten, G., Biletta, I. and Lyly-Yrjanainen, M. (2013). Is job quality becoming more unequal? *International Labor Review*, 66 (4), 753–784.

Greenbury, R. (1995). *Final report of the Study Group on Directors' Remuneration*. London: Confederation of British Industry.

Gregg, P. and Gardiner, L. (2015). *A steady job? The UK's record on labour market security and stability since the millennium* [online]. London: Resolution Foundation. Available at: http://www.resolutionfoundation.org/app/uploads/2015/07/A-steady-job.pdf

Gregg, P., Jewell, S. and Tonks, I. (2005). *Executive pay and performance in the UK 1994–2002*. CPMO Working Paper Series #05/122. Bristol: The Centre for Market and Public Organisation. Available at: http://www.bristol.ac.uk/media-library/sites/cmpo/migrated/documents/wp122.pdf

Gregg, P., Jewell, S. and Tonks, I. (2012). Executive pay and performance: Did bankers' bonuses cause the crisis? *International Review of Finance*, 12 (1), 89–122.

Guest, D.E. (2004). Flexible employment contracts, the psychological contract and employee outcomes: An analysis and review of the evidence. *International Journal of Management Reviews*, 5, 1–19.

Guest, D.E. and Conway, N. (2002). Communicating the psychological contract: An employer perspective. *Human Resource Management Journal*, 12, 22–38.

Guillemard A.-M. (2013). Prolonging working life in an aging world: A cross-national perspective on labor market and welfare policies toward active aging. In J. Field, R. Burke and C. Cooper (eds.), *The SAGE Handbook of Aging, Work and Society*. London: Sage.

Guzzo, R.A., Jette, R.D. and Katzell, R.A. (1985). The effects of psychologically based intervention programs on worker productivity. *Personnel Psychology*, 38, 275–292.

Haldane, A. (2017) *Productivity puzzles*. A speech by Andy Haldane. Available at: www.bankofengland.co.uk/publications/Documents/speeches/2017/speech968.pdf

Hales, C. (2005). Rooted in supervision, branching into management: Continuity and change in the role of the first line manager. *Journal of Management Studies*, 42, 471–506.

Hansson, E., Mattisson, K., Bjork, J., Ostergen, P. and Jakobsson, K. (2011). Relationship between commuting and health outcomes in a cross-sectional population survey in southern Sweden. *BMC Public Health*, 11, 834.

Harris, L., Doughty, D. and Kirk, S. (2002). The devolution of HR responsibilities – perspectives from the UK's public sector. *Journal of European Industrial Training*, 26, 218–229.

Harrop, A. and Jopling, K. (2009). *One voice – Shaping our ageing society*, London: Age UK. Available at: https://www.ageuk.org.uk/documents/en-gb/for-professionals/research/one%20voice%20(2009)_pro.pdf?dtrk=true

Haynes, B. and Price, I. (2004). Quantifying the complex adaptive workplace. *Facilities*, 22 (1/2), 8–18.

Health and Safety Executive (HSE) (2003). *Management Standards on Workplace Stress*. London: HSE.

Health and Safety Executive (HSE) (2015). *Self-reported work-related ill health and workplace injuries*. Runcorn: HSE. Available at: www.hse.gov.uk/statistics/lfs/#illness.

Health and Safety Executive (HSE) (2016). *Appraisal values or 'unit costs'*. London: HSE. Available at: www.hse.gov.uk/economics/eauappraisal.htm (accessed October 2015).

Heron, R., Bevan, S. and Varney, J. (2016). Health and employment. In S. Davies (ed.), *Baby Boomers: Fit for the Future*. Annual Report of the Chief Medical Officer, 2015. London: Department of Health.

Herriot, P., Manning, W.E.G. and Kidd, J.M. (1997). The content of the psychological contract. *British Journal of Management*, 8, 151–162.

Herriot, P. and Pemberton, C. (1997). Facilitating new deals. *Human Resource Management Journal*, 7, 45–56.

Hershey, D., Mowen, J. and Jacobs-Lawson, J. (2003). An experimental comparison of retirement planning intervention seminars. *Journal of Educational Gerontology*, 29 (4), 339–359.

Herzberg, F. (1968). One more time: How do we motivate employees? *Harvard Business Review*, 46 (1), 53–62.

High Pay Centre (2015). *The state of pay: High Pay Centre briefing on executive pay*. London: High Pay Centre. Available at: http://highpaycentre.org/files/The_State_of_Pay_2015.pdf

Hildyard, L. (2013). *Huge executive salaries are vital to UK competitiveness*. London: New Economics Foundation. Available at: http://highpaycentre.org/files/NEF_mythbuster.pdf

Hill, K.B., Burke, F.J.T., Brown, J., Macdonald, E.B., Morris, J.A., White, D.A. and Murray, K. (2010). Dental practitioners and ill health retirement: a qualitative investigation into the causes and effects. *British Dental Journal*, 209 (5), E8.

Hillage, J., Holmes, J., Rickard, C., Marvell, R., Taskila, T., Bajorek, Z., Bevan, S. and Brine, J. (2015). *Workplace policy and management practices to improve the health of employees: Evidence Reviews 1, 2 and 3*. NICE Guideline #NG13. London: National Institute for Health and Care Excellence.

Hitlin, P. (2016). *Research in the crowdsourcing age: A case study* [online]. Washington, DC: Pew Research Center. Available at: http://www.pewinternet.org/2016/07/11/research-in-the-crowdsourcing-age-a-case-study/

Holzer, H. (2015). *Job market polarization and US worker skills: A tale of two middles*. Washing ton, DC: Economic Studies, Brookings Institution. Available at: https://www.brookings.edu/research/job-market-polarization-and-u-s-worker-skills-a-tale-of-two-middles/

Homkes, R. (2014). *What role will leadership play in driving the future of UK manufacturing?* Foresight Future of Manufacturing Project Evidence Paper #15. London: Government Office for Science. Available at: https://www.gov.uk/government/uploads/system/uploads/attachment_data/file/302792/13–825-future-manufacturing-leadership.pdf

Hopley, L. (2014). *Backing Britain . . . The reshoring story continues*. The Engineering Employers Federation [online]. Available at: https://www.eef.org.uk/campaigning/news-blogs-and-publications/blogs/2014/mar/backing-britain--the-reshoring-story-continues

Hsu, Y.-S. (2013). Training older workers: A review. In J. Field, R. Burke and C.L. Cooper (eds.), *The SAGE Handbook of Aging, Work and Society*. London: Sage.

Hurka, T. (2003). Desert: Individualistic and holistic. In S. Olsaretti (ed.), *Desert and Justice* (pp. 45–68). Oxford: Clarendon Press.

Hutchinson, S. (2008). *The role of first line managers in bringing policies to life*. Bristol: Centre for Employment Studies Research, Bristol Business School, University of the West of England.

Hutchinson, S. and Purcell, J. (2007). *Line Managers in Reward, Learning and Development: Research into practice*. London: CIPD.

Hutchinson, S. and Purcell, C. (2010). Managing ward managers for roles in HRM and NHS: Overworked and under-resourced. *Human Resource Management Journal*, 20, 357–374.

Hutchinson, S. and Tailby, S. (2012). Strategic HR and the line: How can front-line managers manage? Paper presented at the 11th World Congress of IFSAM, University of Limerick.

Hutton, W. (2010). *Are We Heading for a Fairer Workplace?* London: The Work Foundation.

Hutton, W. (2011). *Hutton Review of Fair Pay in the Public Sector: Final Report.* London: HMSO.

Hutton, W. and Bevan, S. (2005). Why pure economics cannot work in Europe. *European Business Forum,* Winter, 7–9.

Huwart, J.Y. and Verdier, L. (2013). *Economic Globalisation: Origins and consequences.* OECD Insights. Paris: OECD Publishing.

Institute of Health Equity (2010) *Fair Society, Healthy Lives: Strategic review of health inequalities post 2010.* London: Institute for Health Equity. Available at: http://www.parliament.uk/documents/fair-society-healthy-lives-full-report.pdf

International Labor Organization (ILO) (2015). *World employment and social outlook: The changing nature of jobs.* Geneva: ILO. Available at: http://www.ilo.org/global/research/global-reports/weso/2015-changing-nature-of-jobs/WCMS_368626/lang--en/index.htm

International Labor Organization (ILO) (undated) *Job Security Index.* Available at: http://www.ilo.org/sesame/SESHELP.NoteJSI

International Longevity Centre-UK (ILC-UK) (2015). *The missing million: Pathways back into employment.* Business in the Community Research Report. London: ILC-UK. Available at: http://www.ilcuk.org.uk/index.php/publications/publication_details/the_missing_million_pathways_back_into_employment

Jahoda, M. (1982). *Employment and Unemployment: A social-psychological analysis.* Cambridge: Cambridge University Press.

Jenkins, A.K., Poulston, J. and Davies, E.M.M. (2014). The working lives of older hotel workers: Is there evidence of psychological disengagement in the work-to-retirement transition zone? Presentation to the Council for Hospitality Management Education Annual Research Conference, 28–30 May, Buxton, Derby, UK (unpublished).

Jenkins G.D., Mitra, A., Gupta, N. and Shaw, J.D. (1998). Are financial incentives related to performance? A meta-analytic review of empirical research. *Journal of Applied Psychology,* 83 (5), 777–787.

Jensen, M. and Murphy, K. (1990). Performance pay and top management incentives. *Journal of Political Economy,* 98, 225–264.

Jones, A., Visser, F., Coats, D., Bevan, S. and McVerry, A. (2007). *Transforming Work: Reviewing the case for change and new ways of working.* Manchester: Equal Opportunities Commission.

Jones, A. and Williams, L. (2005). *How ICT? Managing at the Front Line.* London: The Work Foundation.

Jones, M.R. (1955). Introduction. In M.R. Jones (ed.), *Nebraska Symposium on Motivation.* Lincoln, NE: University of Nebraska Press.

Judge, L. and Tomlinson, D. (2016), *Secret agents: Agency workers in the new world of work* [online]. London: Resolution Foundation. Available at: http://www.resolutionfoundation.org/publications/secret-agents-agency-workers-in-the-new-world-of-work/

Kant, I. (1997). *Lectures on Ethics.* Trans. P. Heath. Cambridge: Cambridge University Press.

Katz, L. and Krueger, A. (2016). *The rise and nature of alternative work arrangements in the United States, 1995–2015* [online]. Cambridge, MA: National Bureau of Economic Research. Available at: https://krueger.princeton.edu/sites/default/files/akrueger/files/katz_krueger_cws_-_march_29_20165.pdf

Kessler, I. (2007). Reward choices: Strategy and equity. In J. Storey (ed.) *Resource Management: A Critical Text*. London: Thomson Learning.

Kohn, A. (1993). Why incentive plans cannot work. *Harvard Business Review*, September/ October. Available at: https://hbr.org/1993/09/why-incentive-plans-cannot-work

Kotter, J.P. (1990). What leaders really do? *Harvard Business Review*, December. Available at: http://www.machon-adler.co.il/readers/reader32.pdf

Kotterman, J. (2006). Leadership versus management: What's the difference? *Journal for Quality and Participation*, 29 (2), 13–17.

Koumenta, M., Humphris, A., Kleiner, M. and Pagliero, M. (2014). *Occupational regulation in the EU and the UK: Prevalence and labour market impacts*. London: BIS. Available at: https://www.gov.uk/government/uploads/system/uploads/attachment_data/file/343554/bis-14–999-occupational-regulation-in-the-EU-and-UK.pdf

Kumble, J. and Kelly, N.J. (1999). Leadership versus management. *Supervision*, 61, 8–10.

Kunze, F. and Boehm, S. (2013). Research on age diversity in the workforce: current trends and future research directions. In J. Field, R. Burke and C.L. Cooper (eds.), *The SAGE Handbook of Aging, Work and Society*. London: Sage.

Kunze, F. and Menges, J. (2016). Younger supervisors, older subordinates: An organisational-level study of age differences, emotions, and performance, *Journal of Organisational Behaviour*, 38 (4), 461–486

Labriola, M., Christensen, K.B., Lund, T., Nielsen, M.L. and Diderichsen, F. (2006). Multilevel analysis of workplace and individual risk factors for long-term sickness absence. *Journal of Occupational Environmental Medicine*, 48, 923–929.

Lai, Y., Saridakis, G. and Blackburn, R. (2015). Job stress in the United Kingdom: Are small and medium-sized enterprises and large enterprises different? *Stress Health*, 31 (3), 222–235.

Lambert, R. (2010). Speech to Royal Society of Arts, 30 March.

Lawler E. (1971). *Pay and Organizational Effectiveness: A psychological view*. New York: McGraw-Hill.

Lawler, E.E. (2002). The folly of forced ranking. *Strategy and Business*, 28, 28–32.

Lazear, E.P. (2000). Performance pay and productivity. *America Economic Review*, 90 (5): 1346–1361.

Leigh, A. (2013). The economics and politics of teacher merit pay. *CESifo Economic Studies*, 59 (1), 1–33.

Levine, L. (2012). *Offshoring and job loss among US workers*. Congressional Research Service. Available at: https://www.fas.org/sgp/crs/misc/RL32292.pdf

Locke, E.A. (1968). Toward a theory of task motivation and incentives. *Organizational Behavior and Human Performance*, 3, 157–189.

Locke, E.A., Bryan, J.F. and Kendall, L.M. (1968). Goals and intentions as mediators of the effects of monetary incentives on behavior. *Journal of Applied Psychology*, 52, 104–121.

Locke, E.A., Feren, D.B., McCaleb, V.M., Shaw, K.N. and Denny, A.T. (1980). The relative effectiveness of four methods of motivating employee performance. In K.D. Duncan, M.M. Gruenberg and D. Wallis (eds.), *Changes in Working Life* (pp. 363?388). New York: Wiley.

Locke, E.A. and Latham, G.P. (1990). *A Theory of Goal Setting and Task Performance.* Englewood Cliffs, NJ: Prentice-Hall.

Loretto, W. and White, P. (2006). Employers' attitudes, practices and policies towards older workers. *Human Resource Management Journal*, 16 (3), 313–330.

Los, B., Timmer, M.P. and De Vries, G. (2014). *The demand for skills 1995–2008: A global supply chain perspective.* OECD Economics Department Working Paper #1141. Paris: OECD. Available at: http://www.oecd-ilibrary.org/economics/the-demand-for-skills–1995–2008_5jz123g0f5lp-en?crawler=true

Lunenburg, F.C. (2011). Leadership versus management: A key distinction – at least in theory. *International Journal of Management, Business, and Administration*, 14, 1–4.

MacKenzie, S.B., Podsakoff, P.M. and Fetter, R. (1991). Organizational citizenship behavior and objective productivity as determinants of managers' evaluations of performance. *Organizational Behavior and Human Decision Processes*, 50, 1–28.

MacKenzie, S.B., Podsakoff, P.M. and Fetter, R. (1993). The impact of organizational citizenship behavior on evaluations of salesperson performance. *Journal of Marketing*, 57 (1), 70–80.

Macleod, A., Worman, D., Wilton, P., Woodman, P. and Hutchings, P. (2010). *Managing an ageing workforce: How employers are adapting to an older labour market.* London: CIPD/CMI. Available at: http://www.equality-ne.co.uk/downloads/675_ageing-workforce.pdf

MacLeod, D. and Clarke, N. (2009). *Engaging for Success: Enhancing performance through employee engagement.* London: Department for Business Innovation and Skills.

Mahy, B., Rycx, F. and Volral, M. (2011). Wage dispersion and firm productivity in different working environments. *British Journal of Industrial Relations*, 49 (3), 460–485.

Maitland, A. (2010). *Working better: The over 50s, the new work generation.* London: Equality and Human Rights Commission. Available at: https://www.dcu.ie/sites/default/files/agefriendly/workingbetter_over_50s.pdf

Mangham, I. and Pye, A. (1991). *The Doing of Managing.* Oxford: Blackwell.

Manyika, J., Woetzel, J., Dobbs, R., Remes, J., Labaye, E. and Jordan, A. (2015). *Can long term growth be saved?* New York: McKinsey & Company [online]. Available at: http://www.mckinsey.com/global-themes/employment-and-growth/can-long-term-global-growth-be-saved

Marmot, M. (2006). *Status Syndrome: How your social standing directly affects your health and life expectancy.* London: Bloomsbury.

Marmot, M. (2010). *Fair Society, Healthy Lives: The Marmot Review: Strategic review of health inequalities in England post–2010.* London: Department for International Development.

Marsden, D. and French, S. (1998). *What a performance: Performance related pay in the public services.* Centre for Economic Performance special papers, CEPSP #10. London: Centre for Economic Performance, LSE. Available at: http://eprints.lse.ac.uk/4421/1/what_a_performance.pdf

Martin, G., Dymock, D., Billett, S. and Johnson, G. (2014). In the name of meritocracy: Managers' perceptions of policies and practices for training older workers. *Ageing and Society*, 34 (6), 992–1018.

Marvell, R. and Cox, A. (2017). *Fulfilling work: What do older workers value about work and why?* Brighton: Institute of Employment Studies and Centre for Ageing Better. Available at: https://www.ageing-better.org.uk/publications/fulfilling-work-what-do-older-workers-value-about-work-and-why

Maslach, C., Schaufeli, W.B. and Leiter, M.P. (2001). Job burnout. *Annual Review of Psychology*, 52, 397–422.

Maslow, G.R., Haydon, A., McRee, A.L., Ford, C.A. and Halpern, C.T. (2011). Growing up with a chronic illness: Social success, educational/vocational distress. *Journal of Adolescent Health*, 49 (2), 206–212.

Mayo, E. (1949). *Hawthorne and the Western Electric Company: The social problems of an industrial civilisation*. London: Routledge.

McBain, R., Ghobadian, A., Switzer, J., Wilton, P., Woodman, P. and Pearson, G. (2012). *The Business Benefits of Management and Leadership Development*. London: CMI/Penna.

McConville, T. and Holden, L. (1999). The filling in the sandwich: HRM and middle managers in the health sector. *Personnel Review*, 28, 406–424.

McCulloch, S., Robertson, R. and Kirkpatrick, P. (2016). Sustaining people with dementia or mild cognitive impairment in employment: A systematic review of qualitative evidence. *British Journal of Occupational Therapy*, 79 (11), 682–692.

McEnhill, L. and Steadman, K. (2015). *This won't hurt a bit: Supporting small businesses to be healthy, wealthy and wise.* London: The Work Foundation. Available at: http://www.theworkfoundation.com/wp-content/uploads/2016/11/393_This_wont_hurt-abit-main_report.pdf

McGill University (2016). 'Smart soles' in shoes to help patients recover from a broken hip. *McGill Reporter.* Available at: http://publications.mcgill.ca/reporter/2016/03/smart-soles-in-shoes-to-help-patients-recover-from-a-broken-hip/

McGowan, M., Andrews, D. and Millot. V. (2017). *The walking dead? Zombie firms and productivity performance in* OECD *countries*. Economics Department Working Paper #1372. Paris: OECD. Available at: www.oecd.org/eco/growth/The-Walking-Dead-Zombie-Firms-and-Productivity-Performance-in-OECD-Countries.pdf

McGuinness, R. (2014). Take down that slide: Why wacky office spaces don't always work. *The Metro*, 30 April. Available at: http://metro.co.uk/2014/04/30/take-down-that-slide-why-wacky-office-spaces-dont-always-work–4712558/#ixzz4KPTUmEH8

McKay, S. and Simpson, I. (2016). Work: Attitudes and experiences of work in a changing labour market. *British Social Attitudes*, 33, 1 –24. Available at: http://www.bsa.natcen.ac.uk/media/39061/bsa33_work.pdf

McLean Parks, J., Kidder, D. and Gallagher, D. (1998). Fitting square pegs into round holes: Mapping the domain of contingent work arrangements onto the psychological contract. *Journal of Organizational Behavior*, 19, 697–730.

McNair, S. (2006). How different is the older labour market? Attitudes to work and retirement among older people in Britain. *Social Policy and Society*, 5 (4), 485–494.

Mein, G., Martikainen, P., Hemingway, H., Stansfeld, S. and Marmot, M. (2003). Is retirement good or bad for mental and physical health functioning? Whitehall II

Longitudinal study of civil servants. *Journal of Epidemiology and Community Health*, 57, 46–49.

Metcalf, D. (2005). *British unions: Resurgence or perdition.* London: The Work Foundation. Available at: www.theworkfoundation.com/Reports/68/British-unions-resurgence-or-perdition 2005.

Mintzberg, H. (1990). The manager's job: Folklore and fact. *Harvard Business Review*, 68, 163–176.

Mishel, L. (2006). *CEO-minimum wage ratio soars.* Economic Snapshot, Economic Policy Institute. Available at: http://www.epi.org/publication/webfeatures_snapshots_20060627/

Molloy, R., Smith, C.L., Trezzi, R. and Wozniak, A. (2016) *Understanding declining fluidity in the US labor market.* BPEA Conference Paper, Brookings Papers on Economic Activity. Available at: http://www.brookings.edu/about/projects/bpea/papers/2016/molloy-et-al-declining-fluidity

Morrell, G. and Tennant, R. (2010). *Pathways to retirement: The influence of employer policy and practice on retirement decisions.* DWP Research Report #673. London: Department for Work and Pensions. Available at: https://www.gov.uk/government/uploads/system/uploads/attachment_data/file/214444/rrep673.pdf

Motowidlo, S.J. and Schmit, M.J (1999). Performance assessment in unique jobs. In D.R. Ligen and E.D. Pulakos (eds.), *The Changing Nature of Job Performance: Implications for staffing, motivation, and development* (pp. 56–86). San Francisco, CA: Jossey-Bass.

Mountford, H. (2013). 'I'll take care of you': The use of supportive work practices to retain older workers. *Asia Pacific Journal of Human Resources*, 51 (3), 272–291.

Munir, F., Burr, H., Hansen, J.H., Rugulies, R. and Nielsen, K. (2011). Do positive psychosocial work factors protect against 2-year incidence of long-term sickness absence among employees with and those without depressive symptoms? A prospective study. *Journal of Psychosomatic Research*, 70, 3–9.

Nathan, M. and Doyle, J. (2002). *The State of the Office: The politics and geography of working space.* London: The Work Foundation.

National Institute for Adult and Continuing Learning (NIACE) (2015). *Mid Life Career Review: Pilot Project Outcomes: Phases 1, 2, and 3 (2013–2015).* Final report to the Department for Business, Innovation and Skills. Available at: http://www.learningandwork.org.uk/wp-content/uploads/2017/01/MLCR-Final-Report.pdf

National Institute of Health and Care Excellence (NICE) (2009). *Mental Wellbeing at Work.* Public Health Guideline #PH22. London: NICE.

Naylor, C., Parsonage, M., McDaid, D., Knapp, M., Fossey, M. and Galea, A. (2012) *Long-term conditions and mental health: The cost of co-morbidities.* London: The King's Fund. Available at: https://www.kingsfund.org.uk/sites/default/files/field/field_publication_file/long-term-conditions-mental-health-cost-comorbidities-naylor-feb12.pdf

Neal, D. (2011). *The design of performance pay in education.* NBER Working Paper #16710. Cambridge, MA: National Bureau of Economic Research. Available at: http://www.nber.org/papers/w16710

Nicholson, P., Mayho, G. and Sharp, S. (2015). *Cognitive Enhancing Drugs and the Workplace.* London: British Medical Association.

Noone, J., Alpass, F. and Stephens, C. (2010). Do men and women differ in their retirement planning? Testing a theoretical model of gendered pathways to retirement preparation. *Research on Aging*, 32 (6), 715–738.

Noone, J., O'Loughlin, K and Kendig, H. (2013). Australian baby boomers retiring 'early': Understanding the benefits of retirement preparation for involuntary and voluntary retirees. *Journal of Aging Studies*, 27 (3), 207–217.

Noone, J., Stephens, C. and Alpass, F. (2009). Preretirement planning and well-being in later life: A prospective study. *Research on Aging*, 31 (3), 295–317.

Oakman, J. and Howie, L. (2013). How can organisations influence their older employees' decision of when to retire? *Work*, 45, 389–397.

OECD (1997). *Employment outlook. Economic performance and the structure of collective bargaining*. Paris: OECD. Available at: http://www.keepeek.com/Digital-Asset-Management/oecd/social-issues-migration-health/oecd-employment-outlook–1997_empl_outlook–1997-en#page3

OECD (2007). *Offshoring and employment: Trends and impacts*. Paris: OECD. Available at: http://www.oecd.org/sti/ind/offshoringandemploymenttrendsandimpacts.htm

OECD (2012). *Employment outlook, Figure 3.12*. Paris: OECD. Available at: http://www.keepeek.com/Digital-Asset-Management/oecd/employment/oecd-employment-outlook–2012/labour-losing-to-capital-what-explains-the-declining-labour-share_empl_outlook–2012-4-en

OECD (2013a) *Employment outlook*. Paris: OECD. Available at: http://www.oecd.org/els/employmentoutlook-previouseditions.htm

OECD (2013b). *Trade union membership database*. Paris: OECD. Available at: https://stats.oecd.org/Index.aspx?DataSetCode=UN_DEN 2013

OECD (2014a). *Education at a glance*. Paris: OECD. Available at: http://www.keepeek.com/Digital-Asset-Management/oecd/education/education-at-a-glance–2014_eag–2014-en#page145

OECD (2014b). *Employment outlook*. Paris: OECD. Available at: http://www.oecd-ilibrary.org/employment/oecd-employment-outlook–2014_empl_outlook–2014-en

OECD (2014c). *Non-regular employment, job security and the labour market divide*. Paris: OECD. Available at: http://www.oecd-ilibrary.org/employment/oecd-employment-outlook–2014/non-regular-employment-job-security-and-the-labour-market-divide_empl_outlook–2014-7-en

OECD (2015). *Fit Mind, Fit Job: From evidence to practice in mental health and work*. Paris: OECD.

OECD (2016a). *Education at a glance*. Paris: OECD. Available at: http://www.keepeek.com/Digital-Asset-Management/oecd/education/education-at-a-glance–2016/indicator-a6-what-are-the-earnings-advantages-from-education_eag–2016–12-en#.WcUwp1tSyUl

OECD (2016b). *Entrepreneurship at a glance 2016*. Paris: OECD. Available at: http://www.oecd-ilibrary.org/industry-and-services/entrepreneurship-at-a-glance–2016_entrepreneur_aag–2016-en;jsessionid=1h458blddt9sg.x-oecd-live–03

OECD (2016c). *Health at a Glance*. Paris: OECD.

OECD (2016d). *How good is your job? Measuring and assessing job quality*. Paris: OECD. Available at: http://www.oecd.org/employment/labour-stats/Job-quality-OECD.pdf

OECD (2016e). *International migration outlook.* Paris: OECD. Available at: http://www. keepeek.com/Digital-Asset-Management/oecd/social-issues-migration-health/ international-migration-outlook–2016_migr_outlook–2016-en#page117

OECD (2016f). *The risk of automation for jobs in* OECD *countries.* Social, Employment and Migration Working Papers. Paris: OECD. Available at: http://www.oecd-ilibrary. org/social-issues-migration-health/the-risk-of-automation-for-jobs-in-oecd-countries_5jlz9h56dvq7-en

OECD (2017a). *Gross domestic spending on R&D.* Paris: OECD. Available at: https://data. oecd.org/rd/gross-domestic-spending-on-r-d.htm

OECD (2017b). *Population with tertiary education.* Paris: OECD. Available at: https:// data.oecd.org/eduatt/population-with-tertiary-education.htm

Office for Budget Responsibility (OBR) (2016). *Economic and fiscal outlook.* Cm 9212. London: OGL. Available at: http://cdn.budgetresponsibility.org.uk/March2016EFO.pdf

Office for National Statistics (ONS) (2012). *Older workers in the labour market.* Statistical Release, 13 June, London: ONS.

Office for National Statistics (ONS) (2013). *Cancer registration statistics, England 2013.* London: ONS. Available at: www.ons.gov.uk/ons/dcp171778 _ 4 09714.pdf.

Office for National Statistics (ONS) (2014a). *National statistics: Trade union statistics.* London: ONS. Available at: https://www.gov.uk/government/statistics/trade-union-statistics–2014

Office for National Statistics (ONS) (2014b). *Self-employed workers in the UK – 2014.* London: ONS. Available at: http://webarchive.nationalarchives.gov. uk/20160105210312/http://www.ons.gov.uk/ons/rel/lmac/self-employed-workers-in-the-uk/2014/rep-self-employed-workers-in-the-uk–2014.html

Office for National Statistics (ONS) (2014c). *Sickness absence in the labour market: 24 February – Analysis describing sickness absence rates of employees in the labour market.* London: ONS. Available at: https://www.ons.gov.uk/employmentandlabourmarket/ peopleinwork/labourproductivity/articles/ sicknessabsenceinthelabourmarket/2014–02–25

Office for National Statistics (ONS) (2014d). *Statistical bulletin: Annual survey of hours and earnings: 2014 provisional results.* London: ONS. Available at: http://www.ons.gov. uk/ons/rel/ashe/annual-survey-of-hours-and-earnings/2014-provisional-results/ stb-ashe-statistical-bulletin–2014.html#tab-The-make-up-of-earnings

Office for National Statistics (ONS) (2014e). *Statistical bulletin: International comparisons of productivity – Final estimates: 2012.* London: ONS. Available at: https://www.ons. gov.uk/economy/economicoutputandproductivity/productivitymeasures/bulletins/ internationalcomparisonsofproductivityfinalestimates/2014–02–20

Office for National Statistics (ONS) (2015a). *Labour market release.* London: ONS. Available at: http://www.ons.gov.uk/ons/publications/re-reference-tables. html?edition=tcm%3A77–357108

Office for National Statistics (ONS) (2015b). *Participation rates in the UK – 2014–3. Older people.* London: ONS. Available at: https://www.ons.gov.uk/employmentandlabour market/peopleinwork/employmentandemployeetypes/compendium/participation ratesintheuklabourmarket/2015–03–19/participationratesintheuk20143olderpeople

Office for National Statistics (ONS) (2017). *Contracts that do not guarantee a minimum number of hours*. London: ONS. Available at: https://www.ons.gov.uk/employment andlabourmarket/peopleinwork/earningsandworkinghours/articles/contractsthat donotguaranteeaminimumnumberofhours/may2017

Ogbonnaya, C., Daniels, K., Connolly, S. and Van Veldhoven, M. (2013). Do high performance work practices promote positive employee attitudes or do they intensify work? British Academy of Management Conference, Liverpool.

Oxera Consulting (2007). *Tax-advantaged employee share schemes: Analysis of productivity effects Report 2: Productivity measured using gross value added*. HMRC Research Report #33. London: HM Revenue and Customs.

Pachito, D.V., Eckeli, A.L., Desouky, A.S., Corbett, M.A., Partonen, T., Wilson Rajaratnam, S.M. and Riera, R. (2016). Workplace lighting for improving mood and alertness in daytime workers. *Cochrane Database of Systematic Reviews*, 6: CD012243.

Parker, L. and Bevan, S. (2011). *Good Work and Our Times: Final Report of the Good Work Commission*. London: The Work Foundation.

Perry, J., Engbers, T. and Yun Jun, S. (2009). Back to the future? Performance-related pay, empirical research and the perils of persistence. *Public Administration Review*, 69, 39–51.

Pfeffer, J. (1998). Six dangerous myths about pay. *Harvard Business Review*, 76 (3), 109–119.

Pfeffer, J. and Langton, N. (1993). The effect of wage dispersion on satisfaction, productivity and working collaboratively: Evidence from college and university faculty. *Administrative Science Quarterly*, 38 (3), 382–407.

Pillai, R., Rankin, J. and Stanley, K. (2007). *Disability 2020: Opportunities for the full and equal citizenship of disabled people in Britain in 2020*. London: Institute for Public Policy Research. Available at: https://www.ippr.org/files/images/media/files/publication/2011/05/Disability_2020_full_1568.pdf

Pillay, H.K., Kelly, K. and Tones, M.J. (2010). Supporting the mature aged workforce. *New Zealand Journal of Human Resource Management*, 10 (1), 13–26.

Pond, R., Stephens, C. and Alpass, F. (2010). How health affects retirement decisions: Three pathways taken by middle-older aged New Zealanders. *Ageing and Society*, 30 (3), 527–545.

Porter, L.W. and Lawler, E.E. (1965). Properties of organization structure in relation to job attitudes and job behavior. *Psychological Bulletin*, 64 (1), 23–51.

Porter, L.W and Lawler, E.E. (1968). *Managerial Attitudes and Performance*. Homewood, IL: Dorsey Press.

Porter, M.E. and Ketels, C.H.M. (2003). *UK competitiveness: Moving to the next stage*. DTI Economics Paper #3. London: ESRC. Available at: http://webarchive.nationalarchives.gov.uk/20121205151147/http://www.bis.gov.uk/files/file14771.pdf

PricewaterhouseCoopers (PwC) (2008). *Building the case for wellness*. London: PwC. Available at: http://www.pulsescreening.co.uk/Corporate/dwp-wellness-report-public.pdf

PricewaterhouseCoopers (PwC) (2017). *Workforce of the future: The competing forces shaping 2030*. London: PwC. Available at: http://www.pwc.com/gx/en/services/people-organisation/workforce-of-the-future/workforce-of-the-future-the-competing-forces-shaping–2030-pwc.pdf

Purcell, J. and Hutchinson, S. (2007). Front line managers as agents in the HRM-performance causal chain: theory, analysis and evidence. *Human Resources Journal*, 17 (1), 3–20.

Quine, S., Bernard, D. and Kendig, H. (2006). Understanding baby boomers' expectations and plans for their retirement: Findings from a qualitative study. *Australasian Journal on Ageing*, 25 (3), 145–150.

Ray, K., Foley, B., Tsang, T., Walne, D. and Bajorek, Z. (2014). *A review of the evidence on the impact, effectiveness and value for money of performance-related pay in the public sector.* London: The Work Foundation. Available at: https://www.gov.uk/government/uploads/system/uploads/attachment_data/file/381600/PRP_final_report_TWF_Nov_2014.pdf

Reilly, P. (2003). *The Link between Pay and Performance*. Brighton: Institute for Employment Studies.

Renwick, D. and MacNeil, C.M. (2002). Line manager involvement in careers. *Career Development International*, 7, 407–414.

Reynolds, F., Farrow, A. and Blank, A. (2012). 'Otherwise it would be nothing but cruises': Exploring the subjective benefits of working beyond 65. *International Journal of Ageing in Later Life*, 7 (1), 79–106.

Rhoades, L. and Eisenberger, R. (2002). Perceived organizational support: A review of the literature. *Journal of Applied Psychology*, 87, 698–714.

Rice, N.E., Lang, I.A., Henley, W. and Melzer, D. (2011). Common health predictors of early retirement: Findings from the English Longitudinal Study of Ageing. *Age and Ageing*, 40 (1), 54–61.

Ritchie, L., Banks, P., Danson, M. and Borrowman, F. (2015). Dementia in the workplace: A review. *Journal of Public Mental Health*, 14 (1), 24–34.

Roberts, P. (2010). The offshore outsourcing of American jobs: A greater threat than terrorism. *Global Research* [online]. Available at: https://www.globalresearch.ca/the-offshore-outsourcing-of-american-jobs-a-greater-threat-than-terrorism/18725

Robertson, I. and Cooper, C.L. (2010a). *Well-being: Productivity and happiness at work.* Basingstoke: Palgrave Macmillan.

Robertson, I.T. and Cooper, C.L. (2010b). Full engagement: the integration of employee engagement and psychological well-being. *Leadership and Organization Development Journal*, 31 (4), 324–336.

Robertson, J. (2013). Side by side: A workplace engagement program for people with younger onset dementia. *Dementia*, 12 (5), 666–674.

Robinson, D., Perryman, S. and Hayday, S. (2004). *The Drivers of Employee Engagement.* Brighton: IES.

Robinson, S.L. and Rousseau, D.M. (1994). Violating the psychological contract: Not the exception but the norm. *Journal of Organizational Behavior*, 15, 245–259.

Rolfe, H., Rienzo, C., Lalani, M. and Portes, J. (2013). *Migration and productivity: Employers' practices, public attitudes and statistical evidence.* National Institute of Economic and Social Research. Available at: http://www.niesr.ac.uk/sites/default/files/publications/Migration%20productivity%20final.pdf

Rothaermel, F.T. and Hess, A.M. (2007). Building dynamic capabilities: Innovation driven by individual-, firm-, and network-level effects. *Organization Science*, 18 (6): 898–921.

Rousseau, D.M. (1989). Psychological and implied contracts in organizations. *Employee Responsibilities and Rights Journal*, 2, 121–139.

Rupp, D.E. and Cropanzano, R. (2002). The mediating effects of social exchange relationships in predicting workplace outcomes from multifoci organizational justice. *Organizational Behavior and Human Decision Processes*, 89, 925–946.

Rushton, L. and Hutchings, S. (2015). *The Burden of Occupational Cancer in Great Britain: Cutaneous Malignant Melanoma and Occupational Exposure to Solar Radiation.* IOSH. MRC-HPA Centre for Environment and Health Department of Epidemiology and Biostatistics, Imperial College London.

Sachs, P.R. and Redd, C.A. (1993). The Americans with Disabilities Act and individuals with neurological impairments. *Rehabilitation Psychology*, 38 (2), 87–101.

Saez, E. (2012). *Striking it richer: The evolution of top incomes in the United States.* Berkeley, CA: University of California Berkeley, Department of Economics. Available at: https://eml.berkeley.edu//~saez/saez-UStopincomes–2010.pdf

Sahakian, B. and LaBuzetta, J.N. (2013). *Bad Moves: How decision making goes wrong, and the ethics of smart drugs.* Oxford: Oxford University Press.

Sahakian, B. and Morein-Zamir, S. (2010). Neuroethical issues in cognitive enhancement. *Journal of Psychopharmacology*, 25 (2), 197–204.

Sainsbury Centre for Mental Health (2007). *The Economic and Social Costs of Mental Illness in England.* London: SCMH.

Sapir, A. (2014). *LT challenges and policy perspectives in an interconnected global economy: Discussion of the* OECD *view.* In Joint OECD and ERSI Workshop [online]. Paris: Université libre de Bruxelles. Available at: https://www.oecd.org/eco/growth/SAPIR_OECD_310114.pdf

Schalk, R. and Rousseau, D.M. (2001). Psychological contracts in employment. In N. Anderson (ed.), *Handbook of Industrial, Work and Organizational Psychology* (pp. 133–142). London: Sage.

Schofield, D., Shrestha, R.N., Cunich, M., Tanton, R., Kelly, S., Passey, M.E. and Veerman, L.J. (2015). Lost productive life years caused by chronic conditions in Australians aged 45–64 years, 2010–2030. *Medical Journal of Australia*, 203 (6), 260.

Scottish TUC (2016). *Dementia in the workplace: A guide for trade union reps.* Available at: http://www.stuc.org.uk/files/Dementia/Dementia%20in%20the%20Workplace%20(Final).pdf (accessed 15 December 2016).

Shacklock, K. (2006). Extended working lives? The meaning of working to older university workers in Australia. *International Journal of Human Resources Development and Management*, 6 (2/4), 161–173.

Shaw, J.D., Gupta, N. and Delery, J.E. (2002). Pay dispersion and workforce performance: Moderating effects of incentives and interdependence. *Strategic Management Journal*, 23, 491–512.

Siegrist, J., Benach, J., McKnight, A. and Goldblatt, P. (2010). *Employment arrangements, work conditions and health inequalities: Report on new evidence on health inequality reduction, produced by Task group 2 for the Strategic review of health inequalities post 2010.* London: Institute for Health Equity.

Simms, J. (2006). Small company, big smile. *Director Magazine*, August. Available at: www.director.co.uk/MAGAZINE/2006/8%20Aug/happy_60_1.html (accessed 10 July 2017).

Sinclair, D., Watson, J. and Beach, B. (2013). *Working longer: An* EU *perspective*. London: ILC-UK. Available at: http://www.ilcuk.org.uk/index.php/publications/publication_ details/working_longer_an_eu_perspective

Sissons, P. (2011). *The hourglass and the escalator: Labour market change and mobility*. London: The Work Foundation. Available at: http://www.agcas.org.uk/assets/download ?file=2670&parent=1052

Smeaton, D., Vegeris, S. and Sahin-Dikmen, M. (2009). *Older workers: Employment preferences, barriers and solutions*. EHRC Research Report #43. London: Equality and Human Rights Commission. Available at: https://www.equalityhumanrights.com/sites/ default/files/research-report–43-older-workers-employment-preferences-barriers-and-solutions_0.pdf

Sparrow, P., Wong, W., Otaye, L. and Bevan, S. (2013). *The changing contours of fairness: Can we match individual and organisational perspectives?* Research Report. London: CIPD. Available at: https://www.cipd.co.uk/knowledge/culture/ethics/fairness-report

Stationery Office (2012). *Research and analysis: The 2011 Workplace Employment Relations Study (*WERS*)*. Available at: https://www.gov.uk/government/publications/the–2011-workplace-employment-relations-study-wers

Steadman, K., Wood, M. and Silvester, H. (2015). *Health and wellbeing at work: A survey of employees, 2014*. DWP Research Report #901. London: TSO. Available at: https:// www.gov.uk/government/publications/health-and-wellbeing-at-work-survey-of-employees

Stern, M. (2013). You are already enhanced. *Slate* [online]. Available at: http://www.slate. com/articles/health_and_science/superman/2013/05/history_of_human_enhancement_ how_plastic_surgery_birth_control_aspirin_ivf.2.html

Stone, I., Braidford, P., Houston, M. and Bolger, F. (2012). *Promoting high performance working*. London: Department for Business, Innovation and Skills. Available at: https://www.gov.uk/government/uploads/system/uploads/attachment_data/ file/34638/12–1195-promoting-high-performance-working.pdf

Strack, R., Baier, J., Marchingo, M. and Sharda, S. (2014). *The global workforce crisis: $10 trillion at risk* [online]. Boston Consulting Group. Available at: https://www. bcgperspectives.com/content/articles/management_two_speed_economy_public_ sector_global_workforce_crisis/

Sullivan, J. and Diffley, C. (2003). *Embracing the Way with New Technology*. London: The Work Foundation.

Summers, K., Jinnett, K. and Bevan, S. (2015). *Musculoskeletal disorders, workforce health and productivity in the United States*. London: The Work Foundation. Available at: http://www.theworkfoundation.com/wp-content/uploads/2016/11/385_White-paper-Musculoskeletal-disorders-workforce-health-and-productivity-in-the-USA-final.pdf

Talbot, R., Nicolle, C.A., Maguire, M. and Rackliff, L. (2011). The journey to work – a barrier to older workers. In 6th International Conference on Inclusive Design, Helen Hamlyn Centre, RCA, London, 18–20 April.

Tamkin, P. (2004). *Management capability and performance*. Brighton: IES. Available at: http://www.employment-studies.co.uk/resource/management-capability-and-performance

Tamkin, P. and Ni Luanaigh, A. (2016). *The relationship between* UK *management and leadership and productivity*. Available at: http://www.employmentstudies.co.uk/system/files/resources/files/ukces0816c_0.pdf

Tappura, S., Syvänen, S. and Saarela, K. (2014). Challenges and needs for support in managing occupational health and safety from managers' viewpoints. *Nordic Journal of Working Life Studies*, 4 (3), 31–51.

Taskila, T., Shreeve, V., Laghini, M. and Bevan, S. (2015). *Living long, working well: Supporting older workers with health conditions to remain active at work*. The fourth white paper of the Health at Work Policy Unit. London: The Work Foundation. Available at: http://www.theworkfoundation.com/wp-content/uploads/2016/11/386_Living_long_working_well_Final.pdf

Taylor, P. (2007). *Employment and labour market policies for an ageing workforce and initiatives at the workplace. National overview report: United Kingdom*. Dublin: European Foundation for the Improvement of Living and Working Conditions.

Taylor, P., Mcloughlin, C., Brooke, E., Biase, T.D. and Steinberg, M. (2013). Managing older workers during a period of tight labour supply. *Ageing and Society*, 33 (1), 16–43.

Terkel, S. (1974). Working: *People talk about what they do all day and how they feel about what they do*. New York: New Press.

The Ditchley Foundation (2014). *The future of manufacturing: Is 'reshoring' the new name of the game?* [online]. Available at: http://www.ditchley.co.uk/conferences/past-programme/2010–2019/2014/manufacturing

The Economist (2013a). Has the ideas machine broken down? [online]. Available at: https://www.economist.com/news/briefing/21569381-idea-innovation-and-new-technology-have-stopped-driving-growth-getting-increasing

The Economist (2013b). Here, there and everywhere [online]. Available at: https://www.economist.com/news/special-report/21569572-after-decades-sending-work-across-world-companies-are-rethinking-their-offshoring

The Economist (2013c). Shape up [online]. Available at: https://www.economist.com/news/special-report/21569568-offshored-jobs-return-rich-countries-must-prove-they-have-what-it-takes-shape

The Royal Society (2012). *Human enhancement and the future of work* [online]. London. Available at: https://royalsociety.org/~/media/Royal_Society_Content/policy/projects/human-enhancement/2012–11–06-Human-enhancement.pdf

Thompson, M. (1993). *Pay and performance: The employee experience*. IMS Report #258. Brighton: The Institute of Manpower Studies.

TNS Opinion & Social (2012). *Public attitudes towards robots* [online]. European Commission. Available at: http://ec.europa.eu/commfrontoffice/publicopinion/archives/ebs/ebs_382_en.pdf

Toor, S. and Ofori, G. (2008). Leadership versus management: How they are different and why. *Leadership and Management in Engineering*, 8 (2), 61–72.

Topa, G., Moriano, J., Depolo, J., Alcover, C.-M. and Morales, J. (2009). Antecedents and consequences of retirement planning and decision-making: A meta-analysis and model. *Journal of Vocational Behaviour*, 75 (1), 38–55.

Towers Watson (2013). *Majority of U.S. public companies concerned about complying with proposed* CEO *pay ratio rule, Towers Watson poll finds, October.* Available at: nhttps://www.towerswatson.com/en/Insights/Newsletters/Global/executive-pay-matters/2013/Most-US-Public-Companies-Concerned-About-Complying-With-Proposed-CEO-Pay-Ratio-Rule

Trades Union Congress (TUC) (2014). *More than two in five new jobs created since mid–2010 have been self-employed.* Available at: https://www.tuc.org.uk/news/more-two-five-new-jobs-created-mid–2010-have-been-self-employed

Trades Union Congress (TUC) (2015). *Number of commuters spending more than two hours travelling to and from work up by 72% in last decade, says TUC.* Available at: https://www.tuc.org.uk/news/number-commuters-spending-more-two-hours-travelling-and-work–72-last-decade-says-tuc

Trevor, C.O., Reilly, G. and Gerhart, B. (2012). Reconsidering pay dispersion's effect on the performance of interdependent work: Reconciling sorting and pay inequality. *Academy of Management Journal,* 55 (3), 585–610.

Trist, E. and Bamforth, K. (1951). Some social and psychological consequences of the longwall method of coal getting: An examination of the psychological situation and defences of a work group in relation to the social structure and technological content of the work system. *Human Relations,* 4 (1), 3–38.

Turner, A. (2009). *The Turner Review: A regulatory response to the global banking crisis.* Financial Services Authority, March. Available at: https://uk.practicallaw.thomsonreuters.com/3–500–6175?transitionType=Default&contextData=(sc.Default)&firstPage=true&bhcp=1

Turner, V. (2014). *The digital universe of opportunities: Rich data and the increasing value of the internet of things.* EMC Digital Universe study.

UK Commission for Employment and Skills (UKCES) (2012). *The youth employment challenge.* London: UKCES. Available at: https://www.gov.uk/government/publications/the-youth-employment-challenge

UK Commission for Employment and Skills (UKCES) (2013a). *Management matters: Key findings from the* UKCES *surveys.* London: UKCES. Available at: http://dera.ioe.ac.uk/18244/1/briefing-paper-management-matters.pdf

UK Commission for Employment and Skills (UKCES) (2013b). *Scaling the youth employment challenge.* London: UKCES. Available at: https://www.gov.uk/government/publications/scaling-the-youth-employment-challenge

UK Commission for Employment and Skills (UKCES) (2014a). *Working futures 2014–2024.* Evidence Report #100. London: UKCES. Available at: www.gov.uk/government/uploads/system/uploads/attachment_data/file/513801/Working_Futures_final_evidence_report.pdf

UK Commission for Employment and Skills (UKCES) (2014b). *The future of work: Jobs and skills in 2030.* London: UKCES. Available at: https://www.gov.uk/government/publications/jobs-and-skills-in–2030

UK Commission for Employment and Skills (UKCES) (2015a). *UK skills and international competitiveness 2014.* London: UKCES. Available at: https://www.gov.uk/government/publications/uk-skills-levels-and-international-competitiveness–2014

UK Commission for Employment and Skills (UKCES) (2015b). *The death of the Saturday job: The decline in earning and learning among young people in the UK*. Available at: https://www.gov.uk/government/publications/the-death-of-the-saturday-job-the-decline-in-earning-and-learning-amongst-young-people-in-the-uk

US Bureau of Labor Statistics (2005). *Contingent and alternative employment arrangements* [online]. Washington, DC: BLS. Available at: https://www.bls.gov/news.release/pdf/conemp.pdf

US Government Accountability Office (US GOA) (2015). *Contingent workforce: Size, characteristics, earnings, and benefits* [online]. Washington, DC: US GAO. Available at: https://www.gao.gov/assets/670/669766.pdf

Vahtera, J., Kivimäki, M., Pentti, J. and Theorell, T. (2000). Effect of change in the psychosocial work environment on sickness absence: A seven-year follow-up of initially healthy employees. *Journal of Epidemiology and Community Health*, 54, 484–493.

van Dyne, L., Cummings, L. and Parks, J. (1995). Extra-role behaviors: In pursuit of construct and definitional clarity (a bridge over muddied waters). *Research in Organizational Behavior: An Annual Series of Analytical Essays and Critical Reviews*, 17, 215.

van Mierlo, H., Rutte, C., Vermunt, J., Kompier, M. and Doorewaard, J. (2006). Individual autonomy in work teams: The role of team autonomy, self-efficacy, and social support. *European Journal of Work and Organizational Psychology*, 15 (3), 281–299.

Vaughan-Jones, H. and Barham, L. (2010). *Healthy Work: Evidence into action*. Oxford: The Oxford Health Alliance, The Work Foundation and RAND Europe.

Visser, J. (2013). *Data Base on Institutional Characteristics of Trade Unions, Wage Setting, State Intervention and Social Pacts 1960–2011 (ICTWSS)*. Amsterdam: Amsterdam Institute for Advanced Labour Studies (ALAS). Available at: https://pdfs.semanticscholar.org/1122/77c5ba0d371895358911c7702ce91d135d0e.pdf

Vroom, V. (1964). *Work and Motivation*. New York: Wiley.

Waddell, G. and Burton, A.K. (2006). *Is Work Good for Your Health and Well-Being?* London: Department of Work and Pensions.

Wadsworth, J., Dhingra, S., Ottaviano, G. and Van Reenan, J. (2016). *Brexit and the impact of immigration on the UK*. London: Centre for Economic Performance, LSE. Available at: http://cep.lse.ac.uk/pubs/download/brexit05.pdf

Walker, D. (2009). *A review of corporate governance in UK banks and other financial industry entities: Final recommendations*. London: The Walker Review. Available at: http://webarchive.nationalarchives.gov.uk/+/http:/www.hm-treasury.gov.uk/d/walker_review_261109.pdf

Welfare, S. (2011) *Working harder not smarter: the employee contribution to meeting the UK's productivity challenge*. London: The Smith Institute. Available at: www.smith-institute.org.uk/book/working-harder-not-smarter-employee-contribution-meeting-uks-productivity-challenge

WERS (2004). *Research analysis: The 2004 Workplace Employment Relations Survey (WERS)*. Available at: www.gov.uk/government/publications/the–2004-workplace-employment-relations-survey-wers

WERS (2011). *Research analysis: The 2011 Workplace Employment Relations Survey (WERS)*. Available at: www.gov.uk/government/publications/the–2011-workplace-employment-relations-study-wers

White, M., Hill, S., Mills, C. and Smeaton, D. (2006). Managing to change? British workplaces and the future of work. *British Journal of Industrial Relations*, 44 (2), 374–376.

Williams R. (2002). *Managing Employee Performance: Design and implementation in organizations*. London: Cengage Learning.

Woessman, L. (2011). Cross-country evidence on teacher performance pay. *Economics of Education Review*, 30 (3), 404–418.

Wong, W., Sullivan, J., Albert, A., Hugget, M. and Parkin, J. (2009). *Quality People Management for Quality Outcomes*. London: The Work Foundation.

Woodger, C. (2012). *I want to work there!* London: SCG International. Available at: http://www.scg.international/blog/news/2012/10/i-want-to-work-there/

Woodruffe, C. (1992). What is meant by a competency? In R. Boam and P. Sparrow (eds.), *Designing and Achieving Competency*. Maidenhead: McGraw-Hill.

World Health Organization (WHO) (2010). *Five Keys to Healthy Workplaces*. Geneva: WHO.

World Health Organization (WHO) (2012). *Dementia: A public health priority*. Geneva: WHO.

Worrall, L. and Cooper, C.L. (2013). The quality of working life: Managers' wellbeing, motivation and productivity. *European Business Review*, July, 49–52.

Wright, C. and Brown, W. (2014). *From center stage to bit player: Trade unions and the British economy*. Available at: http://econpapers.repec.org/article/wsiserxxx/v_3a59_3ay_3a2014_3ai_3a04_3an_3as0217590814500301.htm

Yanadori, Y. and Cui, V. (2013). Creating incentives for innovation? The relationship between pay dispersion in R&D groups and firm innovation performance. *Strategic Management Journal*, 34, 1502–1511.

Yang, Y., Cannings, K. and Konrad, A.M. (2012). Pay dispersion and job satisfaction and job attitudes for women and men: A study of Swedish doctors. *Gender in Management: An International Journal*, 27 (4), 249–270.

Yarker, J., Munir, F., Donaldson-Fielder, E. and Hicks, B. (2010). *Managing Rehabilitation: A competency framework for manager to support return to work*. London: British Occupational Health Research Foundation.

Zaleznik, A. (1977). Managers and leaders: Are they different? *Harvard Business Review*, 55, 67–76.

INDEX